50% OFF SSAT Upper Level Prep Course!

Dear Customer,

We consider it an honor and a privilege that you chose our SSAT Upper Level Study Guide. As a way of showing our appreciation and to help us better serve you, we have partnered with Mometrix Test Preparation to offer you **50% off their online SSAT Upper Level Test Prep Course.** Many SSAT courses are needlessly expensive and don't deliver enough value. With their course, you get access to the best SSAT test prep material, and **you only pay half price.**

Mometrix has structured their online course to perfectly complement your printed study guide. The SSAT Upper Level Online Course contains **in-depth lessons** that cover all the most important topics, **220+ video reviews** that explain difficult concepts, over **1,050 practice questions** to ensure you feel prepared, and more than **470 flashcards** for studying on the go.

Online SSAT Upper Level Test Prep Course

Topics Include:

- Quantitative
    - o   Rational Numbers
    - o   Proportions and Ratios
    - o   Inequalities
    - o   Geometry
- Reading Comprehension
    - o   Writing Devices
    - o   Building a Vocabulary
    - o   Literature
    - o   Figurative Language
- Verbal
    - o   Synonyms
    - o   Analogies

Course Features:

- SSAT Upper Level Study Guide
    - o   Get content that complements our best-selling study guide.
- Full-Length Practice Tests
    - o   With over 1,050 practice questions, you can test yourself again and again.
- Mobile Friendly
    - o   If you need to study on the go, the course is easily accessible from your mobile device.
- SSAT Flashcards
    - o   Their course includes a flashcard mode consisting of over 470 content cards to help you study.

To receive this discount, visit their website at mometrix.com/university/ssatu or simply scan this QR code with your smartphone. At the checkout page, enter the discount code: **TPBSSATU50**

If you have any questions or concerns, please contact Mometrix at support@mometrix.com.

Sincerely,

FREE Test Taking Tips Video/DVD Offer

To better serve you, we created videos covering test taking tips that we want to give you for FREE.
These videos cover world-class tips that will help you succeed on your test.

We just ask that you send us feedback about this product. Please let us know what you thought about it—whether good, bad, or indifferent.

To get your **FREE videos**, you can use the QR code below or email freevideos@studyguideteam.com with "Free Videos" in the subject line and the following information in the body of the email:

   a. The title of your product
   b. Your product rating on a scale of 1-5, with 5 being the highest
   c. Your feedback about the product

If you have any questions or concerns, please don't hesitate to contact us at info@studyguideteam.com.

Thank you!

SSAT Upper Level Prep Book 2024-2025
4 SSAT Practice Tests and Study Guide
[9th Edition]

Lydia Morrison

Interested in buying more than 10 copies of our product? Contact us about bulk discounts:
bulkorders@studyguideteam.com

ISBN 13: 9781637750742

Table of Contents

Welcome

Dear Reader,

Welcome to your new Test Prep Books study guide! We are pleased that you chose us to help you prepare for your exam. There are many study options to choose from, and we appreciate you choosing us. Studying can be a daunting task, but we have designed a smart, effective study guide to help prepare you for what lies ahead.

Whether you're a parent helping your child learn and grow, a high school student working hard to get into your dream college, or a nursing student studying for a complex exam, we want to help give you the tools you need to succeed. We hope this study guide gives you the skills and the confidence to thrive, and we can't thank you enough for allowing us to be part of your journey.

In an effort to continue to improve our products, we welcome feedback from our customers. We look forward to hearing from you. Suggestions, success stories, and criticisms can all be communicated by emailing us at info@studyguideteam.com.

Sincerely,
Test Prep Books Team

FREE Videos/DVD OFFER

Doing well on your exam requires both knowing the test content and understanding how to use that knowledge to do well on the test. We offer completely FREE test taking tip videos. **These videos cover world-class tips that you can use to succeed on your test.**

To get your **FREE videos**, you can use the QR code below or email freevideos@studyguideteam.com with "Free Videos" in the subject line and the following information in the body of the email:

   a. The title of your product
   b. Your product rating on a scale of 1-5, with 5 being the highest
   c. Your feedback about the product

If you have any questions or concerns, please don't hesitate to contact us at info@studyguideteam.com.

Quick Overview

As you draw closer to taking your exam, effective preparation becomes more and more important. Thankfully, you have this study guide to help you get ready. Use this guide to help keep your studying on track and refer to it often.

This study guide contains several key sections that will help you be successful on your exam. The guide contains tips for what you should do the night before and the day of the test. Also included are test-taking tips. Knowing the right information is not always enough. Many well-prepared test takers struggle with exams. These tips will help equip you to accurately read, assess, and answer test questions.

A large part of the guide is devoted to showing you what content to expect on the exam and to helping you better understand that content. In this guide are practice test questions so that you can see how well you have grasped the content. Then, answer explanations are provided so that you can understand why you missed certain questions.

Don't try to cram the night before you take your exam. This is not a wise strategy for a few reasons. First, your retention of the information will be low. Your time would be better used by reviewing information you already know rather than trying to learn a lot of new information. Second, you will likely become stressed as you try to gain a large amount of knowledge in a short amount of time. Third, you will be depriving yourself of sleep. So be sure to go to bed at a reasonable time the night before. Being well-rested helps you focus and remain calm.

Be sure to eat a substantial breakfast the morning of the exam. If you are taking the exam in the afternoon, be sure to have a good lunch as well. Being hungry is distracting and can make it difficult to focus. You have hopefully spent lots of time preparing for the exam. Don't let an empty stomach get in the way of success!

When travelling to the testing center, leave earlier than needed. That way, you have a buffer in case you experience any delays. This will help you remain calm and will keep you from missing your appointment time at the testing center.

Be sure to pace yourself during the exam. Don't try to rush through the exam. There is no need to risk performing poorly on the exam just so you can leave the testing center early. Allow yourself to use all of the allotted time if needed.

Remain positive while taking the exam even if you feel like you are performing poorly. Thinking about the content you should have mastered will not help you perform better on the exam.

Once the exam is complete, take some time to relax. Even if you feel that you need to take the exam again, you will be well served by some down time before you begin studying again. It's often easier to convince yourself to study if you know that it will come with a reward!

Test-Taking Strategies

1. Predicting the Answer

When you feel confident in your preparation for a multiple-choice test, try predicting the answer before reading the answer choices. This is especially useful on questions that test objective factual knowledge. By predicting the answer before reading the available choices, you eliminate the possibility that you will be distracted or led astray by an incorrect answer choice. You will feel more confident in your selection if you read the question, predict the answer, and then find your prediction among the answer choices. After using this strategy, be sure to still read all of the answer choices carefully and completely. If you feel unprepared, you should not attempt to predict the answers. This would be a waste of time and an opportunity for your mind to wander in the wrong direction.

2. Reading the Whole Question

Too often, test takers scan a multiple-choice question, recognize a few familiar words, and immediately jump to the answer choices. Test authors are aware of this common impatience, and they will sometimes prey upon it. For instance, a test author might subtly turn the question into a negative, or he or she might redirect the focus of the question right at the end. The only way to avoid falling into these traps is to read the entirety of the question carefully before reading the answer choices.

3. Looking for Wrong Answers

Long and complicated multiple-choice questions can be intimidating. One way to simplify a difficult multiple-choice question is to eliminate all of the answer choices that are clearly wrong. In most sets of answers, there will be at least one selection that can be dismissed right away. If the test is administered on paper, the test taker could draw a line through it to indicate that it may be ignored; otherwise, the test taker will have to perform this operation mentally or on scratch paper. In either case, once the obviously incorrect answers have been eliminated, the remaining choices may be considered. Sometimes identifying the clearly wrong answers will give the test taker some information about the correct answer. For instance, if one of the remaining answer choices is a direct opposite of one of the eliminated answer choices, it may well be the correct answer. The opposite of obviously wrong is obviously right! Of course, this is not always the case. Some answers are obviously incorrect simply because they are irrelevant to the question being asked. Still, identifying and eliminating some incorrect answer choices is a good way to simplify a multiple-choice question.

4. Don't Overanalyze

Anxious test takers often overanalyze questions. When you are nervous, your brain will often run wild, causing you to make associations and discover clues that don't actually exist. If you feel that this may be a problem for you, do whatever you can to slow down during the test. Try taking a deep breath or counting to ten. As you read and consider the question, restrict yourself to the particular words used by the author. Avoid thought tangents about what the author *really* meant, or what he or she was *trying* to say. The only things that matter on a multiple-choice test are the words that are actually in the question. You must avoid reading too much into a multiple-choice question, or supposing that the writer meant something other than what he or she wrote.

3

5. No Need for Panic

It is wise to learn as many strategies as possible before taking a multiple-choice test, but it is likely that you will come across a few questions for which you simply don't know the answer. In this situation, avoid panicking. Because most multiple-choice tests include dozens of questions, the relative value of a single wrong answer is small. As much as possible, you should compartmentalize each question on a multiple-choice test. In other words, you should not allow your feelings about one question to affect your success on the others. When you find a question that you either don't understand or don't know how to answer, just take a deep breath and do your best. Read the entire question slowly and carefully. Try rephrasing the question a couple of different ways. Then, read all of the answer choices carefully. After eliminating obviously wrong answers, make a selection and move on to the next question.

6. Confusing Answer Choices

When working on a difficult multiple-choice question, there may be a tendency to focus on the answer choices that are the easiest to understand. Many people, whether consciously or not, gravitate to the answer choices that require the least concentration, knowledge, and memory. This is a mistake. When you come across an answer choice that is confusing, you should give it extra attention. A question might be confusing because you do not know the subject matter to which it refers. If this is the case, don't eliminate the answer before you have affirmatively settled on another. When you come across an answer choice of this type, set it aside as you look at the remaining choices. If you can confidently assert that one of the other choices is correct, you can leave the confusing answer aside. Otherwise, you will need to take a moment to try to better understand the confusing answer choice. Rephrasing is one way to tease out the sense of a confusing answer choice.

7. Your First Instinct

Many people struggle with multiple-choice tests because they overthink the questions. If you have studied sufficiently for the test, you should be prepared to trust your first instinct once you have carefully and completely read the question and all of the answer choices. There is a great deal of research suggesting that the mind can come to the correct conclusion very quickly once it has obtained all of the relevant information. At times, it may seem to you as if your intuition is working faster even than your reasoning mind. This may in fact be true. The knowledge you obtain while studying may be retrieved from your subconscious before you have a chance to work out the associations that support it. Verify your instinct by working out the reasons that it should be trusted.

8. Key Words

Many test takers struggle with multiple-choice questions because they have poor reading comprehension skills. Quickly reading and understanding a multiple-choice question requires a mixture of skill and experience. To help with this, try jotting down a few key words and phrases on a piece of scrap paper. Doing this concentrates the process of reading and forces the mind to weigh the relative importance of the question's parts. In selecting words and phrases to write down, the test taker thinks

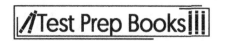

about the question more deeply and carefully. This is especially true for multiple-choice questions that are preceded by a long prompt.

9. Subtle Negatives

One of the oldest tricks in the multiple-choice test writer's book is to subtly reverse the meaning of a question with a word like *not* or *except*. If you are not paying attention to each word in the question, you can easily be led astray by this trick. For instance, a common question format is, "Which of the following is...?" Obviously, if the question instead is, "Which of the following is not...?," then the answer will be quite different. Even worse, the test makers are aware of the potential for this mistake and will include one answer choice that would be correct if the question were not negated or reversed. A test taker who misses the reversal will find what he or she believes to be a correct answer and will be so confident that he or she will fail to reread the question and discover the original error. The only way to avoid this is to practice a wide variety of multiple-choice questions and to pay close attention to each and every word.

10. Reading Every Answer Choice

It may seem obvious, but you should always read every one of the answer choices! Too many test takers fall into the habit of scanning the question and assuming that they understand the question because they recognize a few key words. From there, they pick the first answer choice that answers the question they believe they have read. Test takers who read all of the answer choices might discover that one of the latter answer choices is actually *more* correct. Moreover, reading all of the answer choices can remind you of facts related to the question that can help you arrive at the correct answer. Sometimes, a misstatement or incorrect detail in one of the latter answer choices will trigger your memory of the subject and will enable you to find the right answer. Failing to read all of the answer choices is like not reading all of the items on a restaurant menu: you might miss out on the perfect choice.

11. Spot the Hedges

One of the keys to success on multiple-choice tests is paying close attention to every word. This is never truer than with words like *almost*, *most*, *some*, and *sometimes*. These words are called "hedges" because they indicate that a statement is not totally true or not true in every place and time. An absolute statement will contain no hedges, but in many subjects, the answers are not always straightforward or absolute. There are always exceptions to the rules in these subjects. For this reason, you should favor those multiple-choice questions that contain hedging language. The presence of qualifying words indicates that the author is taking special care with his or her words, which is certainly important when composing the right answer. After all, there are many ways to be wrong, but there is only one way to be right! For this reason, it is wise to avoid answers that are absolute when taking a multiple-choice test. An absolute answer is one that says things are either all one way or all another. They often include words like *every*, *always*, *best*, and *never*. If you are taking a multiple-choice test in a subject that doesn't lend itself to absolute answers, be on your guard if you see any of these words.

12. Long Answers

 In many subject areas, the answers are not simple. As already mentioned, the right answer often requires hedges. Another common feature of the answers to a complex or subjective question are qualifying clauses, which are groups of words that subtly modify the meaning of the sentence. If the question or answer choice describes a rule to which there are exceptions or the subject matter is complicated, ambiguous, or confusing, the correct answer will require many words in order to be expressed clearly and accurately. In essence, you should not be deterred by answer choices that seem excessively long. Oftentimes, the author of the text will not be able to write the correct answer without offering some qualifications and modifications. Your job is to read the answer choices thoroughly and completely and to select the one that most accurately and precisely answers the question.

13. Restating to Understand

Sometimes, a question on a multiple-choice test is difficult not because of what it asks but because of how it is written. If this is the case, restate the question or answer choice in different words. This process serves a couple of important purposes. First, it forces you to concentrate on the core of the question. In order to rephrase the question accurately, you have to understand it well. Rephrasing the question will concentrate your mind on the key words and ideas. Second, it will present the information to your mind in a fresh way. This process may trigger your memory and render some useful scrap of information picked up while studying.

14. True Statements

Sometimes an answer choice will be true in itself, but it does not answer the question. This is one of the main reasons why it is essential to read the question carefully and completely before proceeding to the answer choices. Too often, test takers skip ahead to the answer choices and look for true statements. Having found one of these, they are content to select it without reference to the question above. The savvy test taker will always read the entire question before turning to the answer choices. Then, having settled on a correct answer choice, he or she will refer to the original question and ensure that the selected answer is relevant. The mistake of choosing a correct-but-irrelevant answer choice is especially common on questions related to specific pieces of objective knowledge.

15. No Patterns

One of the more dangerous ideas that circulates about multiple-choice tests is that the correct answers tend to fall into patterns. These erroneous ideas range from a belief that B and C are the most common right answers, to the idea that an unprepared test-taker should answer "A-B-A-C-A-D-A-B-A." It cannot be emphasized enough that pattern-seeking of this type is exactly the WRONG way to approach a multiple-choice test. To begin with, it is highly unlikely that the test maker will plot the correct answers according to some predetermined pattern. The questions are scrambled and delivered in a random order. Furthermore, even if the test maker was following a pattern in the assignation of correct answers, there is no reason why the test taker would know which pattern he or she was using. Any attempt to discern a pattern in the answer choices is a waste of time and a distraction from the real work of taking the test. A test taker would be much better served by extra preparation before the test than by reliance on a pattern in the answers.

6

Bonus Content

We host multiple bonus items online, including all four practice tests in digital format. Scan the QR code or go to this link to access this content:

testprepbooks.com/bonus/ssat-upper

The first time you access the page, you will need to register as a "new user" and verify your email address.

If you have any issues, please email support@testprepbooks.com.

Introduction to the Upper Level SSAT

Function of the Test

The Secondary School Admission Test (SSAT) is a standardized test used for students that are applying to an independent or private school. The Upper Level SSAT is administered to students currently in grades 8 through 11, applying to grades 9 through 12 and beyond to post-graduate opportunities, and it evaluates math, reading, and verbal skills. The test is used in the United States and is also available in several other countries throughout the world to determine if students have the necessary skills for success in a college preparatory program.

Test Administration

The standard SSAT is administered in groups and offered on six Saturdays throughout the year. The standard test is available at hundreds of testing centers in the US and locations throughout the world.

Closed Standard Test

If you are testing with a member school that is not open to the public, you will take a "closed" Standard test, which requires an access code obtained directly from the school for registration.

Open Standard Test

An open Standard test is an administration that is open to the general public. No access code is required for an Open Standard test.

Limited Standard Test

Sunday testing is available to those who observe religious events on Saturdays, but must be approved before registration.

Prometric Test

Upper Level SSAT test-takers can opt to take the Prometric Test. This is a computer-based SSAT administered at a Prometric Test Center.

At-Home SSAT

Upper Level SSAT test-takers may also opt take a SSAT at Home. This is also a computer-based SSAT that is administered online and taken at a student's home or other suitable location.

The SSAT Flex Test

A Flex test is an in-person paper exam that can be taken any day except when the Standard test is administered. The Flex test may be provided in an open or closed format. Same as the Standard test, Open Flex tests are open to the general public and do not require an access code. The Closed Flex test requires an access code.

Students may repeat the standard test without penalty. Students must create an account on the SSAT website in order to register. This account also allows students to print their admission tickets and receive their test scores. Registration opens about 10 weeks prior to a testing date. Late registration begins 3 weeks before the test date and rush registration starts 10 days before the test date. Late and rush registrations incur additional fees.

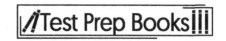

Testing accommodations are available for students with disabilities. Students requiring accommodations must apply and be approved before registering for the test. Approval is only required once in an academic year. The official guidelines for accommodations can be accessed on the SSAT.org website.

Test Format

The Upper Level SSAT consists of multiple-choice questions in Quantitative (Math), Verbal, Reading Comprehension, and Experimental sections, and a writing sample. The writing sample is not scored, but is sent to prospective schools to demonstrate a student's writing ability.

The writing sample asks the student to choose between two writing prompts—a traditional essay or a creative writing stimulus—and to write an original essay or story based on the prompt. The Quantitative section is broken down into two parts, each with 25 questions in the areas of number concepts, geometry, algebra, and probability. A calculator is not permitted. The Verbal section includes 60 questions: 30 synonyms and 30 analogies. The Reading Comprehension section includes a total of 40 questions relating to several short passages that range from approximately 250-350 words. The passages may be pulled from literary fiction, social sciences, humanities, and sciences and the questions focus mainly on reading comprehension skills, including inferences, identifying the main idea, and determining the author's purpose. The Experimental section includes 16 questions (6 Verbal, 5 Reading, and 5 Quantitative) in order to test their reliability for SSAT forms to be used in the future. The Experimental section is not scored. The testing period and sections are broken down as follows:

Section	Number of Questions	Question Type	Time Allotted
Writing Sample	1	Written Response	25 minutes
Break			10 minutes
Quantitative (Part 1)	25	Multiple Choice	30 minutes
Reading	40	Multiple Choice	40 minutes
Break			10 minutes
Verbal	60	Multiple Choice	30 minutes
Quantitative (Part 2)	25	Multiple Choice	30 minutes
Experimental	16	Multiple Choice	15 minutes

Scoring

In the Upper Level SSAT, students are given one point for each correct answer, and they lose a quarter of a point for each incorrect answer. Unanswered questions do not affect the score either way.

A free scoring report is available online through a student's SSAT account roughly 2 weeks after the test date. The report includes a narrative explanation of the scores, along with a raw score, a scaled score, percentile rank, and total scaled score. The possible scaled score ranges from 440 – 710 per section, and the percentile rank is from 1 – 99. The total scaled score range is 1320 – 2130, with a mid-point of 1725.

The SSAT is a norm-referenced test, meaning that the score is compared to a norm group of test takers' scores from the last 3 years. The score report includes the student's scores, as well as the average norm scores in each section for comparison. The percentile rank shows how a student performed relative to the norm group. For example, if a student's percentile is 80, it means he or she scored the same or better than 80% of those in the norm group. Schools use many factors to select students for admission, so a "good score" or passing score is difficult to determine.

Study Prep Plan for the Upper Level SSAT

1 **Schedule -** Use one of our study schedules below or come up with one of your own.

2 **Relax -** Test anxiety can hurt even the best students. There are many ways to reduce stress. Find the one that works best for you.

3 **Execute -** Once you have a good plan in place, be sure to stick to it.

One Week Study Schedule		
	Day 1	Writing Sample
	Day 2	Operations with Fractions, Decimals...
	Day 3	Algebra
	Day 4	Perimeter and Area
	Day 5	Reading Comprehension
	Day 6	Practice Test #1
	Day 7	Take Your Exam!

Two Week Study Schedule				
	Day 1	Writing Sample	Day 8	Data Analysis/Probability
	Day 2	Quantitative Reasoning	Day 9	Reading Comprehension
	Day 3	Operations with Fractions, Decimals...	Day 10	Verbal
	Day 4	Sequences and Series	Day 11	Vocabulary
	Day 5	Algebra	Day 12	Practice Test #1
	Day 6	Equations and Graphing	Day 13	Practice Test #2
	Day 7	Perimeter and Area	Day 14	Take Your Exam!

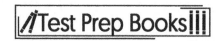

One Month Study Schedule							
Day 1	Writing Sample	Day 11	Conjectures, Predictions...	Day 21	Synonyms
Day 2	Quantitative Reasoning	Day 12	Perimeter and Area	Day 22	Practice Test #1
Day 3	Basic Addition, Subtraction...	Day 13	Lines and Angles	Day 23	Answer Explanations #1
Day 4	Operations with Fractions, Decimals...	Day 14	Data Analysis/ Probability	Day 24	Practice Test #2
Day 5	Factorization	Day 15	Interpreting Displays of Data	Day 25	Answer Explanations #2
Day 6	Sequences and Series	Day 16	Reading Comprehension	Day 26	Practice Test #3
Day 7	The Problem-Solving Process and...	Day 17	Determining the Author's...	Day 27	Answer Explanations #3
Day 8	Algebra	Day 18	Verbal	Day 28	Practice Test #4
Day 9	Solving Simple Algebraic Problems	Day 19	Place the Word in a Sentence	Day 29	Answer Explanations #4
Day 10	Equations and Graphing	Day 20	Vocabulary	Day 30	Take Your Exam!

Build your own prep plan by visiting:

testprepbooks.com/prep

11

As you study for your test, we'd like to take the opportunity to remind you that you are capable of great things! With the right tools and dedication, you truly can do anything you set your mind to. The fact that you are holding this book right now shows how committed you are. In case no one has told you lately, you've got this! Our intention behind including this coloring page is to give you the chance to take some time to engage your creative side when you need a little brain-break from studying. As a company, we want to encourage people like you to achieve their dreams by providing good quality study materials for the tests and certifications that improve careers and change lives. As individuals, many of us have taken such tests in our careers, and we know how challenging this process can be. While we can't come alongside you and cheer you on personally, we can offer you the space to recall your purpose, reconnect with your passion, and refresh your brain through an artistic practice. We wish you every success, and happy studying!

Math Reference Sheet

Symbol	Phrase
+	added to, increased by, sum of, more than
-	decreased by, difference between, less than, take away
×	multiplied by, 3 (4, 5 . . .) times as large, product of
÷	divided by, quotient of, half (third, etc.) of
=	is, the same as, results in, as much as
x, t, n, etc.	a variable which is an unknown value or quantity
<	is under, is below, smaller than, beneath
>	is above, is over, bigger than, exceeds
≤	no more than, at most, maximum; less than or equal to
≥	no less than, at least, minimum; greater than or equal to
√	square root of, exponent divided by 2

Geometry	Description
$P = 2l + 2w$	for perimeter of a rectangle
$P = 4 \times s$	for perimeter of a square
$P = a + b + c$	for perimeter of a triangle
$A = \frac{1}{2} \times b \times h = \frac{bh}{2}$	for area of a triangle
$A = b \times h$	for area of a parallelogram
$A = \frac{1}{2} \times h(b_1 + b_2)$	for area of a trapezoid
$A = \frac{1}{2} \times a \times P$	for area of a regular polygon
$C = 2 \times \pi \times r$	for circumference (perimeter) of a circle
$A = \pi \times r^2$	for area of a circle
$c^2 = a^2 + b^2; c = \sqrt{a^2 + b^2}$	for finding the hypotenuse of a right triangle
$SA = 2xy + 2yz + 2xz$	for finding surface area
$V = \frac{1}{3}xyh$	for finding volume of a rectangular pyramid
$V = \frac{4}{3}\pi r^3; \frac{1}{3}\pi r^2 h; \pi r^2 h$	for volume of a sphere; a cone; and a cylinder

Radical Expressions	Description
$\sqrt[n]{a} = a^{\frac{1}{n}}, \sqrt[n]{a^m} = (\sqrt[n]{a})^m = a^{\frac{m}{n}}$	a is the radicand, n is the index, m is the exponent
$\sqrt{x^2} = (x^2)^{\frac{1}{2}} = x$	to convert square root to exponent
$a^m \times a^n = a^{m+n}$	multiplying radicands with exponents
$(a^m)^n = a^{m \times n}$	multiplying exponents
$(a \times b)^m = a^m \times b^m$	parentheses with exponents

Property	Addition	Multiplication
Commutative	$a + b = b + a$	$a \times b = b \times a$
Associative	$(a + b) + c = a + (b + c)$	$(a \times b) \times c = a \times (b \times c)$
Identity	$a + 0 = a; \ 0 + a = a$	$a \times 1 = a; \ 1 \times a = a$
Inverse	$a + (-a) = 0$	$a \times \frac{1}{a} = 1; \ a \neq 0$
Distributive		$a(b + c) = ab + ac$

Data	Description
Mean	equal to the total of the values of a data set, divided by the number of elements in the data set
Median	middle value in an odd number of ordered values of a data set, or the mean of the two middle values in an even number of ordered values in a data set
Mode	the value that appears most often
Range	the difference between the highest and the lowest values in the set

Graphing	Description
(x, y)	ordered pair, plot points in a graph
$y = mx + b$	slope-intercept form; m represents the slope of the line and b represents the y-intercept
$f(x)$	read as f of x, which means it is a function of x
(x_2, y_2) and (x_2, y_2)	two ordered pairs used to determine the slope of a line
$m = \frac{y_2 - y_1}{x_2 - x_1}$	to find the slope of the line, m, for ordered pairs
$Ax + By = C$	standard form of an equation, also for solving a system of equations through the elimination method
$M = (\frac{x_1 + x_2}{2}, \frac{y_1 + y_2}{2})$	for finding the midpoint of an ordered pair
$y = ax^2 + bx + c$	quadratic function for a parabola
$y = a(x - h)^2 + k$	quadratic function for a parabola with vertex
$y = ab^x; y = a \times b^x$	function for exponential curve
$y = ax^2 + bx + c$	standard form of a quadratic function
$x = \frac{-b}{2a}$	for finding axis of symmetry in a parabola; given quadratic formula in standard form
$f = \sqrt{\frac{\Sigma(x - \bar{x})^2}{n - 1}}$	function for standard deviation of the sample; where $\bar{x}$ = sample mean and n = sample size

Proportions and Percentage	Description
$\frac{gallons}{cost} = \frac{gallons}{cost} : \frac{7\ gallons}{\$14.70} = \frac{x}{\$20}$	written as equal ratios with a variable representing the missing quantity
$\frac{y_1}{x_1} = \frac{y_2}{x_2}$	for direct proportions
$(y_1)(x_1) = (y_2)(x_2)$	for indirect proportions
$\frac{change}{original\ value} \times 100 = percent\ change$	for finding percentage change in value
$\frac{new\ quantity - old\ quantity}{old\ quantity} \times 100$	for calculating the increase or decrease in percentage

14

Writing Sample

The Upper Level SSAT begins with a 25-mintue writing sample section where test takers are asked to write a creative story based on one of two prompts to choose from. While this section is not scored, the writing sample can be provided with the score report to each admission's office for an additional fee. This section gives test takers the opportunity to show their writing ability as well as demonstrate creativity and self-expression. Test takers should be sure that their stories have a beginning, middle, and end.

Planning should occur after looking at the picture or reading the prompt but before beginning any writing. This brainstorming stage is when writers consider their purpose and think of ideas that they can use in their writing. Graphic organizers like story webs are excellent tools to use during the planning stage. Graphic organizers can help connect the writing purpose to supporting details, and they can help begin the process of structuring the writing piece.

Parts of the Essay

The **introduction** has to do a few important things:

- Establish the topic of the essay in original wording (i.e., not just repeating the prompt)

- Clarify the significance/importance of the topic or purpose for writing. This should provide a brief overview rather than share too many details, a brief overview.

- Offer a thesis statement that identifies the writer's own viewpoint on the topic. Typically, the thesis statement is one or two brief sentences that offer a clear, concise explanation of the main point on the topic.

Body paragraphs reflect the ideas developed in the outline. Three or four points is probably sufficient for a short essay, and they should include the following:

- A **topic sentence** that identifies the sub-point (e.g., a reason why, a way how, a cause or effect)

- A detailed **explanation** of each sub-point, explaining why the writer thinks this point is valid

- **Illustrative examples**, such as personal examples or real-world examples, that support and validate the point (i.e., "prove" the point)

- A **concluding sentence** that connects the examples, reasoning, and analysis to the point being made

The **conclusion,** or final paragraph, should be brief and should reiterate the focus, clarifying why the discussion is significant or important. It is important to avoid adding specific details or new ideas to this paragraph. The purpose of the conclusion is to sum up what has been said to bring the discussion to a close.

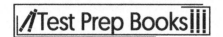

The Short Overview

The essay may seem challenging, but following these steps can help writers focus:

- Take one-two minutes to think about the topic.
- Generate some ideas through brainstorming (three-four minutes).
- Organize ideas into a brief outline, selecting just three-four main points to cover in the essay
- Develop essay in parts:

    o Introduction paragraph, with intro to topic and main points

    o Viewpoint on the subject at the end of the introduction

    o Body paragraphs, based on outline, each should make a main point, explain the viewpoint, and use examples to support the point

    o Brief conclusion highlighting the main points and closing

- Read over the essay (last five minutes).
- Look for any obvious errors, making sure that the writing makes sense.

Writing an essay can be overwhelming, and performance panic is a natural response. The outline serves as a basis for the writing and helps to keep writers focused. Getting stuck can also happen, and it's helpful to remember that brainstorming can be done at any time during the writing process. Following the steps of the writing process is the best defense against writer's block.

Timed essays can be particularly stressful, but assessors are trained to recognize the necessary planning and thinking for these timed efforts. Using the plan above and sticking to it helps with time management. Timing each part of the process helps writers stay on track. Sometimes writers try to cover too much in their essays. If time seems to be running out, this is an opportunity to determine whether all of the ideas in the outline are necessary. Three body paragraphs are sufficient, and more than that is probably too much to cover in a short essay.

More isn't *better* in writing. A strong essay will be clear and concise. It will avoid unnecessary or repetitive details. It is better to have a concise, five-paragraph essay that makes a clear point, than a ten-paragraph essay that doesn't. The goal is to write one-two pages of quality writing. Paragraphs should also reflect balance; if the introduction goes to the bottom of the first page, the writing may be going off-track or be repetitive. It's best to fall into the one-two page range, but a complete, well-developed essay is the ultimate goal.

Applying Basic Knowledge of the Elements of the Writing Process

Practice Makes Prepared Writers

Like any other useful skill, writing only improves with practice. While writing may come more easily to some than others, it is still a skill to be honed and improved. Regardless of a person's natural abilities, there is always room for growth in writing. Practicing the basic skills of writing can aid in preparations for the SSAT.

One way to build vocabulary and enhance exposure to the written word is through reading. This can be through reading books, but reading of any materials such as newspapers, magazines, and even social

16

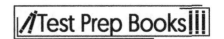

media count towards practice with the written word. This also helps to enhance critical reading and thinking skills, through analysis of the ideas and concepts read. Think of each new reading experience as a chance to sharpen these skills.

Planning

Brainstorming

One of the most important steps in writing an essay is prewriting. Before drafting an essay, it's helpful to think about the topic for a moment or two, in order to gain a more solid understanding of the task. Then, spending about five minutes jotting down the immediate ideas that could work for the essay is recommended. Brainstorming is a way to get some words on the page and offer a reference for ideas when drafting. Scratch paper is provided for writers to use any prewriting techniques such as webbing, free writing, or listing. The goal is to get ideas out of the mind and onto the page.

In the planning stage, it's important to consider all aspects of the topic, including different viewpoints on the subject. There are more than two ways to look at a topic, and a strong argument considers those opposing viewpoints. Considering opposing viewpoints can help writers present a fair, balanced, and informed essay that shows consideration for all readers. This approach can also strengthen an argument by recognizing and potentially refuting opposing viewpoint(s).

Drawing from personal experience may help to support ideas. For example, if the goal for writing is a personal narrative, then the story should come from the writer's own life. Many writers find it helpful to draw from personal experience, even in an essay that is not strictly narrative. Personal anecdotes or short stories can help to illustrate a point in other types of essays as well.

Once the ideas are on the page, it's time to turn them into a solid plan for the essay. The best ideas from the brainstorming results can then be developed into a more formal outline.

Outlining

An **outline** is a system used to organize writing. When reading texts, outlining is important because it helps readers organize important information in a logical pattern using Roman numerals. Usually, outlines start out with the main idea(s) and then branch out into subgroups or subsidiary thoughts or subjects. The outline should be methodical, with at least two main points follow each by at least two subpoints. Not only do outlines provide a visual tool for readers to reflect on how events, characters, settings, or other key parts of the text or passage relate to one another, but they can also lead readers to a stronger conclusion. The sample below demonstrates what a general outline looks like.

    I. Main Topic 1
        a. Subtopic 1
        b. Subtopic 2
            1. Detail 1
            2. Detail 2
   II. Main Topic 2
        a. Subtopic 1
        b. Subtopic 2
            1. Detail 1
            2. Detail 2

Free Writing

Like brainstorming, **free writing** is another prewriting activity to help the writer generate ideas. This method involves setting a timer for 2 or 3 minutes and writing down all ideas that come to mind about the topic using complete sentences. Once time is up, review the sentences to see what observations have been made and how these ideas might translate into a more coherent direction for the topic. Even if sentences lack sense as a whole, this is an excellent way to get ideas onto the page in the very beginning stages of writing. Using complete sentences can make this a bit more challenging than brainstorming, but overall it is a worthwhile exercise, as it may force the writer to come up with more complete thoughts about the topic.

Writing

Now it comes time to actually write your essay. Follow the outline you developed in the brainstorming process and try to incorporate the sentences you wrote in the free writing exercise.

Basing the essay on the outline aids in both organization and coherence. The goal is to ensure that there is enough time to develop each sub-point in the essay, roughly spending an equal amount of time on each idea. Keeping an eye on the time will help. If there are fifteen minutes left to draft the essay, then it makes sense to spend about 5 minutes on each of the ideas. Staying on task is critical to success, and timing out the parts of the essay can help writers avoid feeling overwhelmed.

Remember that your work here does not have to be perfect. This process is often referred to as **drafting** because you're just creating a rough draft of your work.

Don't get bogged down on the small details. For instance, if you're not sure whether or not a word should be capitalized, mark it somehow and look up the capitalization rule while in the revision process if not in a testing situation. The same goes for referencing sources. That should not be focused on until after the writing process.

Forming Paragraphs

A good **paragraph** should have the following characteristics:

- Be logical with organized sentences
- Have a unified purpose within itself
- Use sentences as building blocks
- Be a distinct section of a piece of writing
- Present a single theme introduced by a topic sentence
- Maintain a consistent flow through subsequent, relevant, well-placed sentences
- Tell a story of its own or have its own purpose, yet connect with what is written before and after
- Enlighten, entertain, and/or inform

Though certainly not set in stone, the length should be a consideration for the reader's sake, not merely for the sake of the topic. When paragraphs are especially short, the reader might experience an irregular, uneven effect; when they're much longer than 250 words, the reader's attention span, and probably their retention, is challenged. While a paragraph can technically be a sentence long, a good rule of thumb is for paragraphs to be at least three sentences long and no more than ten sentence long. An optimal word length is 100 to 250 words.

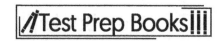

Coherent Paragraphs

Coherence is simply defined as the quality of being logical and consistent. In order to have coherent paragraphs, therefore, authors must be logical and consistent in their writing, whatever the document might be. Two words are helpful to understanding coherence: flow and relationship. Earlier, transitions were referred to as being the "glue" to put organized thoughts together. Now, let's look at the topic sentence from which flow and relationship originate.

The **topic sentence**, usually the first in a paragraph, holds the essential features that will be brought forth in the paragraph. It is also here that authors either grab or lose readers. It may be the only writing that a reader encounters from that writer, so it is a good idea to summarize and represent ideas accurately.

The coherent paragraph has a logical order. It utilizes transitional words and phrases, parallel sentence structure, clear pronoun references, and reasonable repetition of key words and phrases. Use common sense for repetition. Consider synonyms for variety. Be consistent in verb tense whenever possible.

When writers have accomplished their paragraph's purpose, they prepare it to receive the next paragraph. While writing, read the paragraph over, edit, examine, evaluate, and make changes accordingly. Possibly, a paragraph has gone on too long. If that occurs, it needs to be broken up into other paragraphs, or the length should be reduced. If a paragraph didn't fully accomplish its purpose, consider revising it.

Main Point of a Paragraph

What is the main point of a paragraph? It is *the* point all of the other important and lesser important points should lead up to, and it should be summed up in the topic sentence.

Sometimes there is a fine line between a paragraph's topic sentence and its main point. In fact, they actually might be one and the same. Often, though, they are two separate, but closely related, aspects of the same paragraph.

Depending upon the writer's purpose, the topic sentence or the paragraph's main point might not be fully revealed until the paragraph's conclusion.

Sometimes, while developing paragraphs, authors deviate from the main point, which means they have to delete and rework their materials to stay on point.

Examining Paragraphs

Throughout this text, composing and combining sentences, using basic grammar skills, employing rules and guidelines, identifying differing points of view, using appropriate context, constructing accurate word usage, and discerning correct punctuation have all been discussed. Whew! The types of sentences, patterns, transitions, and overall structure have been covered as well.

While authors write, thoughts coalesce to form words on "paper" (aka a computer screen). Authors strategically place those thoughts in sentences to give them "voice" in an orderly manner, and then they manipulate them into cohesive sentences for cohesion to express ideas. Like a hunk of modeling clay (thanks to computers, people are no longer bound to erasers and whiteout), sentences can be worked and reworked until they cooperate and say what was originally intended.

Before calling a paragraph complete, identify its main point, making sure that related sentences stay on point. Pose questions such as, "Did I sufficiently develop the main point? Did I say it succinctly enough? Did I give it time to develop? *Is* it developed?"

Let's examine the following two paragraphs, each an example of a movie review. Read them and form a critique.

> Example 1: *Eddie the Eagle* is a movie about a struggling athlete. Eddie was crippled at birth. He had a lot of therapy and he had a dream. Eddie trained himself for the Olympics. He went far away to learn how to ski jump. It was hard for him, but he persevered. He got a coach and kept trying. He qualified for the Olympics. He was the only one from Britain who could jump. When he succeeded, they named him, "Eddie the Eagle."

> Example 2: The last movie I saw in the theater was *Eddie the Eagle,* a story of extraordinary perseverance inspired by real life events. Eddie was born in England with a birth defect that he slowly but surely overcame, but not without trial and error (not the least of which was his father's perpetual *dis*couragement). In fact, the old man did everything to get him to give up, but Eddie was dogged beyond anyone in the neighborhood; in fact, maybe beyond anyone in the whole town or even the whole world! Eddie, simply, did not know to quit. As he grew up, so did his dream; a strange one, indeed, for someone so unaccomplished: to compete in the Winter Olympics as a ski jumper (which he knew absolutely nothing about). Eddie didn't just keep on dreaming about it. He actually went to Germany and *worked* at it, facing unbelievable odds, defeats, and put-downs by Dad and the other Men in Charge, aka the Olympic decision-makers. Did that stop him? No way! Eddie got a coach and persevered. Then, when he failed, he persevered some more, again and again. You should be able to open up a dictionary, look at the word "persevere," and see a picture of Eddie the Eagle because, when everybody told him he couldn't, he did. The result? He is forever dubbed, "Eddie the Eagle."

Both reviews tell something about the movie *Eddie the Eagle*. Does one motivate the reader to want to see the movie more than the other? Does one just provide a few facts while the other paints a virtual picture of the movie? Does one give a carrot and the other a rib eye steak, mashed potatoes, and chocolate silk pie?

Paragraphs sometimes only give facts. Sometimes that's appropriate and all that is needed. Sometimes, though, writers want to use the blank documents on their computer screens to paint a picture. Writers must "see" the painting come to life. To do so, pick a familiar topic, write a simple sentence, and add to it. Pretend, for instance, there's a lovely view. What does one see? Is it a lake? Try again—picture it as though it were the sea! Visualize a big ship sailing out there. Is it sailing away or approaching ? Who is on it? Is it dangerous? Is it night and are there crazy pirates on board? Uh-oh! Did one just jump ship and start swimming toward shore?

Referencing Sources

Anytime you quote or paraphrase another piece of writing you will need to include a citation. A **citation** is a short description of the work that your quote or information came from. The manual of style your teacher wants you to follow will dictate exactly how to format that citation. For example, this is how you would cite a book according to the APA manual of style:

- *Format*: Last name, First initial, Middle initial. (Year Published) *Book Title*. City, State: Publisher.
- Example: Sampson, M. R. (1989). Diaries from an Alien Invasion. Springfield, IL: Campbell Press.

20

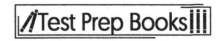

Revising

Revising and proofreading offers an opportunity for writers to polish things up. Putting one's self in the reader's shoes and focusing on what the essay actually says helps writers identify problems—it's a movement from the mindset of writer to the mindset of editor. The goal is to have a clean, clear copy of the essay.

During the essay portion of a test, leaving a few minutes at the end to revise and proofread offers an opportunity for writers to polish things up. Putting one's self in the reader's shoes and focusing on what the essay actually says helps writers identify problems—it's a movement from the mindset of writer to the mindset of editor. The goal is to have a clean, clear copy of the essay. The following areas should be considered when proofreading:

- Sentence fragments
- Awkward sentence structure
- Run-on sentences
- Incorrect word choice
- Grammatical agreement errors
- Spelling errors
- Punctuation errors
- Capitalization errors

Recursive Writing Process

While the writing process may have specific steps, the good news is that the process is recursive, meaning the steps need not be completed in a particular order. Many writers find that they complete steps at the same time such as drafting and revising, where the writing and rearranging of ideas occur simultaneously or in very close order. Similarly, a writer may find that a particular section of a draft needs more development, and will go back to the prewriting stage to generate new ideas. The steps can be repeated at any time, and the more these steps of the recursive writing process are employed, the better the final product will be.

Writing Prompts

In the SSAT Upper Level Writing Sample, you will have a choice between two prompts. One prompt will be a traditional essay, and one will be a creative essay. The organization of your ideas is very important for both these essays. The essay should be clear and coherent regardless of which prompt you choose. Two sample prompts are available below.

Argument Prompt

Write an argumentative essay. Take a side on the following question:

> Currently, what is the biggest issue we face as human beings and how should we go about solving it?

Creative Prompt

Write a creative essay that begins with the phrase below.

> The air inside had suddenly become chilly...

Quantitative Reasoning

Number Concepts and Operations

The Position of Numbers Relative to Each Other

Place Value of a Digit

Numbers count in groups of 10. This means that the number in the 10's place will remain the same throughout the set of natural and whole numbers. This is referred to as working within a base 10 numeration system. Only the numbers from zero to nine are used to represent any number. The foundation for doing this involves **place value**. Numbers are written side by side. This is to show the amount in each place value.

For place value, let's look at how the number 10 is different from the numbers zero to 9. Ten has two digits instead of just one. The one is in the tens' place, and the zero is in the ones' place. Therefore, there is one group of tens and zero ones. 11 has one 10 and one 1. Considering numbers from 11 to 19 should be the next step in understanding place value. Each value within this range of numbers consists of one group of 10 and a specific number of leftover ones. Counting by tens can be practiced once the tens column is understood. This process consists of increasing the number in the tens' place by one. For example, counting by 10 starting at 17 would result in the next four values being 27, 37, 47, and 57.

A place value chart can be used for understanding and learning about numbers that have more digits. Here is an example of a place value chart:

	MILLIONS			THOUSANDS			ONES			.	DECIMALS		
billions	hundred millions	ten millions	millions	hundred thousands	ten thousands	thousands	hundreds	tens	ones		tenths	hundredths	thousandths

In the number 1,234, there are 4 ones and 3 tens. The 2 is in the hundreds' place, and the one is in the thousands' place. Note that each group of three digits is separated by a comma. The 2 has a value that is 10 times greater than the 3. Every place to the left has a value 10 times greater than the place to its right. Also, each group of three digits is also known as a **period**. 234 is in the ones' period.

The number 1,234 can be written out as *one-thousand, two hundred thirty-four*. The process of writing out numbers is known as the **decimal system**. It is also based on groups of 10. The place value chart is a helpful tool in using this system. In order to write out a number, it always starts with the digit(s) in the highest period. For example, in the number 23,815,467, the 23 is in highest place and is in the millions'

22

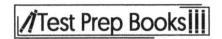

period. The number is read *twenty-three million, eight hundred fifteen thousand, four hundred sixty-seven*. Each period is written separately through the use of commas. Also, no "ands" are used within the number. Another way to think about the number 23,815,467 is through the use of an addition problem. For example,

$$23,815,467 = 20,000,000 + 3,000,000 + 800,000 + 10,000 + 5,000 + 400 + 60 + 7$$

This expression is known as **expanded form**. The actual number 23,815,467 is considered to be in **standard form**.

In order to compare whole numbers with many digits, place value can be used. In each number to be compared, it is necessary to find the highest place value in which the numbers differ and to compare the value within that place value. For example,

$$4,523,345 < 4,532,456$$

because of the values in the ten thousands' place. A similar process can be used for decimals. However, number lines can also be used. Tick marks can be placed between two whole numbers on the number line that represent tenths, hundredths, etc. Each number being compared can then be plotted. The value farthest to the right on the number line is the largest.

Classifying Real Numbers

The mathematical number system is made up of two general types of numbers: real and complex. **Real numbers** are both irrational and rational numbers, while **complex numbers** are those composed of both a real number and an imaginary one. Imaginary numbers are the result of taking the square root of -1, and $\sqrt{-1} = i$.

The real number system is often explained using a Venn diagram similar to the one below. After a number has been labeled as a real number, further classification occurs when considering the other groups in this diagram. If a number is a never-ending, non-repeating decimal, it falls in the **irrational** category. Otherwise, it is **rational**. Furthermore, if a number does not have a fractional part, it is classified as an **integer**, such as -2, 75, or 0. **Whole numbers** are an even smaller group that only includes positive integers and 0. The last group, **natural numbers**, is made up of only positive integers, such as 2, 56, or 12.

23

Integers are the whole numbers together with their negatives. They include numbers like 5, -24, 0, -6, and 15. They do not include fractions or numbers that have digits after the decimal point.

Rational numbers are all numbers that can be written as a fraction using integers. They are inclusive of integers, fractions, and decimals that terminate, or end (1.7, 0.04213) or repeat (0.136$\overline{5}$). A **fraction** is written as $\frac{x}{y}$ and represents the quotient of x being divided by y. More practically, it means dividing the whole into y equal parts, then taking x of those parts.

Examples of rational numbers include $\frac{1}{2}$ and $\frac{5}{4}$. The **numerator** is the number on the top of the fraction, while the **denominator** is the number on the bottom. Because every integer can be written as a fraction with a denominator of 1, (e.g., $\frac{3}{1} = 3$), every integer is also a rational number.

A **number line** typically consists of integers (...3, 2, 1, 0, -1, -2, -3...), and is used to visually represent the value of a rational number. Each rational number has a distinct position on the line determined by comparing its value with the displayed values on the line. For example, if plotting -1.5 on the number line below, it is necessary to recognize that the value of -1.5 is .5 less than -1 and .5 greater than -2. Therefore, -1.5 is plotted halfway between -1 and -2.

The number system that is used consists of only ten different digits or characters. However, this system is used to represent an infinite number of values. As mentioned, the **place value system** makes this infinite number of values possible. The position in which a digit is written corresponds to a given value. Starting from the decimal point (which is implied, if not physically present), each subsequent place value to the left represents a value greater than the one before it. Conversely, starting from the decimal point, each subsequent place value to the right represents a value less than the one before it.

In accordance with the **base-10 system**, the value of a digit increases by a factor of ten each place it moves to the left. For example, consider the number 7. Moving the digit one place to the left (70), increases its value by a factor of 10 ($7 \times 10 = 70$). Moving the digit two places to the left (700) increases its value by a factor of 10 twice ($7 \times 10 \times 10 = 700$). Moving the digit three places to the left (7,000) increases its value by a factor of 10 three times ($7 \times 10 \times 10 \times 10 = 7,000$), and so on.

Conversely, the value of a digit decreases by a factor of ten each place it moves to the right. (Note that multiplying by $\frac{1}{10}$ is equivalent to dividing by 10). For example, consider the number 40. Moving the digit one place to the right (4) decreases its value by a factor of 10 ($40 \div 10 = 4$). Moving the digit two places to the right (0.4), decreases its value by a factor of 10 twice ($40 \div 10 \div 10 = 0.4$) or:

$$40 \times \frac{1}{10} \times \frac{1}{10} = 0.4$$

Moving the digit three places to the right (0.04) decreases its value by a factor of 10 three times:

$$40 \div 10 \div 10 \div 10 = 0.04 \text{ or } 40 \times \frac{1}{10} \times \frac{1}{10} \times \frac{1}{10} = 0.04$$

24

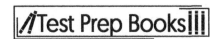

Prime and Composite Numbers

Whole numbers are classified as either prime or composite. A **prime number** can only be divided evenly by itself and one. For example, the number 11 can only be divided evenly by 11 and one; therefore, 11 is a prime number. A helpful way to visualize a prime number is to use concrete objects and try to divide them into equal piles. If dividing 11 coins, the only way to divide them into equal piles is to create 1 pile of 11 coins or to create 11 piles of 1 coin each. Other examples of prime numbers include 2, 3, 5, 7, 13, 17, and 19.

A **composite number** is any whole number that is not a prime number. A composite number is a number that can be divided evenly by one or more numbers other than itself and one. For example, the number 6 can be divided evenly by 2 and 3. Therefore, 6 is a composite number. If dividing 6 coins into equal piles, the possibilities are 1 pile of 6 coins, 2 piles of 3 coins, 3 piles of 2 coins, or 6 piles of 1 coin. Other examples of composite numbers include 4, 8, 9, 10, 12, 14, 15, 16, 18, and 20.

To determine if a number is a prime or composite number, the number is divided by every whole number greater than one and less than its own value. If it divides evenly by any of these numbers, then the number is composite. If it does not divide evenly by any of these numbers, then the number is prime. For example, 5 cannot be divided evenly by 2, 3, or 4. Therefore, 5 must be a prime number.

Ordering Numbers

A common question type asks to order rational numbers from least to greatest or greatest to least. The numbers will come in a variety of formats, including decimals, percentages, roots, fractions, and whole numbers. These questions test for knowledge of different types of numbers and the ability to determine their respective values.

Before discussing ordering all numbers, let's start with decimals.

To compare decimals and order them by their value, utilize a method similar to that of ordering large numbers.

The main difference is where the comparison will start. Assuming that any numbers to left of the decimal point are equal, the next numbers to be compared are those immediately to the right of the decimal point. If those are equal, then move on to compare the values in the next decimal place to the right.

For example,

Which number is greater, 12.35 or 12.38?

Check that the values to the left of the decimal point are equal:

$$12 = 12$$

Next, compare the values of the decimal place to the right of the decimal:

$$12.3 = 12.3$$

Those are also equal in value.

Finally, compare the value of the numbers in the next decimal place to the right on both numbers:

$$12.35 \text{ and } 12.38$$

Here the 5 is less than the 8, so the final way to express this inequality is:

$$12.35 < 12.38$$

Comparing decimals is regularly exemplified with money because the "cents" portion of money ends in the hundredths' place. When paying for gasoline or meals in restaurants, and even in bank accounts, if enough errors are made when calculating numbers to the hundredths place, they can add up to dollars and larger amounts of money over time.

Now that decimal ordering has been explained, let's expand and consider all real numbers. Whether the question asks to order the numbers from greatest to least or least to greatest, the crux of the question is the same—convert the numbers into a common format. Generally, it's easiest to write the numbers as whole numbers and decimals so they can be placed on a number line. Follow these examples to understand this strategy.

1) Order the following rational numbers from greatest to least:

$$\sqrt{36}, 0.65, 78\%, \frac{3}{4}, 7, 90\%, \frac{5}{2}$$

Of the seven numbers, the whole number (7) and decimal (0.65) are already in an accessible form, so concentrate on the other five.

First, the square root of 36 equals 6. (If the test asks for the root of a non-perfect root, determine which two whole numbers the root lies between.) Next, convert the percentages to decimals. A percentage means "per hundred," so this conversion requires moving the decimal point two places to the left, leaving 0.78 and 0.9.

Lastly, evaluate the fractions:

$$\frac{3}{4} = \frac{75}{100} = 0.75 \; ; \frac{5}{2} = 2\frac{1}{2} = 2.5$$

Now, the only step left is to list the numbers in the requested order:

$$7, \sqrt{36}, \frac{5}{2}, 90\%, 78\%, \frac{3}{4}, 0.65$$

2) Order the following rational numbers from least to greatest:

$$2.5, \sqrt{9}, \text{-}10.5, 0.853, 175\%, \sqrt{4}, \frac{4}{5}$$

$$\sqrt{9} = 3$$

$$175\% = 1.75$$

$$\sqrt{4} = 2$$

$$\frac{4}{5} = 0.8$$

26

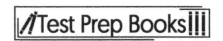

From least to greatest, the answer is:

$$-10.5, \frac{4}{5}, 0.853, 175\%, \sqrt{4}, 2.5, \sqrt{9}$$

When comparing or ordering numbers, the numbers should be written in the same format (decimal or fraction), if possible. For example, $\sqrt{49}$, 7.3, and $\frac{15}{2}$ are easier to order if each one is converted to a decimal, such as 7, 7.3, and 7.5 (converting fractions and decimals is covered in a subsequent section). A number line is used to order and compare the numbers. Any number that is to the right of another number is greater than that number. Conversely, a number positioned to the left of a given number is less than that number.

Basic Addition, Subtraction, Multiplication, and Division

Gaining more of something is related to addition, while taking something away relates to subtraction. Vocabulary words such as *total, more, less, left,* and *remain* are common when working with these problems. The $+$ sign means *plus.* This shows that addition is happening. The $-$ sign means *minus.* This shows that subtraction is happening. The symbols will be important when you write out equations.

Addition
Addition can also be defined in equation form. For example, $4 + 5 = 9$ shows that $4 + 5$ is the same as 9. Therefore, $9 = 9$, and "four plus five equals nine." When two quantities are being added together, the result is called the **sum**. Therefore, the sum of 4 and 5 is 9. The numbers being added, such as 4 and 5, are known as the **addends**.

Subtraction
Subtraction can also be in equation form. For example, $9 - 5 = 4$ shows that $9 - 5$ is the same as 4 and that "9 minus 5 is 4." The result of subtraction is known as a **difference.** The difference of $9 - 5$ is 4. 4 represents the amount that is left once the subtraction is done. The order in which subtraction is completed does matter. For example, $9 - 5$ and $5 - 9$ do not result in the same answer. $5 - 9$ results in a negative number. So, subtraction does not adhere to the commutative or associative property. The order in which subtraction is completed is important.

Multiplication
Multiplication is when we add equal amounts. The answer to a multiplication problem is called a **product**. Products stand for the total number of items within different groups. The symbol for multiplication is $\times$ or $\cdot$. We say 2×3 or $2 \cdot 3$ means "2 times 3."

As an example, there are three sets of four apples. The goal is to know how many apples there are in total. Three sets of four apples gives:

$$4 + 4 + 4 = 12$$

Also, three times four apples gives $3 \times 4 = 12$. Therefore, for any whole numbers a and b, where a is not equal to zero, $a \times b = b + b + \cdots b$, where b is added a times. Also, $a \times b$ can be thought of as the

27

number of units in a rectangular block consisting of a rows and b columns. For example, 3×7 is equal to the number of squares in the following rectangle:

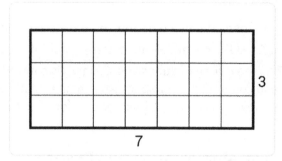

The answer is 21, and there are 21 squares in the rectangle.

When any number is multiplied by one (for example, $8 \times 1 = 8$), the value of original number does not change. Therefore, 1 is the **multiplicative identity**. For any whole number a, $1 \times a = a$. Also, any number multiplied by zero results in zero. Therefore, for any whole number a, $0 \times a = 0$.

Another method of multiplication can be done with the use of an **area model**. An area model is a rectangle that is divided into rows and columns that match up to the number of place values within each number. Take the example 29×65. These two numbers can be split into simpler numbers:

$$29 = 25 + 4 \text{ and } 65 = 60 + 5$$

The products of those 4 numbers are found within the rectangle and then summed up to get the answer. The entire process is:

$$(60 \times 25) + (5 \times 25) + (60 \times 4) + (5 \times 4)$$

$$1,500 + 240 + 125 + 20$$

$$1,885$$

Here is the actual area model:

	25	**4**
60	60x25 1,500	60x4 240
5	5x25 125	5x4 20

$$
\begin{array}{r}
1,500 \\
240 \\
125 \\
+\quad 20 \\
\hline
1,885
\end{array}
$$

28

Division

Division is based on dividing a given number into parts. The simplest problem involves dividing a number into equal parts. For example, if a pack of 20 pencils is to be divided among 10 children, you would have to divide 20 by 10. In this example, each child would receive 2 pencils.

The symbol for division is ÷ or /. The equation above is written as

$$20 \div 10 = 2, \text{ or } \frac{20}{10} = 2$$

This means "20 divided by 10 is equal to 2." Division can be explained as the following: for any whole numbers a and b, where b is not equal to zero, $a \div b = c$ if—and only if—$a = b \times c$. This means, division can be thought of as a multiplication problem with a missing part. For instance, calculating $20 \div 10$ is the same as asking the following: "If there are 20 items in total with 10 in each group, how many are in each group?" Therefore, 20 is equal to ten times what value? This question is the same as asking, "If there are 20 items in total with 2 in each group, how many groups are there?" The answer to each question is 2.

In a division problem, a is known as the **dividend**, b is the **divisor**, and c is the **quotient**. Zero cannot be divided into parts. Therefore, for any nonzero whole number a, $0 \div a = 0$. Also, division by zero is undefined. Dividing an amount into zero parts is not possible.

More difficult division problems involve dividing a number into equal parts, but having some left over. An example is dividing a pack of 20 pencils among 8 friends so that each friend receives the same number of pencils. In this setting, each friend receives 2 pencils, but there are 4 pencils leftover. 20 is the dividend, 8 is the divisor, 2 is the quotient, and 4 is known as the **remainder**. Within this type of division problem, for whole numbers a, b, c, and d, $a \div b = c$ with a remainder of d.

This is true if and only if:

$$a = (b \times c) + d$$

When calculating $a \div b$, if there is no remainder, a is said to be *divisible* by b. **Even numbers** are all divisible by the number 2. **Odd numbers** are not divisible by 2. An odd number of items cannot be paired up into groups of 2 without having one item leftover.

Dividing a number by a single digit or two digits can be turned into repeated subtraction problems. An area model can be used throughout the problem that represents multiples of the divisor. For example, the answer to $8,580 \div 55$ can be found by subtracting 55 from 8580 one at a time and counting the total number of subtractions necessary.

However, a simpler process involves using larger multiples of 55. First, $100 \times 55 = 5,500$ is subtracted from 8,580, and 3,080 is leftover. Next, $50 \times 55 = 2,750$ is subtracted from 3,080 to obtain 380. $5 \times 55 = 275$ is subtracted from 330 to obtain 55, and finally: $1 \times 55 = 55$ is subtracted from 55 to obtain zero. Therefore, there is no remainder, and the answer is:

$$100 + 50 + 5 + 1 = 156$$

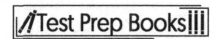

Here is a picture of the area model and the repeated subtraction process:

$$8580 \div 55$$

	55
100	5500
50	2750
5	275
1	55

```
      55 | 8580
           -5500   (100 x 55)
            3080
           -2750   (50 x 55)
             330
            -275   (5 x 55)
              55
             -55   (1 x 55)
               0
```

If you want to check the answer of a division problem, multiply the answer by the divisor. This will help you check to see if the dividend is obtained. If there is a remainder, the same process is done, but the remainder is added on at the end to try to match the dividend. In the previous example, $156 \times 55 = 8,580$ would be the checking procedure. Dividing decimals involves the same repeated subtraction process. The only difference would be that the subtractions would involve numbers that include values in the decimal places. Lining up decimal places is crucial in this type of problem.

Using Operations in Math and Real-World Problems

Addition and subtraction are "inverse operations." Adding a number and then subtracting the same number will cancel each other out. This results in the original number, and vice versa. For example,

$$8 + 7 - 7 = 8$$

and

$$137 - 100 + 100 = 137$$

Multiplication and division are also **inverse operations**. So, multiplying by a number and then dividing by the same number results in the original number. For example,

$$8 \times 2 \div 2 = 8 \text{ and } 12 \div 4 \times 4 = 12$$

Inverse operations are used to work backwards to solve problems. In the case that 7 and a number add to 18, the inverse operation of subtraction is used to find the unknown value:

$$18 - 7 = 11$$

If a school's entire 4th grade was divided evenly into 3 classes each with 22 students, the inverse operation of multiplication is used to determine the total students in the grade:

$$22 \times 3 = 66$$

More scenarios involving inverse operations are listed in the tables below.

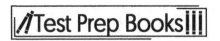

Word problems take concepts that are learned in the classroom and turn them into real-life situations. Some parts of the problem are known and at least one part is unknown. There are three types of instances in which something can be unknown: the starting point, the change, or the final result. These can all be missing from the information that is given.

For an addition problem, the change is the quantity of a new amount added to the starting point.

For a subtraction problem, the change is the quantity taken away from the starting point.

Regarding addition, the given equation is $3 + 7 = 10$.

The number 3 is the starting point. 7 is the change, and 10 is the result from adding a new amount to the starting point. Different word problems can arise from this same equation, depending on which value is the unknown. For example, here are three problems:

- If a boy had 3 pencils and was given 7 more, how many would he have in total?

- If a boy had 3 pencils and a girl gave him more so that he had 10 in total, how did she give to him?

- A boy was given 7 pencils so that he had 10 in total. How many did he start with?

All three problems involve the same equation. Finding out which part of the equation is missing is the key to solving each word problem. The missing answers would be 10, 7, and 3, respectively.

In terms of subtraction, the same three scenarios can occur. Imagine the given equation is $6 - 4 = 2$.

The number 6 is the starting point, 4 is the change, and 2 is the new amount that is the result from taking away an amount from the starting point. Again, different types of word problems can arise from this equation. For example, here are three possible problems:

- If a girl had 6 quarters and 2 were taken away, how many would be left over?
- If a girl had 6 quarters, purchased a pencil, and had 2 quarters left over, how many did she pay with?
- If a girl paid for a pencil with 4 quarters and had 2 quarters left over, how many did she start with?

The three question types follow the structure of the addition word problems. Finding out whether the starting point, the change, or the final result is missing is the goal in solving the problem. The missing answers would be 2, 4, and 6, respectively.

The three addition problems and the three subtraction word problems can be solved by using a picture, a number line, or an algebraic equation. If an equation is used, a question mark can be used to show the number we don't know. For example, $6 - 4 = ?$ can be written to show that the missing value is the result. Using equation form shows us what part of the addition or subtraction problem is missing.

Key words within a multiplication problem involve *times, product, doubled,* and *tripled.* Key words within a division problem involve *split, quotient, divided, shared, groups,* and *half.* Like addition and subtraction, multiplication and division problems also have three different types of missing values.

Multiplication consists of a certain number of groups, with the same number of items within each group, and the total amount within all groups. Therefore, each one of these amounts can be the missing value.

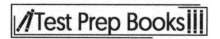

For example, the given equation is $5 \times 3 = 15$.

5 and 3 are interchangeable, so either amount can be the number of groups or the number of items within each group. 15 is the total number of items. Again, different types of word problems can arise from this equation. For example, here are three problems:

- If a classroom is serving 5 different types of apples for lunch and has 3 apples of each type, how many total apples are there to give to the students?

- If a classroom has 15 apples with 5 different types, how many of each type are there?

- If a classroom has 15 apples total with 3 of each type, how many types are there to choose from?

Each question involves using the same equation to solve. It is important to decide which part of the equation is the missing value. The answers to the problems are 15, 3, and 5, respectively.

Similar to multiplication, division problems involve a total amount, a number of groups having the same amount, and a number of items within each group. The difference between multiplication and division is that the starting point in a division problem is the total amount. This then gets divided into equal amounts.

For example, the equation is $48 \div 8 = 6$.

48 is the total number of items, which is being divided into 8 different groups. In order to do so, 6 items go into each group. Also, 8 and 6 are interchangeable. So, the 48 items could be divided into 6 groups of 8 items each. Therefore, different types of word problems can arise from this equation. For example, here are three types of problems:

- A boy needs 48 pieces of chalk. If there are 8 pieces in each box, how many boxes should he buy?

- A boy has 48 pieces of chalk. If each box has 6 pieces in it, how many boxes did he buy?

- A boy has partitioned all of his chalk into 8 piles, with 6 pieces in each pile. How many pieces does he have in total?

Each one of these questions involves the same equation. The third question can easily utilize the multiplication equation $8 \times 6 = ?$ instead of division. The answers are 6, 8, and 48.

Order of Operations
When reviewing calculations consisting of more than one operation, the order in which the operations are performed affects the resulting answer. Consider $5 \times 2 + 7$. Performing multiplication then addition results in an answer of 17 because:

$$5 \times 2 = 10; 10 + 7 = 17$$

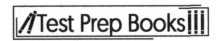

However, if the problem is written $5 \times (2 + 7)$, the order of operations dictates that the operation inside the parentheses must be performed first. The resulting answer is 45 because:

$$2 + 7 = 9, \text{then } 5 \times 9 = 45$$

The order in which operations should be performed is remembered using the acronym PEMDAS. PEMDAS stands for parentheses, exponents, multiplication/division, addition/subtraction. Multiplication and division are performed in the same step, working from left to right with whichever comes first. Addition and subtraction are performed in the same step, working from left to right with whichever comes first.

Consider the following example:

$$8 \div 4 + 8(7 - 7)$$

Performing the operation inside the parentheses produces:

$$8 \div 4 + 8(0) \text{ or } 8 \div 4 + 8 \times 0$$

There are no exponents, so multiplication and division are performed next from left to right resulting in:

$$2 + 8 \times 0, \text{then } 2 + 0$$

Finally, addition and subtraction are performed to obtain an answer of 2. Now consider the following example:

$$6 \times 3 + 3^2 - 6$$

Parentheses are not applicable. Exponents are evaluated first, which brings us to:

$$6 \times 3 + 9 - 6$$

Then multiplication/division forms:

$$18 + 9 - 6$$

At last, addition/subtraction leads to the final answer of 21.

Properties of Operations

Properties of operations exist that make calculations easier and solve problems for missing values. The following table summarizes commonly used properties of real numbers.

Property	Addition	Multiplication
Commutative	$a + b = b + a$	$a \times b = b \times a$
Associative	$(a + b) + c = a + (b + c)$	$(a \times b) \times c = a \times (b \times c)$
Identity	$a + 0 = a; \; 0 + a = a$	$a \times 1 = a; \; 1 \times a = a$
Inverse	$a + (-a) = 0$	$a \times \dfrac{1}{a} = 1; \; a \neq 0$
Distributive	$a(b + c) = ab + ac$	

The **commutative property of addition** states that the order in which numbers are added does not change the sum. Similarly, the **commutative property of multiplication** states that the order in which

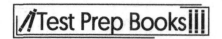

numbers are multiplied does not change the product. The **associative property** of addition and multiplication state that the grouping of numbers being added or multiplied does not change the sum or product, respectively. The commutative and associative properties are useful for performing calculations. For example, $(47 + 25) + 3$ is equivalent to $(47 + 3) + 25$, which is easier to calculate.

The **identity property of addition** states that adding zero to any number does not change its value. The **identity property of multiplication** states that multiplying a number by 1 does not change its value. The **inverse property of addition** states that the sum of a number and its opposite equals zero. Opposites are numbers that are the same with different signs (ex. 5 and -5; $-\frac{1}{2}$ and $\frac{1}{2}$). The **inverse property of multiplication** states that the product of a number (other than 0) and its reciprocal equals 1. **Reciprocal numbers** have numerators and denominators that are inverted (ex. $\frac{2}{5}$ and $\frac{5}{2}$). Inverse properties are useful for canceling quantities to find missing values (see algebra content). For example, $a + 7 = 12$ is solved by adding the inverse of 7 (which is -7) to both sides in order to isolate a.

The **distributive property** states that multiplying a sum (or difference) by a number produces the same result as multiplying each value in the sum (or difference) by the number and adding (or subtracting) the products. Consider the following scenario: You are buying three tickets for a baseball game. Each ticket costs $18. You are also charged a fee of $2 per ticket for purchasing the tickets online.

The cost is calculated:
$$3 \times 18 + 3 \times 2$$

Using the distributive property, the cost can also be calculated $3(18 + 2)$.

Adding and Subtracting Positive and Negative Numbers

Some problems require adding positive and negative numbers or subtracting positive and negative numbers. Adding a negative number to a positive one can be thought of a reducing or subtracting from the positive number, and the result should be less than the original positive number. For example, adding 8 and -3 is the same is subtracting 3 from 8; the result is 5. This can be visualized by imagining that the positive number (8) represents 8 apples that a student has in her basket. The negative number (-3) indicates the number of apples she is in debt or owes to her friend.

In order to pay off her debt and "settle the score," she essentially is in possession of three fewer apples than in her basket $(8 - 3 = 5)$, so she actually has five apples that are hers to keep. Should the negative addend be of higher magnitude than the positive addend (for example $-9 + 3$), the result will be negative, but "less negative" or closer to zero than the large negative number. This is because adding a positive value, even if relatively smaller, to a negative value, reduces the magnitude of the negative in the total. Considering the apple example again, if the girl owed 9 apples to her friend (-9) but she picked 3 $(+3)$ off a tree and gave them to her friend, she now would only owe him six apples (-6), which reduced her debt burden (her negative number of apples) by three.

Subtracting positive and negative numbers works the same way with one key distinction: subtracting a negative number from a negative number yields a "less negative" or more positive result because again, this can be considered as removing or alleviating some debt. For example, if the student with the apples owed 5 apples to her friend, she essentially has -5 apples. If her mom gives that friend 10 apples on behalf of the girl, she now has removed the need to pay back the 5 apples and surpassed neutral (no net apples owed) and now her friend owes *her* five apples $(+5)$.

34

Stated mathematically: $-5 - (-10) = +5$

When subtracting integers and negative rational numbers, one has to change the problem to adding the opposite and then apply the rules of addition.

Subtracting two positive numbers is the same as adding one positive and one negative number.

> For example, $4.9 - 7.1$ is the same as $4.9 + (-7.1)$. The solution is -2.2 since the absolute value of -7.1 is greater than 4.9. Another example is $8.5 - 6.4$ which is the same as $8.5 + (-6.4)$. The solution is 2.1 since the absolute value of 8.5 is greater than 6.4.

- Subtracting a positive number from a negative number results in negative value.

> For example, $(-12) - 7$ is the same as $(-12) + (-7)$ with a solution of -19.

- Subtracting a negative number from a positive number results in a positive value.

> For example, $12 - (-7)$ is the same as $12 + 7$ with a solution of 19.

- For multiplication and division of integers and rational numbers, if both numbers are positive or both numbers are negative, the result is a positive value.

> For example, $(-1.7) \times (-4)$ has a solution of 6.8 since both numbers are negative values.

If one number is positive and another number is negative, the result is a negative value.

- For example, $(-15) \div 5$ has a solution of -3 since there is one negative number.

Adding one positive and one negative number requires taking the absolute values and finding the difference between them. Then, the sign of the number that has the higher absolute value for the final solution is used.

Operations with Fractions, Decimals, and Percentages

Fractions

A **fraction** is a part of something that is whole. Items such as apples can be cut into parts to help visualize fractions. If an apple is cut into 2 equal parts, each part represents $\frac{1}{2}$ of the apple. If each half is then cut into two parts, the apple now is cut into quarters. Each piece now represents $\frac{1}{4}$ of the apple. In this example, each part is equal because they all have the same size. Geometric shapes, such as circles and squares, can also be utilized to help visualize the idea of fractions. For example, a circle can be drawn on the board and divided into 6 equal parts:

35

Shading can be used to represent parts of the circle that can be translated into fractions. The top of the fraction, the **numerator,** can represent how many segments are shaded. The bottom of the fraction, the **denominator,** can represent the number of segments that the circle is broken into. A pie is a good analogy to use in this example. If one piece of the circle is shaded, or one piece of pie is cut out, $1/_6$ of the object is being referred to. An apple, a pie, or a circle can be utilized in order to compare simple fractions. For example, showing that $\frac{1}{2}$ is larger than $\frac{1}{4}$ and that $\frac{1}{4}$ is smaller than $\frac{1}{3}$ can be accomplished through shading. A **unit fraction** is a fraction in which the numerator is 1, and the denominator is a positive whole number. It represents one part of a whole—one piece of pie.

Imagine that an apple pie has been baked for a holiday party, and the full pie has eight slices. After the party, there are five slices left. How could the amount of the pie that remains be expressed as a fraction? The numerator is 5 since there are 5 pieces left, and the denominator is 8 since there were eight total slices in the whole pie. Thus, expressed as a fraction, the leftover pie totals $\frac{5}{8}$ of the original amount.

Fractions come in three different varieties: proper fractions, improper fractions, and mixed numbers. **Proper fractions** have a numerator less than the denominator, such as $\frac{3}{8}$, but **improper fractions** have a numerator greater than the denominator, such as $\frac{7}{2}$. **Mixed numbers** combine a whole number with a proper fraction, such as $3\frac{1}{2}$. Any mixed number can be written as an improper fraction by multiplying the integer by the denominator, adding the product to the value of the numerator, and dividing the sum by the original denominator. For example:

$$3\frac{1}{2} = \frac{3 \times 2 + 1}{2} = \frac{7}{2}$$

Whole numbers can also be converted into fractions by placing the whole number as the numerator and making the denominator 1. For example, $3 = \frac{3}{1}$.

The bar in a fraction represents division. Therefore $^6/_5$ is the same as $6 \div 5$. In order to rewrite it as a mixed number, division is performed to obtain:

$$6 \div 5 = 1\,\text{R}\,1$$

The remainder is then converted into fraction form. The actual remainder becomes the numerator of a fraction, and the divisor becomes the denominator. Therefore, 1 R 1 is written as $1\frac{1}{5}$, a mixed number. A mixed number can also decompose into the addition of a whole number and a fraction. For example,

$$1\frac{1}{5} = 1 + \frac{1}{5} \text{ and } 4\frac{5}{6} = 4 + \frac{1}{6} + \frac{1}{6} + \frac{1}{6} + \frac{1}{6} + \frac{1}{6}$$

Every fraction can be built from a combination of unit fractions.

One of the most fundamental concepts of fractions is their ability to be manipulated by multiplication or division. This is possible since $\frac{n}{n} = 1$ for any non-zero integer. As a result, multiplying or dividing by $\frac{n}{n}$ will not alter the original fraction since any number multiplied or divided by 1 doesn't change the value of that number. Fractions of the same value are known as equivalent fractions. For example, $\frac{2}{8}$, $\frac{25}{100}$, and $\frac{40}{160}$ are equivalent, as they are all equal to $\frac{1}{4}$.

Like fractions, or **equivalent fractions**, are the terms used to describe these fractions that are made up of different numbers but represent the same quantity. For example, the given fractions are $\frac{4}{8}$ and $\frac{3}{6}$. If a pie was cut into 8 pieces and 4 pieces were removed, half of the pie would remain. Also, if a pie was split into 6 pieces and 3 pieces were eaten, half of the pie would also remain. Therefore, both of the fractions represent half of a pie. These two fractions are referred to as like fractions. **Unlike fractions** are fractions that are different and do not represent equal quantities. When working with fractions in mathematical expressions, like fractions should be simplified. Both $\frac{4}{8}$ and $\frac{3}{6}$ can be simplified into $\frac{1}{2}$.

Comparing fractions can be completed through the use of a number line. For example, if $\frac{3}{5}$ and $\frac{6}{10}$ need to be compared, each fraction should be plotted on a number line. To plot $\frac{3}{5}$, the area from 0 to 1 should be broken into 5 equal segments, and the fraction represents 3 of them. To plot $\frac{6}{10}$, the area from 0 to 1 should be broken into 10 equal segments, and the fraction represents 6 of them.

It can be seen that $\frac{3}{5} = \frac{6}{10}$

Like fractions are plotted at the same point on a number line. Unit fractions can also be used to compare fractions. For example, if it is known that:

$$\frac{4}{5} > \frac{1}{2}$$

and

$$\frac{1}{2} > \frac{4}{10}$$

It is also known that:

$$\frac{4}{5} > \frac{4}{10}$$

37

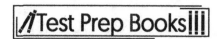

Also, converting improper fractions to mixed numbers can be helpful in comparing fractions because the whole number portion of the number is more visible.

Adding and subtracting mixed numbers and fractions can be completed by decomposing fractions into a sum of whole numbers and unit fractions. For example, the given problem is:

$$5\frac{3}{7} + 2\frac{1}{7}$$

Decomposing into:

$$5 + \frac{1}{7} + \frac{1}{7} + \frac{1}{7} + 2 + \frac{1}{7}$$

This shows that the whole numbers can be added separately from the unit fractions. The answer is:

$$5 + 2 + \frac{1}{7} + \frac{1}{7} + \frac{1}{7} + \frac{1}{7}$$

$$7 + \frac{4}{7}$$

$$7\frac{4}{7}$$

Although many equivalent fractions exist, they are easier to compare and interpret when reduced or simplified. The numerator and denominator of a simple fraction will have no factors in common other than 1. When reducing or simplifying fractions, divide the numerator and denominator by the greatest common factor. A simple strategy is to divide the numerator and denominator by low numbers, like 2, 3, or 5 until arriving at a simple fraction, but the same thing could be achieved by determining the greatest common factor for both the numerator and denominator and dividing each by it. Using the first method is preferable when both the numerator and denominator are even, end in 5, or are obviously a multiple of another number. However, if no numbers seem to work, it will be necessary to factor the numerator and denominator to find the GCF. For example:

1) Simplify the fraction $\frac{6}{8}$:

Dividing the numerator and denominator by 2 results in $\frac{3}{4}$, which is a simple fraction.

2) Simplify the fraction $\frac{12}{36}$:

Dividing the numerator and denominator by 2 leaves $\frac{6}{18}$. This isn't a simple fraction, as both the numerator and denominator have factors in common. Dividing each by 3 results in $\frac{2}{6}$, but this can be further simplified by dividing by 2 to get $\frac{1}{3}$. This is the simplest fraction, as the numerator is 1. In cases like this, multiple division operations can be avoided by determining the greatest common factor (12, in this case) between the numerator and denominator.

3) Simplify the fraction $\frac{18}{54}$ by dividing by the greatest common factor:

First, determine the factors for the numerator and denominator. The factors of 18 are 1, 2, 3, 6, 9, and 18. The factors of 54 are 1, 2, 3, 6, 9, 18, 27, and 54. Thus, the greatest common factor is 18. Dividing $\frac{18}{54}$ by 18 leaves $\frac{1}{3}$, which is the simplest fraction. This method takes slightly more work, but it definitively arrives at the simplest fraction.

Adding and Subtracting Fractions

Adding and subtracting fractions that have the same denominators involves adding or subtracting the numerators. The denominator will stay the same. Therefore, the decomposition process can be made simpler, and the fractions do not have to be broken into unit fractions.

For example, the given problem is:

$$4\frac{7}{8} - 2\frac{6}{8}$$

The answer is found by adding the answers to both:

$$4 - 2 \text{ and } \frac{7}{8} - \frac{6}{8}$$

$$2 + \frac{1}{8} = 2\frac{1}{8}$$

A common mistake would be to add the denominators so that:

$$\frac{1}{4} + \frac{1}{4} = \frac{1}{8}$$

or to add numerators and denominators so that:

$$\frac{1}{4} + \frac{1}{4} = \frac{2}{8}$$

However, conceptually, it is known that two quarters make a half, so neither one of these are correct.

If two fractions have different denominators, equivalent fractions must be used to add or subtract them. The fractions must be converted into fractions that have common denominators. A **least common denominator** or the product of the two denominators can be used as the common denominator. For example, in the problem $\frac{5}{6} + \frac{2}{3}$, either 6, which is the least common denominator, or 18, which is the product of the denominators, can be used. In order to use 6, $\frac{2}{3}$ must be converted to sixths. A number line can be used to show the equivalent fraction is $\frac{4}{6}$. What happens is that $\frac{2}{3}$ is multiplied by a fractional form of 1 to obtain a denominator of 6. Hence,

$$\frac{2}{3} \times \frac{2}{2} = \frac{4}{6}$$

Therefore, the problem is now $\frac{5}{6} + \frac{4}{6} = \frac{9}{6}$, which can be simplified into $\frac{3}{2}$. In order to use 18, both fractions must be converted into having 18 as their denominator. $\frac{5}{6}$ would have to be multiplied by $\frac{3}{3}$,

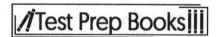

and $\frac{2}{3}$ would need to be multiplied by $\frac{6}{6}$. The addition problem would be $\frac{15}{18} + \frac{12}{18} = \frac{27}{18}$, which reduces into $\frac{3}{2}$.

It is always possible to find a common denominator by multiplying the denominators. However, when the denominators are large numbers, this method is unwieldy, especially if the answer must be provided in its simplest form. Thus, it's beneficial to find the **least common denominator** of the fractions—the least common denominator is incidentally also the **least common multiple**.

Once equivalent fractions have been found with common denominators, simply add or subtract the numerators to arrive at the answer:

$$1) \frac{1}{2} + \frac{3}{4} = \frac{2}{4} + \frac{3}{4} = \frac{5}{4}$$

$$2) \frac{3}{12} + \frac{11}{20} = \frac{15}{60} + \frac{33}{60} = \frac{48}{60} = \frac{4}{5}$$

$$3) \frac{7}{9} - \frac{4}{15} = \frac{35}{45} - \frac{12}{45} = \frac{23}{45}$$

$$4) \frac{5}{6} - \frac{7}{18} = \frac{15}{18} - \frac{7}{18} = \frac{8}{18} = \frac{4}{9}$$

Multiplying and Dividing Fractions

Of the four basic operations that can be performed on fractions, the one that involves the least amount of work is multiplication. To multiply two fractions, simply multiply the numerators together, multiply the denominators together, and place the products of each as a fraction. Whole numbers and mixed numbers can also be expressed as a fraction, as described above, to multiply with a fraction.

Because multiplication is commutative, multiplying a fraction by a whole number is the same as multiplying a whole number by a fraction. The problem involves adding a fraction a specific number of times. The problem $3 \times \frac{1}{4}$ can be translated into adding the unit fraction three times:

$$\frac{1}{4} + \frac{1}{4} + \frac{1}{4} = \frac{3}{4}$$

In the problem $4 \times \frac{2}{5}$, the fraction can be decomposed into $\frac{1}{5} + \frac{1}{5}$ and then added four times to obtain $\frac{8}{5}$. Also, both of these answers can be found by just multiplying the whole number by the numerator of the fraction being multiplied.

The whole numbers can be written in fraction form as:

$$\frac{3}{1} \times \frac{1}{4} = \frac{3}{4}$$

$$\frac{4}{1} \times \frac{2}{5} = \frac{8}{5}$$

Multiplying a fraction times a fraction involves multiplying the numerators together separately and the denominators together separately. For example:

$$\frac{3}{8} \times \frac{2}{3} = \frac{3 \times 2}{8 \times 3} = \frac{6}{24}$$

This can then be reduced to $\frac{1}{4}$.

Dividing a fraction by a fraction is actually a multiplication problem. It involves flipping the divisor and then multiplying normally. For example:

$$\frac{22}{5} \div \frac{1}{2} = \frac{22}{5} \times \frac{2}{1} = \frac{44}{5}$$

The same procedure can be implemented for division problems involving fractions and whole numbers. The whole number can be rewritten as a fraction over a denominator of 1, and then division can be completed.

A common denominator approach can also be used in dividing fractions. Considering the same problem $\frac{22}{5} \div \frac{1}{2}$ a common denominator between the two fractions is 10. $\frac{22}{5}$ would be rewritten as $\frac{22}{5} \times \frac{2}{2} = \frac{44}{10}$ and $\frac{1}{2}$ would be rewritten as:

$$\frac{1}{2} \times \frac{5}{5} = \frac{5}{10}$$

Dividing both numbers straight across results in:

$$\frac{44}{10} \div \frac{5}{10} = \frac{44/5}{10/10} = \frac{44/5}{1} = 44/5$$

Many real-world problems will involve the use of fractions. Key words include actual fraction values, such as *half, quarter, third, fourth*, etc. The best approach to solving word problems involving fractions is to draw a picture or diagram that represents the scenario being discussed, while deciding which type of operation is necessary in order to solve the problem. A phrase such as "one fourth of 60 pounds of coal" creates a scenario in which multiplication should be used, and the mathematical form of the phrase is $\frac{1}{4} \times 60$.

Decimals

The **decimal system** is a way of writing out numbers that uses ten different numerals: 0, 1, 2, 3, 4, 5, 6, 7, 8, and 9. This is also called a "base ten" or "base 10" system. Other bases are also used. For example, computers work with a base of 2. This means they only use the numerals 0 and 1.

The **decimal place** denotes how far to the right of the decimal point a numeral is. The first digit to the right of the decimal point is in the **tenths'** place. The next is the **hundredths'** place. The third is the **thousandths'** place.

So, 3.142 has a 1 in the tenths place, a 4 in the hundredths place, and a 2 in the thousandths place.

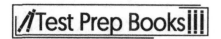
The **decimal point** is a period used to separate the **ones'** place from the **tenths'** place when writing out a number as a decimal.

A **decimal number** is a number written out with a decimal point instead of as a fraction, for example, 1.25 instead of $\frac{5}{4}$. Depending on the situation, it may be easier to work with fractions, while other times, it may be easier to work with decimal numbers.

A decimal number is **terminating** if it stops at some point. It is called **repeating** if it never stops but repeats over and over. It is important to note that every rational number can be written as a terminating decimal or as a repeating decimal.

Addition with Decimals

To add decimal numbers, each number needs to be lined up by the decimal point in vertical columns. For each number being added, the zeros to the right of the last number need to be filled in so that each of the numbers has the same number of places to the right of the decimal. Then, the columns can be added together. Here is an example of $2.45 + 1.3 + 8.891$ written in column form:

$$
\begin{array}{r}
2.450 \\
1.300 \\
+\ 8.891 \\
\end{array}
$$

Zeros have been added in the columns so that each number has the same number of places to the right of the decimal.

Added together, the correct answer is 12.641:

$$
\begin{array}{r}
2.450 \\
1.300 \\
+\ 8.891 \\
\hline
12.641 \\
\end{array}
$$

Subtraction with Decimals

Subtracting decimal numbers is the same process as adding decimals. Here is $7.89 - 4.235$ written in column form:

$$
\begin{array}{r}
7.890 \\
-\ 4.235 \\
\hline
3.655 \\
\end{array}
$$

A zero has been added in the column so that each number has the same number of places to the right of the decimal.

Multiplication with Decimals

The simplest way to multiply decimals is to calculate the product as if the decimals are not there, then count the number of decimal places in the original problem. Use that total to place the decimal the same number of places over in your answer, counting from right to left. For example, 0.5×1.25 can be rewritten and multiplied as 5×125, which equals 625. Then the decimal is added three places from the right for .625.

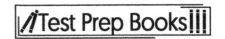

The final answer will have the same number of decimal places as the total number of decimal places in the problem. The first number has one decimal place, and the second number has two decimal places. Therefore, the final answer will contain three decimal places:

$$0.5 \times 1.25 = 0.625$$

Division with Decimals
Dividing a decimal by a whole number entails using long division first by ignoring the decimal point. Then, the decimal point is moved the number of places given in the problem.

For example, $6.8 \div 4$ can be rewritten as $68 \div 4$, which is 17. There is one non-zero integer to the right of the decimal point, so the final solution would have one decimal place to the right of the solution. In this case, the solution is 1.7.

Dividing a decimal by another decimal requires changing the divisor to a whole number by moving its decimal point. The decimal place of the dividend should be moved by the same number of places as the divisor. Then, the problem is the same as dividing a decimal by a whole number.

For example, $5.72 \div 1.1$ has a divisor with one decimal point in the denominator. The expression can be rewritten as $57.2 \div 11$ by moving each number one decimal place to the right to eliminate the decimal. The long division can be completed as $572 \div 11$ with a result of 52. Since there is one non-zero integer to the right of the decimal point in the problem, the final solution is 5.2.

In another example, $8 \div 0.16$ has a divisor with two decimal points in the denominator. The expression can be rewritten as $800 \div 16$ by moving each number two decimal places to the right to eliminate the decimal in the divisor. The long division can be completed with a result of 50.

Percentages
Think of percentages as fractions with a denominator of 100. In fact, **percentage** means "per hundred." Problems often require converting numbers from percentages, fractions, and decimals.

The basic percent equation is the following:

$$\frac{is}{of} = \frac{\%}{100}$$

The placement of numbers in the equation depends on what the question asks.

Example 1
Find 40% of 80.

Basically, the problem is asking, "What is 40% of 80?" The 40% is the percent, and 80 is the number to find the percent "of." The equation is:

$$\frac{x}{80} = \frac{40}{100}$$

After cross-multiplying, the problem becomes $100x = 80(40)$. Solving for x produces the answer:

$$x = 32$$

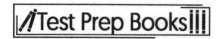

Example 2
What percent of 90 is 20?

The 20 fills in the "is" portion, while 90 fills in the "of." The question asks for the percent, so that will be x, the unknown. The following equation is set up:

$$\frac{20}{90} = \frac{x}{100}$$

Cross-multiplying yields the equation $90x = 20(100)$. Solving for x gives the answer of 22.2%.

Example 3
30% of what number is 30?

The following equation uses the clues and numbers in the problem:

$$\frac{30}{x} = \frac{30}{100}$$

Cross-multiplying results in the equation $30(100) = 30x$. Solving for x gives the answer $x = 100$.

Conversions
Decimals and Percentages
Since a percentage is based on "per hundred," decimals and percentages can be converted by multiplying or dividing by 100. Practically speaking, this always involves moving the decimal point two places to the right or left, depending on the conversion. To convert a percentage to a decimal, move the decimal point two places to the left and remove the % sign. To convert a decimal to a percentage, move the decimal point two places to the right and add a % sign. Here are some examples:

$65\% = 0.65$
$0.33 = 33\%$
$0.215 = 21.5\%$
$99.99\% = 0.9999$
$500\% = 5.00$
$7.55 = 755\%$

Fractions and Percentages
Remember that a percentage is a number per one hundred. So, a percentage can be converted to a fraction by making the number in the percentage the numerator and putting 100 as the denominator:

$$43\% = \frac{43}{100}$$

$$97\% = \frac{97}{100}$$

Note that the percent symbol (%) kind of looks like a 0, a 1, and another 0. So, think of a percentage like 54% as 54 over 100.

44

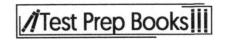

To convert a fraction to a percent, follow the same logic. If the fraction happens to have 100 in the denominator, you're in luck. Just take the numerator and add a percent symbol:

$$\frac{28}{100} = 28\%$$

Otherwise, divide the numerator by the denominator to get a decimal:

$$\frac{9}{12} = 0.75$$

Then convert the decimal to a percentage:

$$0.75 = 75\%$$

Another option is to make the denominator equal to 100. Be sure to multiply the numerator and the denominator by the same number. For example:

$$\frac{3}{20} \times \frac{5}{5} = \frac{15}{100}$$

$$\frac{15}{100} = 15\%$$

Changing Fractions to Decimals
To change a fraction into a decimal, divide the denominator into the numerator until there are no remainders. There may be repeating decimals, so rounding is often acceptable. A straight line above the repeating portion denotes that the decimal repeats.

Example: Express $\frac{4}{5}$ as a decimal.

Set up the division problem.

$$5\overline{)4}$$

5 does not go into 4, so place the decimal and add a zero.

$$5\overline{)4.0}$$

5 goes into 40 eight times. There is no remainder.

$$\begin{array}{r} 0.8 \\ 5\overline{)4.0} \\ -4.0 \\ \hline 0 \end{array}$$

The solution is 0.8.

Example: Express $33\frac{1}{3}$ as a decimal.

Since the whole portion of the number is known, set it aside to calculate the decimal from the fraction portion.

45

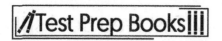

Set up the division problem.

$$3\overline{)1}$$

3 does not go into 1, so place the decimal and add zeros. 3 goes into 10 three times.

$$\begin{array}{r} 0.3 \\ 3\overline{)1.0} \end{array}$$

This will repeat with a remainder of 1.

$$\begin{array}{r} 0.333 \\ 3\overline{)1.000} \\ -9 \\ \hline 10 \\ -9 \\ \hline 10 \end{array}$$

So, we will place a line over the 3 to denote the repetition. The solution is written $0.\overline{3}$.

Changing Decimals to Fractions

To change decimals to fractions, place the decimal portion of the number—the numerator—over the respective place value—the denominator—then reduce, if possible.

Example: Express 0.25 as a fraction.

This is read as twenty-five hundredths, so put 25 over 100. Then reduce to find the solution.

$$\frac{25}{100} = \frac{1}{4}$$

Example: Express 0.455 as a fraction

This is read as four hundred fifty-five thousandths, so put 455 over 1,000. Then reduce to find the solution.

$$\frac{455}{1,000} = \frac{91}{200}$$

There are two types of problems that commonly involve percentages. The first is to calculate some percentage of a given quantity, where you convert the percentage to a decimal, and multiply the quantity by that decimal. Secondly, you are given a quantity and told it is a fixed percent of an unknown quantity. In this case, convert to a decimal, then divide the given quantity by that decimal.

Example: What is 30% of 760?

Convert the percent into a useable number. "Of" means to multiply.

$$30\% = 0.30$$

46

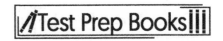

Set up the problem based on the givens, and solve.

$$0.30 \times 760 = 228$$

Example: 8.4 is 20% of what number?

Convert the percent into a useable number.

$$20\% = 0.20$$

The given number is a percent of the answer needed, so divide the given number by this decimal rather than multiplying it.

$$\frac{8.4}{0.20} = 42$$

Factorization

Factors are the numbers multiplied to achieve a product. Thus, every product in a multiplication equation has, at minimum, two factors. Of course, some products will have more than two factors. For the sake of most discussions, assume that factors are positive integers.

To find a number's factors, start with 1 and the number itself. Then divide the number by 2, 3, 4, and so on, seeing if any divisors can divide the number without a remainder, keeping a list of those that do. Stop upon reaching either the number itself or another factor.

Let's find the factors of 45. Start with 1 and 45. Then try to divide 45 by 2, which fails. Now divide 45 by 3. The answer is 15, so 3 and 15 are now factors. Dividing by 4 doesn't work, and dividing by 5 leaves 9. Lastly, dividing 45 by 6, 7, and 8 all don't work. The next integer to try is 9, but this is already known to be a factor, so the factorization is complete. The factors of 45 are 1, 3, 5, 9, 15 and 45.

Prime Factorization

Prime factorization involves an additional step after breaking a number down to its factors: breaking down the factors until they are all prime numbers. A **prime number** is any number that can only be divided by 1 and itself. The prime numbers between 1 and 20 are 2, 3, 5, 7, 11, 13, 17, and 19. As a simple test, numbers that are even or end in 5 are not prime, though there are other numbers that are not prime, but are odd and do not end in 5. For example, 21 is odd and divisible by 1, 3, 7, and 21, so it is not prime.

Let's break 129 down into its prime factors. First, the factors are 3 and 43. Both 3 and 43 are prime numbers, so we're done. But if 43 was not a prime number, then it would also need to be factorized until all of the factors are expressed as prime numbers.

Common Factor

A **common factor** is a factor shared by two numbers. Let's take 45 and 30 and find the common factors:

The factors of 45 are: 1, 3, 5, 9, 15, and 45.
The factors of 30 are: 1, 2, 3, 5, 6, 10, 15, and 30.
Thus, the common factors are 1, 3, 5, and 15.

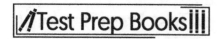

Greatest Common Factor

The **greatest common factor** is the largest number among the shared, common factors. From the factors of 45 and 30, the common factors are 3, 5, and 15. Therefore, 15 is the greatest common factor, as it's the largest number.

Least Common Multiple

The **least common multiple** is the smallest number that's a multiple of two numbers. Let's try to find the least common multiple of 4 and 9. The multiples of 4 are 4, 8, 12, 16, 20, 24, 28, 32, 36, and so on. For 9, the multiples are 9, 18, 27, 36, 45, 54, etc. Thus, the least common multiple of 4 and 9 is 36 because this is the lowest number where 4 and 9 share multiples.

If two numbers share no factors besides 1 in common, then their least common multiple will be simply their product. If two numbers have common factors, then their least common multiple will be their product divided by their greatest common factor. This can be visualized by the formula:

$$LCM = \frac{x \times y}{GCF}$$

where x and y are some integers, and LCM and GCF are their least common multiple and greatest common factor, respectively.

Exponents

Exponents are used in mathematics to express a number or variable multiplied by itself a certain number of times. For example, x^3 means x is multiplied by itself three times. In this expression, x is called the **base**, and 3 is the **exponent**. Exponents can be used in more complex problems when they contain fractions and negative numbers.

Fractional exponents can be explained by looking first at the inverse of exponents, which are **roots**. Given the expression x^2, the square root can be taken, $\sqrt{x^2}$, cancelling out the 2 and leaving x by itself, if x is positive. Cancellation occurs because $\sqrt{x}$ can be written with exponents, instead of roots, as $x^{\frac{1}{2}}$. The numerator of 1 is the exponent, and the denominator of 2 is called the **root** (which is why it's referred to as a **square root**). Taking the square root of x^2 is the same as raising it to the $\frac{1}{2}$ power. Written out in mathematical form, it takes the following progression:

$$\sqrt{x^2} = (x^2)^{\frac{1}{2}} = x$$

From properties of exponents, $2 \times \frac{1}{2} = 1$ is the actual exponent of x. Another example can be seen with $x^{\frac{4}{7}}$. The variable x, raised to four-sevenths, is equal to the seventh root of x to the fourth power: $\sqrt[7]{x^4}$. In general:

$$x^{\frac{1}{n}} = \sqrt[n]{x}$$

and

$$x^{\frac{m}{n}} = \sqrt[n]{x^m}$$

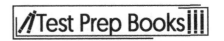

Negative exponents also involve fractions. Whereas y^3 can also be rewritten as $\frac{y^3}{1}$, y^{-3} can be rewritten as $\frac{1}{y^3}$. A negative exponent means the exponential expression must be moved to the opposite spot in a fraction to make the exponent positive. If the negative appears in the numerator, it moves to the denominator. If the negative appears in the denominator, it is moved to the numerator. In general, $a^{-n} = \frac{1}{a^n}$, and a^{-n} and a^n are reciprocals.

Take, for example, the following expression:

$$\frac{a^{-4}b^2}{c^{-5}}$$

Since a is raised to the negative fourth power, it can be moved to the denominator. Since c is raised to the negative fifth power, it can be moved to the numerator. The b variable is raised to the positive second power, so it does not move.

The simplified expression is as follows:

$$\frac{b^2c^5}{a^4}$$

In mathematical expressions containing exponents and other operations, the order of operations must be followed. **PEMDAS** states that exponents are calculated after any parentheses and grouping symbols but before any multiplication, division, addition, and subtraction.

Roots

The **square root symbol** is expressed as $\sqrt{\ }$ and is commonly known as the **radical**. Taking the root of a number is the inverse operation of multiplying that number by itself some number of times. For example, squaring the number 7 is equal to 7×7, or 49. Finding the square root is the opposite of finding an exponent, as the operation seeks a number that when multiplied by itself, equals the number in the square root symbol.

For example, $\sqrt{36} = 6$ because 6 multiplied by 6 equals 36. Note, the square root of 36 is also -6 since:

$$-6 \times -6 = 36$$

This can be indicated using a plus/minus symbol like this: ± 6. However, square roots are often just expressed as a positive number for simplicity, with it being understood that the true value can be either positive or negative.

Perfect squares are numbers with whole number square roots. The list of perfect squares begins with 0, 1, 4, 9, 16, 25, 36, 49, 64, 81, and 100.

Determining the square root of imperfect squares requires a calculator to reach an exact figure. It's possible, however, to approximate the answer by finding the two perfect squares that the number fits between. For example, the square root of 40 is between 6 and 7 since the squares of those numbers are 36 and 49, respectively.

Square roots are the most common root operation. If the radical doesn't have a number to the upper left of the symbol $\sqrt{\ }$, then it's a square root. Sometimes a radical includes a number in the upper left, like $\sqrt[3]{27}$, as in the other common root type—the cube root. Calculating complicated roots, like the cube root, often requires the use of a calculator.

Scientific Notation

Scientific Notation is used to represent numbers that are either very small or very large. For example, the distance to the Sun is approximately 150,000,000,000 meters. Instead of writing this number with so many zeros, it can be written in scientific notation as 1.5×10^{11} meters. The same is true for very small numbers, but the exponent becomes negative. If the mass of a human cell is 0.000000000001 kilograms, that measurement can be easily represented by 1.0×10^{-12} kilograms. In both situations, scientific notation makes the measurement easier to read and understand. Each number is translated to an expression with ones and tenths places multiplied by an expression corresponding to the zeros.

When two measurements are given and both involve scientific notation, it is important to know how these interact with each other:

- In addition and subtraction, the exponent on the ten must be the same before any operations are performed on the numbers. For example, $(1.3 \times 10^4) + (3.0 \times 10^3)$ cannot be added until one of the exponents on the ten is changed. The 3.0×10^3 can be changed to 0.3×10^4, then the 1.3 and 0.3 can be added. The answer comes out to be 1.6×10^4.

- For multiplication, the first numbers can be multiplied and then the exponents on the tens can be added. Once an answer is formed, it may have to be converted into scientific notation again depending on the change that occurred.

- The following is an example of multiplication with scientific notation:

$$(4.5 \times 10^3) \times (3.0 \times 10^{-5}) = 13.5 \times 10^{-2}$$

- Since this answer is not in scientific notation, the decimal is moved over to the left one unit, and 1 is added to the ten's exponent. This results in the final answer: 1.35×10^{-1}.

- For division, the first numbers are divided, and the exponents on the tens are subtracted. Again, the answer may need to be converted into scientific notation form, depending on the type of changes that occurred during the problem.

- **Order of magnitude** relates to scientific notation and is the total count of powers of 10 in a number. For example, there are 6 orders of magnitude in 1,000,000. If a number is raised by an order of magnitude, it is multiplied by 10. Order of magnitude can be helpful in estimating results using very large or small numbers. An answer should make sense in terms of its order of magnitude. For example, if area is calculated using two dimensions with 6 orders of magnitude, because area involves multiplication, the answer should have around 12 orders of magnitude. Also, answers can be estimated by rounding to the largest place value in each number. For example, $5,493,302 \times 2,523,100$ can be estimated by $5 \times 3 = 15$ with 12 orders of magnitude.

Estimation

Estimation is finding a value that is close to a solution but is not the exact answer. For example, if there are values in the thousands to be multiplied, then each value can be estimated to the nearest thousand

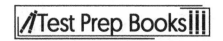

and the calculation performed. This value provides an approximate solution that can be determined very quickly.

Rounding is the process of either bumping a number up or leaving it the same, based on a specified place value. First, the place value is specified. Then, the digit to its right is looked at. For example, if rounding to the nearest hundreds place, the digit in the tens place is used. If it is a 0, 1, 2, 3, or 4, the digit being rounded to is left alone. If it is a 5, 6, 7, 8 or 9, the digit being rounded to is increased by one. All other digits before the decimal point are then changed to zeros, and the digits in decimal places are dropped. If a decimal place is being rounded to, all subsequent digits are just dropped. For example, if 845,231.45 was to be rounded to the nearest thousands place, the answer would be 845,000. The 5 would remain the same due to the 2 in the hundreds place. Also, if 4.567 was to be rounded to the nearest tenths place, the answer would be 4.6. The 5 increased to 6 due to the 6 in the hundredths place, and the rest of the decimal is dropped.

Sometimes when performing operations such as multiplying numbers, the result can be estimated by rounding. For example, to estimate the value of 11.2×2.01, each number can be rounded to the nearest integer. This will yield a result of 22.

Rounding numbers helps with estimation because it changes the given number to a simpler, although less accurate, number than the exact given number. Rounding allows for easier calculations, which estimate the results of using the exact given number. The accuracy of the estimate and ease of use depends on the place value to which the number is rounded. Rounding numbers consists of:

- Determining what place value the number is being rounded to
- Examining the digit to the right of the desired place value to decide whether to round up or keep the digit, and
- Replacing all digits to the right of the desired place value with zeros.

To round 746,311 to the nearest ten thousand, the digit in the ten thousands place should be located first. In this case, this digit is 4 (7<u>4</u>6,311). Then, the digit to its right is examined. If this digit is 5 or greater, the number will be rounded up by increasing the digit in the desired place by one. If the digit to the right of the place value being rounded is 4 or less, the number will be kept the same. For the given example, the digit being examined is a 6, which means that the number will be rounded up by increasing the digit to the left by one.

Therefore, the digit 4 is changed to a 5. Finally, to write the rounded number, any digits to the left of the place value being rounded remain the same and any to its right are replaced with zeros. For the given example, rounding 746,311 to the nearest ten thousand will produce 750,000. To round 746,311 to the nearest hundred, the digit to the right of the three in the hundreds place is examined to determine whether to round up or keep the same number. In this case, that digit is a 1, so the number will be kept the same and any digits to its right will be replaced with zeros. The resulting rounded number is 746,300.

Rounding place values to the right of the decimal follows the same procedure, but digits being replaced by zeros can simply be dropped. To round 3.752891 to the nearest thousandth, the desired place value is located (3.75<u>2</u>891) and the digit to the right is examined. In this case, the digit 8 indicates that the number will be rounded up, and the 2 in the thousandths place will increase to a 3. Rounding up and replacing the digits to the right of the thousandths place produces 3.753000 which is equivalent to 3.753. Therefore, the zeros are not necessary, and the rounded number should be written as 3.753.

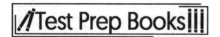
When rounding up, if the digit to be increased is a 9, the digit to its left is increased by 1 and the digit in the desired place value is changed to a zero. For example, the number 1,598 rounded to the nearest ten is 1,600. Another example shows the number 43.72961 rounded to the nearest thousandth is 43.730 or 43.73.

Mental math should always be considered as problems are worked through, and the ability to work through problems in one's head helps save time. If a problem is simple enough, such as $15 + 3 = 18$, it should be completed mentally. The ability to do this will increase once addition and subtraction in higher place values are grasped. Also, mental math is important in multiplication and division. The times tables multiplying all numbers from 1 to 12 should be memorized. This will allow for division within those numbers to be memorized as well. For example, we should know easily that $121 \div 11 = 11$ because it should be memorized that $11 \times 11 = 121$.

Here is the multiplication table to be memorized:

x	1	2	3	4	5	6	7	8	9	10	11	12	13	14	15
1	1	2	3	4	5	6	7	8	9	10	11	12	13	14	15
2	2	4	6	8	10	12	14	16	18	20	22	24	26	28	30
3	3	6	9	12	15	18	21	24	27	30	33	36	39	42	45
4	4	8	12	16	20	24	28	32	36	40	44	48	52	56	60
5	5	10	15	20	25	30	35	40	45	50	55	60	65	70	75
6	6	12	18	24	30	36	42	48	54	60	66	72	78	84	90
7	7	14	21	28	35	42	49	56	63	70	77	84	91	98	105
8	8	16	24	32	40	48	56	64	72	80	88	96	104	112	120
9	9	18	27	36	45	54	63	72	81	90	99	108	117	126	135
10	10	20	30	40	50	60	70	80	90	100	110	120	130	140	150
11	11	22	33	44	55	66	77	88	99	110	121	132	143	154	165
12	12	24	36	48	60	72	84	96	108	120	132	144	156	168	180
13	13	26	39	52	65	78	91	104	117	130	143	156	169	182	195
14	14	28	42	56	70	84	98	112	126	140	154	168	182	196	210
15	15	30	45	60	75	90	105	120	135	150	165	180	195	210	225

The values in gray along the diagonal of the table consist of **perfect squares**. A perfect square is the product of two of the same numbers.

Sequences and Series

Patterns within a sequence can come in 2 distinct forms: the items (shapes, numbers, etc.) either repeat in a constant order, or the items change from one step to another in some consistent way. The **core** is the smallest unit, or number of items, that repeats in a repeating pattern. For example, the pattern

○○▲○○▲○...

has a core that is ○○▲. Knowing only the core, the pattern can be extended. Knowing the number of steps in the core allows the identification of an item in each step without drawing/writing the entire pattern out. For example, suppose the tenth item in the previous pattern must be determined. Because

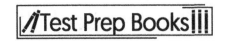

the core consists of three items (oo▲), the core repeats in multiples of 3. In other words, steps 3, 6, 9, 12, etc. will be ▲ completing the core with the core starting over on the next step. For the above example, the 9th step will be ▲ and the 10th will be o.

The most common patterns in which each item changes from one step to the next are arithmetic and geometric sequences. An **arithmetic sequence** is one in which the items increase or decrease by a constant difference. In other words, the same thing is added or subtracted to each item or step to produce the next. To determine if a sequence is arithmetic, determine what must be added or subtracted to step one to produce step two.

Then, check if the same thing is added/subtracted to step two to produce step three. The same thing must be added/subtracted to step three to produce step four, and so on. Consider the pattern 13, 10, 7, 4... To get from step one (13) to step two (10) by adding or subtracting requires subtracting by 3. The next step is checking if subtracting 3 from step two (10) will produce step three (7), and subtracting 3 from step three (7) will produce step four (4). In this case, the pattern holds true. Therefore, this is an arithmetic sequence in which each step is produced by subtracting 3 from the previous step. To extend the sequence, 3 is subtracted from the last step to produce the next. The next three numbers in the sequence are 1, −2, −5.

A **geometric sequence** is one in which each step is produced by multiplying or dividing the previous step by the same number. To determine if a sequence is geometric, decide what step one must be multiplied or divided by to produce step two. Then check if multiplying or dividing step two by the same number produces step three, and so on. Consider the pattern 2, 8, 32, 128... To get from step one (2) to step two (8) requires multiplication by 4. The next step determines if multiplying step two (8) by 4 produces step three (32), and multiplying step three (32) by 4 produces step four (128). In this case, the pattern holds true. Therefore, this is a geometric sequence in which each step is produced by multiplying the previous step by 4. To extend the sequence, the last step is multiplied by 4 and repeated. The next three numbers in the sequence are 512, 2,048, and 8,192.

Although arithmetic and geometric sequences typically use numbers, these sequences can also be represented by shapes. For example, an arithmetic sequence could consist of shapes with three sides, four sides, and five sides (add one side to the previous step to produce the next). A geometric sequence could consist of eight blocks, four blocks, and two blocks (each step is produced by dividing the number of blocks in the previous step by 2).

Frequencies

In mathematics, **frequencies** refer to how often an event occurs or the number of times a particular quantity appears in a given series. To find the number of times a specific value appears, frequency tables are used to record the occurrences, which can then be summed. To construct a frequency table, one simply inputs the values into a tabular format with a column denoting each value, typically in ascending order, with a second column to tally up the number of occurrences for each value, and a third column to give a numerical frequency based on the number of tallies.

A **frequency distribution** communicates the number of outcomes of a given value or number in a data set. When displayed as a bar graph or histogram, a frequency distribution can visually indicate the spread and distribution of the data. A histogram resembling a bell curve approximates a normal distribution.

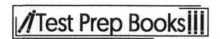

A frequency distribution can also be displayed as a **stem-and-leaf plot**, which arranges data in numerical order and displays values similar to a tally chart with the stem being a range within the set and the leaf indicating the exact value (i.e., stems are whole numbers and leaves are tenths).

	Movie Ratings
4	7
5	2 6 9
6	1 4 6 8 8
7	0 3 5 9
8	1 3 5 6 8 8 9
9	0 0 1 3 4 6 6 9

Key	6 ǀ 1 represents 61

Stem	Leaf
2	0 2 3 6 8 8 9
3	2 6 7 7
4	7 9
5	4 6 9

This plot provides more detail about individual data points and allows for easy identification of the median, as well as any repeated values in the set.

Data that isn't described using numbers is known as **categorical data.** For example, age is numerical data but hair color is categorical data. Categorical data can also be summarized using two-way frequency tables. A **two-way frequency table** counts the relationship between two sets of categorical data. There are rows and columns for each category, and each cell represents frequency information that shows the actual data count between each combination. For example, below is a two-way frequency table showing the gender and breed of cats in an animal shelter:

	Domestic Shorthair	Persian	Domestic Longhair	Total
Male	12	2	7	21
Female	8	4	5	17
Total	20	6	12	38

Entries in the middle of the table are known as the **joint frequencies**. For example, the number of females that are Persians is 4, which is a joint frequency. The totals are the **marginal frequencies**. For example, the total number of males is 21, which is a marginal frequency. If the frequencies are changed into percentages based on totals, the table is known as a **two-way relative frequency table**. Percentages can be calculated using the table total, the row totals, or the column totals. Two-way frequency tables can help in making conclusions about the data.

Solving Word Problems

Word problems, or story problems, are math problems that have a real-world context. In word problems, multiple quantities are often provided with a request to find some kind of relation between them. This often will mean that one variable (the dependent variable whose value needs to be found) can be written as a function of another variable (the independent variable whose value can be figured from the given information). The usual procedure for solving these problems is to start by giving each quantity in the problem a variable, and then figuring the relationship between these variables.

For example, suppose a car gets 25 miles per gallon. How far will the car travel if it uses 2.4 gallons of fuel? In this case, y would be the distance the car has traveled in miles, and x would be the amount of fuel burned in gallons (2.4). Then the relationship between these variables can be written as an algebraic equation, $y = 25x$. In this case, the equation is:

$$y = 25 \times 2.4 = 60$$

So, the car has traveled 60 miles.

Translating Verbal Relationships into Algebraic Equations or Expressions

When attempting to solve a math problem, it's important to apply the correct algorithm. It is much more difficult to determine what algorithm is necessary when solving word problems, because the necessary operations and equations are typically not provided. In these instances, the test taker must translate the words in the problem into true mathematical statements that can be solved.

55

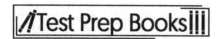

The following are examples:

Symbol	Phrase
$+$	Added to; increased by; sum of; more than
$-$	Decreased by; difference between; less than; take away
$\times$	Multiplied by; 3(4,5...) times as large; product of
$\div$	Divided by; quotient of; half (third, etc.) of
$=$	Is; the same as; results in; as much as; equal to
x, t, n, etc.	A number; unknown quantity; value of; variable

As mentioned, addition and subtraction are **inverse operations**. Adding a number and then subtracting the same number will cancel each other out, resulting in the original number, and vice versa. For example:

$$8 + 7 - 7 = 8 \text{ and } 137 - 100 + 100 = 137$$

Similarly, multiplication and division are inverse operations. Therefore, multiplying by a number and then dividing by the same number results in the original number, and vice versa. For example,

$$8 \times 2 \div 2 = 8 \text{ and } 12 \div 4 \times 4 = 12$$

Inverse operations are used to work backwards to solve problems. In the case that 7 and a number add to 18, the inverse operation of subtraction is used to find the unknown value ($18 - 7 = 11$). If a school's entire 4th grade was divided evenly into 3 classes each with 22 students, the inverse operation of multiplication is used to determine the total students in the grade:

$$22 \times 3 = 66$$

Additional scenarios involving inverse operations are included in the tables below.

There are a variety of real-world situations in which one or more of the operators is used to solve a problem. The tables below display the most common scenarios.

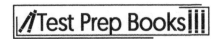

Addition & Subtraction

	Unknown Result	**Unknown Change**	**Unknown Start**
Adding to	5 students were in class. 4 more students arrived. How many students are in class? $5 + 4 =?$	8 students were in class. More students arrived late. There are now 18 students in class. How many students arrived late? $8+? = 18$ Solved by inverse operations $18-8 =?$	Some students were in class early. 11 more students arrived. There are now 17 students in class. How many students were in class early? $?+11 = 17$ Solved by inverse operations $17-11 =?$
Taking from	15 students were in class. 5 students left class. How many students are in class now? $15-5 =?$	12 students were in class. Some students left class. There are now 8 students in class. How many students left class? $12-? = 8$ Solved by inverse operations $8+? = 12 \rightarrow 12-8 =?$	Some students were in class. 3 students left class. Then there were 13 students in class. How many students were in class before? $?-3 = 13$ Solved by inverse operations $13 + 3 =?$

	Unknown Total	**Unknown Addends (Both)**	**Unknown Addends (One)**
Putting together/ taking apart	The homework assignment is 10 addition problems and 8 subtraction problems. How many problems are in the homework assignment? $10 + 8 =?$	Bobby has $9. How much can Bobby spend on candy and how much can Bobby spend on toys? $9 =? +?$	Bobby has 12 pairs of pants. 5 pairs of pants are shorts, and the rest are long. How many pairs of long pants does he have? $12 = 5+?$ Solved by inverse operations $12-5 =?$

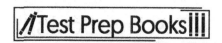
	Unknown Difference	Unknown Larger Value	Unknown Smaller Value
Comparing	Bobby has 5 toys. Tommy has 8 toys. How many more toys does Tommy have than Bobby? $$5 + ? = 8$$ Solved by inverse operations $8 - 5 = ?$ Bobby has $6. Tommy has $10. How many fewer dollars does Bobby have than Tommy? $$10 - 6 = ?$$	Tommy has 2 more toys than Bobby. Bobby has 4 toys. How many toys does Tommy have? $$2 + 4 = ?$$ Bobby has 3 fewer dollars than Tommy. Bobby has $8. How many dollars does Tommy have? $$? - 3 = 8$$ Solved by inverse operations $8 + 3 = ?$	Tommy has 6 more toys than Bobby. Tommy has 10 toys. How many toys does Bobby have? $$? + 6 = 10$$ Solved by inverse operations $10 - 6 = ?$ Bobby has $5 less than Tommy. Tommy has $9. How many dollars does Bobby have? $$9 - 5 = ?$$

Multiplication and Division

	Unknown Product	Unknown Group Size	Unknown Number of Groups
Equal groups	There are 5 students, and each student has 4 pieces of candy. How many pieces of candy are there in all? $$5 \times 4 = ?$$	14 pieces of candy are shared equally by 7 students. How many pieces of candy does each student have? $$7 \times ? = 14$$ Solved by inverse operations $14 \div 7 = ?$	If 18 pieces of candy are to be given out 3 to each student, how many students will get candy? $$? \times 3 = 18$$ Solved by inverse operations $18 \div 3 = ?$

	Unknown Product	Unknown Factor	Unknown Factor
Arrays	There are 5 rows of students with 3 students in each row. How many students are there? $$5 \times 3 = ?$$	If 16 students are arranged into 4 equal rows, how many students will be in each row? $$4 \times ? = 16$$ Solved by inverse operations $16 \div 4 = ?$	If 24 students are arranged into an array with 6 columns, how many rows are there? $$? \times 6 = 24$$ Solved by inverse operations $24 \div 6 = ?$

	Larger Unknown	Smaller Unknown	Multiplier Unknown
Comparing	A small popcorn costs $1.50. A large popcorn costs 3 times as much as a small popcorn. How much does a large popcorn cost? $1.50 \times 3 = ?$	A large soda costs $6 and that is 2 times as much as a small soda costs. How much does a small soda cost? $2 \times ? = 6$ Solved by inverse operations $6 \div 2 = ?$	A large pretzel costs $3 and a small pretzel costs $2. How many times as much does the large pretzel cost as the small pretzel? $? \times 2 = 3$ Solved by inverse operations $3 \div 2 = ?$

Modeling and Solving Word Problems

Word problems can appear daunting, but don't let the wording intimidate you. No matter the scenario or specifics, the key to answering them is to translate the words into a math problem. Always keep in mind what the question is asking and what operations could lead to that answer.

Some word problems require more than just one simple equation to be written and solved. Consider the following situations and the linear equations used to model them.

Suppose Margaret is 2 miles to the east of John at noon. Margaret walks to the east at 3 miles per hour. How far apart will they be at 3 p.m.? To solve this, x would represent the time in hours past noon, and y would represent the distance between Margaret and John. Now, noon corresponds to the equation where x is 0, so the y-intercept is going to be 2. It's also known that the slope will be the rate at which the distance is changing, which is 3 miles per hour. This means that the slope will be 3 (be careful at this point: if units were used, other than miles and hours, for x- and y-variables, a conversion of the given information to the appropriate units would be required first). The simplest way to write an equation given the y-intercept, and the slope is the Slope-Intercept form, which is $y = mx + b$. Recall that m here is the slope and b is the y-intercept. So, $m = 3$ and $b = 2$. Therefore, the equation will be:

$$y = 3x + 2$$

The word problem asks how far to the east Margaret will be from John at 3 p.m., which means when x is 3. So, substitute $x = 3$ into this equation to obtain:

$$y = 3 \cdot 3 + 2 = 9 + 2 = 11$$

Therefore, she will be 11 miles to the east of him at 3 p.m.

For another example, suppose that a box with 4 cans in it weighs 6 lbs., while a box with 8 cans in it weighs 12 lbs. Find out how much a single can weighs. To do this, let x denote the number of cans in the box, and y denote the weight of the box with the cans in lbs. This line touches two pairs: $(4, 6)$ and $(8, 12)$. A formula for this relation could be written using the two-point form, with:

$$x_1 = 4, y_1 = 6, x_2 = 8, y_2 = 12$$

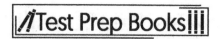

This would yield:

$$\frac{y-6}{x-4} = \frac{12-6}{8-4}$$

$$\frac{y-6}{x-4} = \frac{6}{4} = \frac{3}{2}$$

However, only the slope is needed to solve this problem, since the slope will be the weight of a single can. From the computation, the slope is $\frac{3}{2}$. Therefore, each can weighs $\frac{3}{2}$ lb.

The Problem-Solving Process and Determining If Enough Information Is Provided to Solve a Problem

Overall, the problem-solving process in mathematics involves a step-by-step procedure that one must follow when deciding what approach to take. First, one must understand the problem by deciding what is being sought, then if enough information is given, and what units are necessary in the solution. This is a crucial, but sometimes difficult step. It involves carefully reading the entire problem, identifying (perhaps even underlining) the facts or information that *is* known, and then deciphering the question words to determine what the problem is asking. In this way, math problems require students to be detectives, evaluating the "clues" or facts given in the problem, deciding what the problem is looking for, and evaluating whether sufficient information or "clues" are presented in the problem to solve the posed question.

In general, when solving word problems (also called story problems), it's important to understand what is being asked and to properly set up the initial equation. Always read the entire problem through, and then separate out what information is given in the statement. Decide what you are being asked to find and label each quantity with a variable or constant. Then write an equation to determine the unknown variable. Remember to label answers; sometimes knowing what the answers' units should can help eliminate other possible solutions.

When trying to solve any word problem, look for a series of key words indicating addition, subtraction, multiplication, or division to help you determine how to set up the problem:

> **Addition**: *add, altogether, together, plus, increased by, more than, in all, sum,* and *total*

> **Subtraction**: *minus, less than, difference, decreased by, fewer than, remain,* and *take away*

> **Multiplication**: *times, twice, of, double,* and *triple*

> **Division**: *divided by, cut up, half, quotient of, split,* and *shared equally*

If a question asks to give words to a mathematical expression and says "equals," then an = sign must be included in the answer. Similarly, "less than or equal to" is expressed by the inequality symbol ≤, and "greater than or equal" to is expressed as ≥. Furthermore, "less than" is represented by <, and "greater than" is expressed by >.

These strategies are applicable to other question types. For example, calculating salary after deductions, balancing a checkbook, and calculating a dinner bill are common word problems similar to business planning. Just remember to use the correct operations. When a balance is increased, use addition.

When a balance is decreased, use subtraction. Common sense and organization are your greatest assets when answering word problems.

For example, suppose the following word problem is encountered:

Walter's Coffee Shop sells a variety of drinks and breakfast treats.

Price List	
Hot Coffee	$2.00
Slow-Drip Iced Coffee	$3.00
Latte	$4.00
Muffin	$2.00
Crepe	$4.00
Egg Sandwich	$5.00

Costs	
Hot Coffee	$0.25
Slow-Drip Iced Coffee	$0.75
Latte	$1.00
Muffin	$1.00
Crepe	$2.00
Egg Sandwich	$3.00

Walter's utilities, rent, and labor costs him $500 per day. Today, Walter sold 200 hot coffees, 100 slow-drip iced coffees, 50 lattes, 75 muffins, 45 crepes, and 60 egg sandwiches. What was Walter's total profit today?

First, it is necessary to establish what is known (the "facts"), what one wants to know, (the question), how to determine the answer (the process), and if there is enough information to solve (sufficient "clues"). The problem clearly asks: "what was Walter's total profit today," so to accurately answer this type of question, the total cost of making his drinks and treats must be calculated, then the total revenue he earned from selling those products must be determined. After arriving at these two totals, the profit is measured found by deducting the total cost from the total revenue.

Now that the question and steps are identified, the provided facts are evaluated. Walter's costs for today:

Item	Quantity	Cost Per Unit	Total Cost
Hot Coffee	200	$0.25	$50
Slow-Drip Iced Coffee	100	$0.75	$75
Latte	50	$1.00	$50
Muffin	75	$1.00	$75
Crepe	45	$2.00	$90
Egg Sandwich	60	$3.00	$180
Utilities, rent, and labor			$500
Total Costs			$1,020

Walter's revenue for today:

Item	Quantity	Revenue Per Unit	Total Revenue
Hot Coffee	200	$2.00	$400
Slow-Drip Iced Coffee	100	$3.00	$300
Latte	50	$4.00	$200
Muffin	75	$2.00	$150
Crepe	45	$4.00	$180
Egg Sandwich	60	$5.00	$300
Total Revenue			$1,530

$$Walter's\ Profit = Revenue - Costs = \$1,530 - \$1,020 = \$510$$

In this case, enough information was given in the problem to adequately solve it. If, however, the number of sandwiches and drinks or Walter's cost per unit sold were not provided, insufficient information would prevent one from arriving at the answer.

Alternative Methods for Solving Mathematical Problems

When solving a math problem, once the question is identified and the clues are evaluated, the plan of action must be determined. In some cases, there might be many options. Therefore, one should begin with one approach and if the strategy does not fit, he or she should move on to another. In some cases, a combination of approaches can be used. A beginning estimate is always useful for comparison once a solution is found. The answer must be reasonable and must fulfill all requirements of the problem.

Just as there are different types of learners (visual, kinesthetic, etc.), so too are there particular problem-solving approaches that different students prefer or grasp more easily than others. Skilled mathematicians are versed in multiple methods to tackle various problems, with each method bolstering their toolbox with a strategy that can be employed for ease and efficiency when encountering math work.

Instead of focusing on the "right" way to solve a problem, students strive to learn multiple methods and understand the pros, cons, and appropriate applications for each method. For example, when trying to find the zeros in a binomial expression, one might be able to factor the expression, complete the square, use the quadratic equation, or make a rough sketch of the graph and identify the x-intercepts. In some cases, one method may not be possible and another may be "easiest," but by learning the various strategies, students become critical thinkers and select the method they deem most appropriate.

The following two examples demonstrate how different methods can be used for the same problem:

Example:

A store is having a spring sale, where everything is 70% off. You have $45.00 to spend. A jacket is regularly priced at $80.00. Do you have enough to buy the jacket and a pair of gloves, regularly priced at $20.00?

There are two ways to approach this.

62

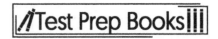

Method 1:

Set up the equations to find the sale prices: the original price minus the amount discounted.

$$\$80.00 - (\$80.00\ (0.70)) = sale\ cost\ of\ the\ jacket$$
$$\$20.00 - (\$20.00\ (0.70)) = sale\ cost\ of\ the\ gloves$$

Solve for the sale cost.

$$\$24.00 = sale\ cost\ of\ the\ jacket$$
$$\$6.00 = sale\ cost\ of\ the\ gloves$$

Determine if you have enough money for both.

$$\$24.00 + \$6.00 = total\ sale\ cost$$

$30.00 is less than $45.00, so you can afford to purchase both.

Method 2:

Determine the percent of the original price that you will pay.

$$100\% - 70\% = 30\%$$

Set up the equations to find the sale prices.

$$\$80.00\ (0.30) = cost\ of\ the\ jacket$$
$$\$20.00\ (0.30) = cost\ of\ the\ gloves$$

Solve.

$$\$24.00 = cost\ of\ the\ jacket$$
$$\$6.00 = cost\ of\ the\ gloves$$

Determine if you have enough money for both.

$$\$24.00 + \$6.00 = total\ sale\ cost$$

$30.00 is less than $45.00, so you can afford to purchase both.

Here's another example:

Mary and Dottie team up to mow neighborhood lawns. If Mary mows 2 lawns per hour and the two of them can mow 17.5 lawns in 5 hours, how many lawns does Dottie mow per hour?

Given rate for Mary.

$$Mary = \frac{2\ lawns}{1\ hour}$$

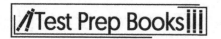

Unknown rate of D for Dottie.

$$Dottie = \frac{D \text{ lawns}}{1 \text{ hour}}$$

Given rate for both.

$$Total \ mowed \ together = \frac{17.5 \text{ lawns}}{5 \text{ hours}}$$

Set up the equation for what is being asked.

$$Mary + Dottie = total \ together.$$

Fill in the givens.

$$2 + D = \frac{17.5}{5}$$

Divide.

$$2 + D = 3.5$$

Subtract 2 from both sides to isolate the variable.

$$2 - 2 + D = 3.5 - 2$$

Solve and label Dottie's mowing rate.

$$D = 1.5 \text{ lawns per hour}$$

Algebra

Algebraic Expressions and Equations

An **algebraic expression** is a statement about an unknown quantity expressed in mathematical symbols. A **variable** is used to represent the unknown quantity, usually denoted by a letter. An equation is a statement in which two expressions (at least one containing a variable) are equal to each other. An algebraic expression can be thought of as a mathematical phrase and an equation can be thought of as a mathematical sentence.

Algebraic expressions and equations both contain numbers, variables, and mathematical operations. The following are examples of algebraic expressions:

$$5x + 3, 7xy - 8(x^2 + y)$$

and

$$\sqrt{a^2 + b^2}$$

64

An expression can be simplified or evaluated for given values of variables. The following are examples of equations:

$$2x + 3 = 7$$

$$a^2 + b^2 = c^2$$

$$2x + 5 = 3x - 2$$

An equation contains two sides separated by an equal sign. Equations can be solved to determine the value(s) of the variable for which the statement is true.

Parts of Expressions

Algebraic expressions consist of variables, numbers, and operations. A **term** of an expression is any combination of numbers and/or variables, and terms are separated by addition and subtraction. For example, the expression $5x^2 - 3xy + 4 - 2$ consists of 4 terms: $5x^2$, $-3xy$, $4y$, and -2. Note that each term includes its given sign (+ or −). The **variable** part of a term is a letter that represents an unknown quantity. The **coefficient** of a term is the number by which the variable is multiplied. For the term $4y$, the variable is y, and the coefficient is 4. Terms are identified by the power (or exponent) of its variable.

A number without a variable is referred to as a **constant**. If the variable is to the first power (x^1 or simply x), it is referred to as a linear term. A term with a variable to the second power (x^2) is quadratic, and a term to the third power (x^3) is cubic. Consider the expression:

$$x^3 + 3x - 1$$

The constant is -1. The linear term is $3x$. There is no quadratic term. The cubic term is x^3.

An algebraic expression can also be classified by how many terms exist in the expression. Any like terms should be combined before classifying. A **monomial** is an expression consisting of only one term. Examples of monomials are: 17, $2x$, and $-5ab^2$. A **binomial** is an expression consisting of two terms separated by addition or subtraction. Examples include:

$$2x - 4 \text{ and } -3y^2 + 2y$$

A **trinomial** consists of 3 terms. For example, $5x^2 - 2x + 1$ is a trinomial.

Adding and Subtracting Linear Algebraic Expressions

An algebraic expression is simplified by combining like terms. As mentioned, term is a number, variable, or product of a number and variables separated by addition and subtraction. For the algebraic expression:

$$3x^2 - 4x + 5 - 5x^2 + x - 3$$

the terms are $3x^2$, $-4x$, 5, $-5x^2$, x, and -3. Like terms have the same variables raised to the same powers (exponents). The like terms for the previous example are $3x^2$ and $-5x^2$, $-4x$ and x, 5 and -3. To combine like terms, the coefficients (numerical factor of the term including sign) are added, and the variables and their powers are kept the same. Note that if a coefficient is not written, it is an implied coefficient of 1 ($x = 1x$). The previous example will simplify to:

$$-2x^2 - 3x + 2$$

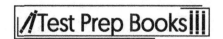
When adding or subtracting algebraic expressions, each expression is written in parentheses. The negative sign is distributed when necessary, and like terms are combined. Consider the following: add

$$2a + 5b - 2 \text{ to } a - 2b + 8c - 4$$

The sum is set as follows:

$$(a - 2b + 8c - 4) + (2a + 5b - 2)$$

In front of each set of parentheses is an implied positive one, which, when distributed, does not change any of the terms. Therefore, the parentheses are dropped and like terms are combined:

$$a - 2b + 8c - 4 + 2a + 5b - 2$$

$$3a + 3b + 8c - 6$$

Consider the following problem: Subtract $2a + 5b - 2$ from $a - 2b + 8c - 4$. The difference is set as follows:

$$(a - 2b + 8c - 4) - (2a + 5b - 2)$$

The implied one in front of the first set of parentheses will not change those four terms. However, distributing the implied -1 in front of the second set of parentheses will change the sign of each of those three terms:

$$a - 2b + 8c - 4 - 2a - 5b + 2$$

Combining like terms yields the simplified expression:

$$-a - 7b + 8c - 2$$

Distributive Property

The distributive property states that multiplying a sum (or difference) by a number produces the same result as multiplying each value in the sum (or difference) by the number and adding (or subtracting) the products. Using mathematical symbols, the distributive property states:

$$a(b + c) = ab + ac$$

The expression $4(3 + 2)$ is simplified using the order of operations. Simplifying inside the parentheses first produces 4×5, which equals 20.

The expression $4(3 + 2)$ can also be simplified using the distributive property:

$$4(3 + 2)$$

$$4 \times 3 + 4 \times 2$$

$$12 + 8 = 20$$

Consider the following example: $4(3x - 2)$. The expression cannot be simplified inside the parentheses because $3x$ and -2 are not like terms and therefore cannot be combined. However, the expression can be simplified by using the distributive property and multiplying each term inside of the parentheses by

66

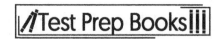

the term outside of the parentheses: $12x - 8$. The resulting equivalent expression contains no like terms, so it cannot be further simplified.

Consider the expression:

$$(3x + 2y + 1) - (5x - 3) + 2(3y + 4)$$

Again, there are no like terms, but the distributive property is used to simplify the expression. Note there is an implied one in front of the first set of parentheses and an implied -1 in front of the second set of parentheses. Distributing the 1, -1, and 2 produces:

$$1(3x) + 1(2y) + 1(1) - 1(5x) - 1(-3) + 2(3y) + 2(4)$$

$$3x + 2y + 1 - 5x + 3 + 6y + 8$$

This expression contains like terms that are combined to produce the simplified expression:

$$-2x + 8y + 12$$

Algebraic expressions are tested to be equivalent by choosing values for the variables and evaluating both expressions. For example, $4(3x - 2)$ and $12x - 8$ are tested by substituting 3 for the variable x and calculating to determine if equivalent values result.

Evaluating Expressions for Given Values

An algebraic expression is a statement written in mathematical symbols, typically including one or more unknown values represented by variables. For example, the expression $2x + 3$ states that an unknown number (x) is multiplied by 2 and added to 3. If given a value for the unknown number, or variable, the value of the expression is determined. For example, if the value of the variable x is 4, the value of the expression 4 is multiplied by 2, and 3 is added. This results in a value of 11 for the expression.

When given an algebraic expression and values for the variable(s), the expression is evaluated to determine its numerical value. To evaluate the expression, the given values for the variables are substituted (or replaced), and the expression is simplified using the order of operations. Parentheses should be used when substituting. Consider the following: Evaluate $a - 2b + ab$ for $a = 3$ and $b = -1$. To evaluate, any variable a is replaced with 3 and any variable b with -1, producing:

$$3 - 2(-1) + 3(-1)$$

Next, the order of operations is used to calculate the value of the expression, which is 2.

Verbal Statements and Algebraic Expressions

As mentioned, an algebraic expression is a statement about unknown quantities expressed in mathematical symbols. The statement *five times a number added to forty* is expressed as $5x + 40$. An equation is a statement in which two expressions (with at least one containing a variable) are equal to one another. The statement *five times a number added to forty is equal to ten* is expressed as:

$$5x + 40 = 10$$

Real world scenarios can also be expressed mathematically. Suppose a job pays its employees $300 per week and $40 for each sale made. The weekly pay is represented by the expression $40x + 300$ where x is the number of sales made during the week.

67

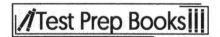

Consider the following scenario: Bob had $20 and Tom had $4. After selling 4 ice cream cones to Bob, Tom has as much money as Bob. The cost of an ice cream cone is an unknown quantity and can be represented by a variable (x). The amount of money Bob has after his purchase is four times the cost of an ice cream cone subtracted from his original:

$$\$20 \rightarrow 20 - 4x$$

The amount of money Tom has after his sale is four times the cost of an ice cream cone added to his original:

$$\$4 \rightarrow 4x + 4$$

After the sale, the amount of money that Bob and Tom have is equal:

$$\rightarrow 20 - 4x = 4x + 4$$

Solving for x yields $x = 2$.

Use of Formulas

Formulas are mathematical expressions that define the value of one quantity, given the value of one or more different quantities. Formulas look like equations because they contain variables, numbers, operators, and an equal sign. All formulas are equations, but not all equations are formulas. A formula must have more than one variable. For example, $2x + 7 = y$ is an equation and a formula (it relates the unknown quantities x and y). However, $2x + 7 = 3$ is an equation but not a formula (it only expresses the value of the unknown quantity x).

Formulas are typically written with one variable alone (or isolated) on one side of the equal sign. This variable can be thought of as the *subject* in that the formula is stating the value of the *subject* in terms of the relationship between the other variables. Consider the distance formula: $distance = rate \times time$ or $d = rt$. The value of the subject variable d (distance) is the product of the variable r and t (rate and time). Given the rate and time, the distance traveled can easily be determined by substituting the values into the formula and evaluating.

The formula $P = 2l + 2w$ expresses how to calculate the perimeter of a rectangle (P) given its length (l) and width (w). To find the perimeter of a rectangle with a length of 3 ft and a width of 2 ft, these values are substituted into the formula for l and w:
$$P = 2(3ft) + 2(2ft)$$

Following the order of operations, the perimeter is determined to be 10 ft. When working with formulas such as these, including units is an important step.

Given a formula expressed in terms of one variable, the formula can be manipulated to express the relationship in terms of any other variable. In other words, the formula can be rearranged to change which variable is the **subject.** To solve for a variable of interest by manipulating a formula, the equation may be solved as if all other variables were numbers. The same steps for solving are followed, leaving operations in terms of the variables instead of calculating numerical values. For the formula $P = 2l + 2w$, the perimeter is the subject expressed in terms of the length and width. To write a formula to calculate the width of a rectangle, given its length and perimeter, the previous formula relating the three variables is solved for the variable w. If P and l were numerical values, this is a two-step linear

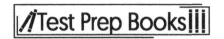

equation solved by subtraction and division. To solve the equation $P = 2l + 2w$ for w, $2l$ is first subtracted from both sides:

$$P - 2l = 2w$$

Then both sides are divided by 2:

$$\frac{P - 2l}{2} = w$$

Dependent and Independent Variables

A **variable** represents an unknown quantity and, in the case of a formula, a specific relationship exists between the variables. Within a given scenario, variables are the quantities that are changing. If two variables exist, one is dependent and one is independent. The value of one variable depends on the other variable. If a scenario describes distance traveled and time traveled at a given speed, distance is dependent and time is independent. The distance traveled depends on the time spent traveling. If a scenario describes the cost of a cab ride and the distance traveled, the cost is dependent and the distance is independent. The cost of a cab ride depends on the distance travelled. Formulas often contain more than two variables and are typically written with the dependent variable alone on one side of the equation. This lone variable is the *subject* of the statement. If a formula contains three or more variables, one variable is dependent and the rest are independent. The values of all independent variables are needed to determine the value of the dependent variable.

The formula $C = 2\pi r$ expresses the dependent variable C, the circumference of a circle, in terms of the independent variables, r—the radius. The circumference of a circle depends on its radius. The formula $d = rt$ ($distance = rate \times time$) expresses the dependent variable d in terms of the independent variables, r and t. The distance traveled depends on the rate (or speed) and the time traveled.

Solving Simple Algebraic Problems

Linear equations and **linear inequalities** are both comparisons of two algebraic expressions. However, unlike equations in which the expressions are equal, linear inequalities compare expressions that may be unequal. Linear equations typically have one value for the variable that makes the statement true. Linear inequalities generally have an infinite number of values that make the statement true.

When solving a linear equation, the desired result requires determining a numerical value for the unknown **variable**. If given a linear equation involving addition, subtraction, multiplication, or division, working backwards isolates the variable. Addition and subtraction are inverse operations, as are multiplication and division. Therefore, they can be used to cancel each other out.

Since variables are the letters that represent an unknown number, you must solve for that unknown number in single variable problems. The main thing to remember is that you can do anything to one side of an equation as long as you do it to the other.

The first steps to solving linear equations are distributing, if necessary, and combining any like terms on the same side of the equation. Sides of an equation are separated by an **equal sign**. Next, the equation is manipulated to show the variable on one side. Again, whatever is done to one side of the equation must be done to the other side of the equation to remain equal. Inverse operations are then used to isolate

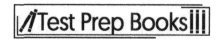

the variable and undo the order of operations backwards. Addition and subtraction are undone, then multiplication and division are undone.

For example, solve $4(t - 2) + 2t - 4 = 2(9 - 2t)$

Distribute: $4t - 8 + 2t - 4 = 18 - 4t$

Combine like terms: $6t - 12 = 18 - 4t$

Add $4t$ to each side to move the variable: $10t - 12 = 18$

Add 12 to each side to isolate the variable: $10t = 30$

Divide each side by 10 to isolate the variable: $t = 3$

The answer can be checked by substituting the value for the variable into the original equation, ensuring that both sides calculate to be equal.

Linear inequalities express the relationship between unequal values. More specifically, they describe in what way the values are unequal. A value can be greater than ($>$), less than ($<$), greater than or equal to ($\geq$), or less than or equal to ($\leq$) another value. $5x + 40 > 65$ is read as *five times a number added to forty is greater than sixty-five.*

When solving a linear inequality, the solution is the set of all numbers that make the statement true. The inequality $x + 2 \geq 6$ has a solution set of 4 and every number greater than 4 (4.01; 5; 12; 107; etc.). Adding 2 to 4 or any number greater than 4 results in a value that is greater than or equal to 6. Therefore, $x \geq 4$ is the solution set.

To algebraically solve a linear inequality, follow the same steps as those for solving a linear equation. The inequality symbol stays the same for all operations except when multiplying or dividing by a negative number. If multiplying or dividing by a negative number while solving an inequality, the relationship reverses (the sign flips). In other words, $>$ switches to $<$ and vice versa. Multiplying or dividing by a positive number does not change the relationship, so the sign stays the same.

An example is shown below.

Solve $-2x - 8 \leq 22$ for the value of x.

Add 8 to both sides to isolate the variable:

$$-2x \leq 30$$

Divide both sides by -2 to solve for x:

$$x \geq -15$$

Although linear equations generally have one solution, this is not always the case. If there is no value for the variable that makes the statement true, there is no solution to the equation. Consider the equation:

$$x + 3 = x - 1$$

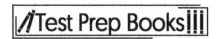

There is no value for x in which adding 3 to the value produces the same result as subtracting one from the value. Conversely, if any value for the variable makes a true statement, the equation has an infinite number of solutions. Consider the equation:

$$3x + 6 = 3(x + 2)$$

Any number substituted for x will result in a true statement (both sides of the equation are equal).

By manipulating equations like the two above, the variable of the equation will cancel out completely. If the remaining constants express a true statement (ex. $6 = 6$), then all real numbers are solutions to the equation. If the constants left express a false statement (ex. $3 = -1$), then no solution exists for the equation.

Solving a linear inequality requires all values that make the statement true to be determined. For example, solving:

$$3x - 7 \geq -13$$

produces the solution $x \geq -2$. This means that -2 and any number greater than -2 produces a true statement. Solution sets for linear inequalities will often be displayed using a number line. If a value is included in the set ($\geq$ or $\leq$), a shaded dot is placed on that value and an arrow extending in the direction of the solutions. For a variable $>$ or $\geq$ a number, the arrow will point right on a number line, the direction where the numbers increase. If a variable is $<$ or $\leq$ a number, the arrow will point left on a number line, which is the direction where the numbers decrease. If the value is not included in the set ($>$ or $<$), an open (unshaded) circle on that value is used with an arrow in the appropriate direction.

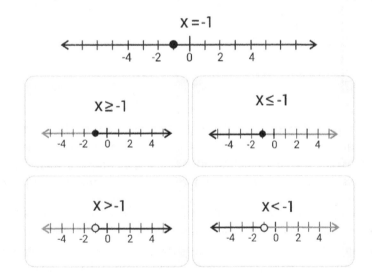

Similar to linear equations, a linear inequality may have a solution set consisting of all real numbers, or can contain no solution. When solved algebraically, a linear inequality in which the variable cancels out and results in a true statement (ex. $7 \geq 2$) has a solution set of all real numbers. A linear inequality in which the variable cancels out and results in a false statement (ex. $7 \leq 2$) has no solution.

Equations and inequalities in two variables represent a relationship. Jim owns a car wash and charges $40 per car. The rent for the facility is $350 per month. An equation can be written to relate the number of cars Jim cleans to the money he makes per month. Let x represent the number of cars and y represent the profit Jim makes each month from the car wash. The equation $y = 40x - 350$ can be used to show Jim's profit or loss. Since this equation has two variables, the coordinate plane can be used to show the relationship and predict profit or loss for Jim. The following graph shows that Jim must wash at least nine cars to pay the rent, where $x = 9$. Anything nine cars and above yield a profit shown in the value on the y-axis.

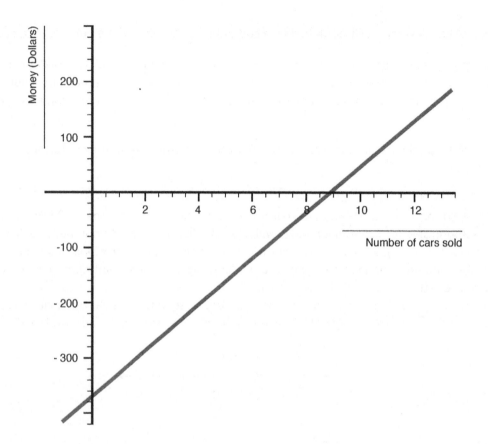

With a single equation in two variables, the solutions are limited only by the situation the equation represents. When two equations or inequalities are used, more constraints are added. For example, in a system of linear equations, there is often—although not always—only one answer. The point of intersection of two lines is the solution. For a system of inequalities, there are infinitely many answers.

The intersection of two solution sets gives the solution set of the system of inequalities. In the following graph, the darker shaded region is where two inequalities overlap. Any set of x and y found in that region satisfies both inequalities. The line with the positive slope is solid, meaning the values on that line are included in the solution. The line with the negative slope is dotted, so the coordinates on that line are not included.

Here's an example:

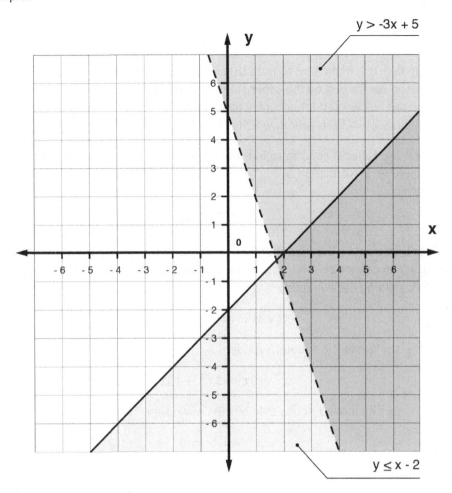

Formulas with two variables are equations used to represent a specific relationship. For example, the formula $d = rt$ represents the relationship between distance, rate, and time. If Bob travels at a rate of 35 miles per hour on his road trip from Westminster to Seneca, the formula $d = 35t$ can be used to represent his distance traveled in a specific length of time. Formulas can also be used to show different roles of the variables, transformed without any given numbers. Solving for r, the formula becomes $\frac{d}{t} = r$. The t is moved over by division so that rate is a function of distance and time.

Solving Equations

Solving equations in one variable involves isolating that variable on one side of the equation. The letters in an equation are variables as they stand for unknown quantities that you are trying to solve for. The numbers attached to the variables by multiplication are called coefficients. For example, in $3x - 7 = 20$, the variable x needs to be isolated. Using opposite operations, the -7 is moved to the right side of the equation by adding seven to both sides:

$$3x - 7 + 7 = 20 + 7$$

$$3x = 27$$

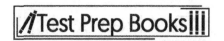

Dividing by three on each side:

$$\frac{3x}{3} = \frac{27}{3}$$

This isolates the variable. It is important to note that if an operation is performed on one side of the equals sign, it has to be performed on the other side to maintain equality. The solution is found to be $x = 9$. This solution can be checked for accuracy by plugging $x = 9$ in the original equation. After simplifying the equation, $20 = 20$ is found, which is a true statement.

When solving radical and rational equations, extraneous solutions must be accounted for when finding the answers. For example, the equation:

$$\frac{x}{x-5} = \frac{3x}{x+3}$$

This has two values that create a 0 denominator: $x \neq 5, -3$. When solving for x, these values must be considered because they cannot be solutions. In the given equation, solving for x can be done using cross-multiplication, yielding the equation:

$$x(x+3) = 3x(x-5)$$

Distributing results in the quadratic equation yields:

$$x^2 + 3x = 3x^2 - 15x$$

Therefore, all terms must be moved to one side of the equals sign. This results in:

$$2x^2 - 18x = 0$$

In factored form is:

$$2x(x-9) = 0$$

Setting each factor equal to zero, the apparent solutions are $x = 0$ and $x = 9$. These two solutions are neither 5 nor −3, so they are viable solutions. Neither 0 nor 9 create a 0 denominator in the original equation.

A similar process exists when solving radical equations. One must check to make sure the solutions are defined in the original equations. Solving an equation containing a square root involves isolating the root and then squaring both sides of the equals sign. Solving a cube root equation involves isolating the radical and then cubing both sides. In either case, the variable can then be solved for because there are no longer radicals in the equation.

Equations with one variable can be solved using the addition principle and multiplication principle. If $a = b$, then $a + c = b + c$, and $ac = bc$. Given the equation:

$$2x - 3 = 5x + 7$$

The first step is to combine the variable terms and the constant terms. Using the principles, expressions can be added and subtracted onto and off both sides of the equals sign, so the equation turns into

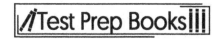

$-10 = 3x$. Dividing by 3 on both sides through the multiplication principle with $c = \frac{1}{3}$ results in the final answer of $x = \frac{-10}{3}$.

Some equations have a higher degree and are not solved by simply using opposite operations. When an equation has a degree of 2, completing the square is an option. For example, the quadratic equation:

$$x^2 - 6x + 2 = 0$$

This can be rewritten by completing the square. A **quadratic equation** is an equation in the form:

$$ax^2 + bx + c = 0$$

The goal of completing the square is to get the equation into the form:

$$(x - p)^2 = q$$

Using the example, the constant term 2 first needs to be moved over to the opposite side by subtracting. Then, the square can be completed by adding 9 to both sides, which is the square of half of the coefficient of the middle term $-6x$. The current equation is:

$$x^2 - 6x + 9 = 7$$

The left side can be factored into a square of a binomial, resulting in:

$$(x - 3)^2 = 7$$

To solve for x, the square root of both sides should be taken, resulting in:

$$(x - 3) = \pm\sqrt{7}$$

$$x = 3 \pm \sqrt{7}$$

Other ways of solving quadratic equations include graphing, factoring, and using the quadratic formula. The equation $y = x^2 - 4x + 3$ can be graphed on the coordinate plane, and the solutions can be observed where the graph crosses the x-axis. The graph will be a parabola that opens up with two solutions at 1 and 3.

The equation can also be factored to find the solutions. The original equation:

$$y = x^2 - 4x + 3$$

This can be factored into:

$$y = (x - 1)(x - 3)$$

Setting this equal to zero, the x-values are found to be 1 and 3, just as on the graph. Solving by factoring and graphing are not always possible. The **quadratic formula** is a method of solving quadratic equations that always results in exact solutions.

The formula is:

$$x = \frac{-b \pm \sqrt{b^2 - 4ac}}{2a}$$

a, b, and c are the coefficients in the original equation in standard form:

$$y = ax^2 + bx + c$$

For this example,

$$x = \frac{4 \pm \sqrt{(-4)^2 - 4(1)(3)}}{2(1)}$$

$$\frac{4 \pm \sqrt{16 - 12}}{2}$$

$$\frac{4 \pm 2}{2}$$

$$1, 3$$

Multistep One-Variable Linear Equations and Inequalities

Solutions of a linear equation or a linear inequality are the values of the variable that make a statement true. In the case of a linear equation, the solution set (list of all possible solutions) typically consists of a single numerical value. To find the solution, the equation is solved by isolating the variable. For example, solving the equation $3x - 7 = -13$ produces the solution $x = -2$. The only value for x which produces a true statement is -2. This can be checked by substituting -2 into the original equation to check that both sides are equal. In this case:

$$3(-2) - 7 = -13 \rightarrow -13 = -13$$

Therefore, -2 is a solution.

Although linear equations generally have one solution, this is not always the case. If there is no value for the variable that makes the statement true, there is no solution to the equation. Consider the equation:

$$x + 3 = x - 1$$

There is no value for x in which adding 3 to the value produces the same result as subtracting one from the value. Conversely, if any value for the variable makes a true statement, the equation has an infinite number of solutions. Consider the equation:

$$3x + 6 = 3(x + 2)$$

Any number substituted for x will result in a true statement (both sides of the equation are equal).

By manipulating equations like the two above, the variable of the equation will cancel out completely. If the remaining constants express a true statement (ex. $6 = 6$), then all real numbers are solutions to the equation. If the constants left express a false statement (ex. $3 = -1$), then no solution exists for the equation.

Linear Relationships

Linear relationships describe the way two quantities change with respect to each other. The relationship is defined as **linear** because a line is produced if all the sets of corresponding values are graphed on a coordinate grid. When expressing the linear relationship as an equation, the equation is often written in the form:

$$y = mx + b \text{ (slope-intercept form)}$$

m and b are numerical values and x and y are variables (for example, $y = 5x + 10$). Given a linear equation and the value of either variable (x or y), the value of the other variable can be determined.

Suppose a teacher is grading a test containing 20 questions with 5 points given for each correct answer, adding a curve of 10 points to each test. This linear relationship can be expressed as the equation:

$$y = 5x + 10$$

x represents the number of correct answers, and y represents the test score. To determine the score of a test with a given number of correct answers, the number of correct answers is substituted into the equation for x and evaluated. For example, for 10 correct answers, 10 is substituted for x:

$$y = 5(10) + 10 \rightarrow y = 60$$

Therefore, 10 correct answers will result in a score of 60. The number of correct answers needed to obtain a certain score can also be determined. To determine the number of correct answers needed to score a 90, 90 is substituted for y in the equation (y represents the test score) and solved:

$$90 = 5x + 10 \rightarrow 80 = 5x \rightarrow 16 = x$$

Therefore, 16 correct answers are needed to score a 90.

Linear relationships may be represented by a table of 2 corresponding values. Certain tables may determine the relationship between the values and predict other corresponding sets. Consider the table below, which displays the money in a checking account that charges a monthly fee:

Month	0	1	2	3	4
Balance	$210	$195	$180	$165	$150

An examination of the values reveals that the account loses $15 every month (the month increases by one and the balance decreases by 15). This information can be used to predict future values. To determine what the value will be in month 6, the pattern can be continued, and it can be concluded that the balance will be $120. To determine which month the balance will be $0, $210 is divided by $15 (since the balance decreases $15 every month), resulting in month 14.

Similar to a table, a graph can display corresponding values of a linear relationship.

The graph above represents the relationship between distance traveled and time. To find the distance traveled in 80 minutes, the mark for 80 minutes is located at the bottom of the graph. By following this mark directly up on the graph, the corresponding point for 80 minutes is directly across from the 160-kilometer mark. This information indicates that the distance travelled in 80 minutes is 160 kilometers. To predict information not displayed on the graph, the way in which the variables change with respect to one another is determined. In this case, distance increases by 40 kilometers as time increases by 20 minutes. This information can be used to continue the data in the graph or convert the values to a table.

Equations and Graphing

As mentioned, a function is called **linear** if it can take the form of the equation:

$$f(x) = ax + b$$

Also, $y = ax + b$ for any two numbers a and b. A linear equation forms a straight line when graphed on the coordinate plane. An example of a linear function is shown below on the graph.

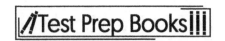

This is a graph of the following function:

$$y = \frac{2}{5}x - 1$$

A table of values that satisfies this function is shown below.

x	y
-5	-3
0	-1
5	1
10	3

These points can be found on the graph using the form (x, y).

To graph relations and functions, the **Cartesian plane** is used. The plane can be visualized as a grid of squares, with one direction being the x-axis and the other direction the y-axis. Generally, the independent variable is placed along the horizontal (x) axis, and the dependent variable is placed along the vertical (y) axis. Any point on the plane can be specified with a pair of numbers (x, y) that represent how far to go along the x-axis and how far to go up or down the y-axis. Specific values for these pairs can be given names such as $C = (-1, 3)$. Negative values mean to move left or down; positive values mean to move right or up. The point where the axes cross one another is called the **origin**. The origin has coordinates $(0, 0)$ and is usually called O when given a specific label.

An illustration of the Cartesian plane, along with the plotted points $(2, 1)$ and $(-1, -1)$, is below.

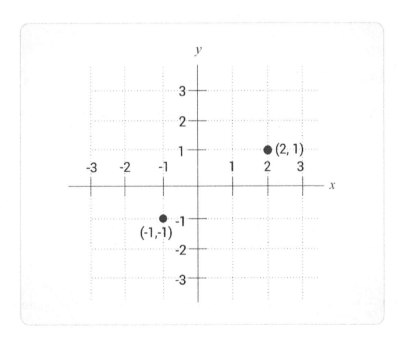

Relations also can be graphed by marking each point whose coordinates satisfy the relation. If the relation is a function, then there is only one value of y for any given value of x. This leads to the **vertical**

79

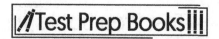

line test: if a relation is graphed, then the relation is a function if any possible vertical line drawn anywhere along the graph would only touch the graph of the relation in no more than one place. Conversely, when graphing a function, then any possible vertical line drawn will not touch the graph of the function at any point or will touch the function at just one point. This test is made from the definition of a function, where each x-value must be mapped to one and only one y-value.

When graphing a linear function, note that the ratio of the change of the y coordinate to the change in the x-coordinate is constant between any two points on the resulting line, no matter which two points are chosen. In other words, in a pair of points on a line, (x_1, y_1) and (x_2, y_2), with $x_1 \neq x_2$ so that the two points are distinct, then the ratio:

$$\frac{y_2 - y_1}{x_2 - x_1}$$

This will be the same, regardless of which particular pair of points are chosen. The ratio below is called the **slope**:

$$\frac{y_2 - y_1}{x_2 - x_1}$$

The slope of the line and is frequently denoted with the letter m. If slope m is positive, then the line goes upward when moving to the right, while if slope m is negative, then the line goes downward when moving to the right. If the slope is 0, then the line is called **horizontal,** and the y-coordinate is constant along the entire line. In lines where the x-coordinate is constant along the entire line, y is not actually a function of x. For such lines, the slope is not defined. These lines are called **vertical** lines.

Linear functions may take forms other than $y = ax + b$. The most common forms of linear equations are explained below:

1. Standard Form: $Ax + By = C$, in which the slope is given by $m = \frac{-A}{B}$, and the y-intercept is given by $\frac{C}{B}$.

2. Slope-Intercept Form: $y = mx + b$, where the slope is m and the y-intercept is b.

3. Point-Slope Form: $y - y_1 = m(x - x_1)$, where the slope is m and (x_1, y_1) is any point on the chosen line.

4. Two-Point Form:

$$\frac{y - y_1}{x - x_1} = \frac{y_2 - y_1}{x_2 - x_1}$$

(x_1, y_1) and (x_2, y_2) are any two distinct points on the chosen line. Note that the slope is given by:

$$m = \frac{y_2 - y_1}{x_2 - x_1}$$

5. Intercept Form: $\frac{x}{x_1} + \frac{y}{y_1} = 1$, in which x_1 is the x-intercept and y_1 is the y-intercept.

These five ways to write linear equations are all useful in different circumstances. Depending on the given information, it may be easier to write one of the forms over another.

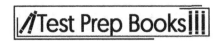
If $y = mx$, y is directly proportional to x. In this case, changing x by a factor changes y by that same factor. If $y = \frac{m}{x}$, y is inversely proportional to x. For example, if x is increased by a factor of 3, then y will be decreased by the same factor, 3.

The **midpoint** between two points, (x_1, y_1) and (x_2, y_2), is given by taking the average of the x-coordinates and the average of the y-coordinates:

$$\left(\frac{x_1 + x_2}{2}, \frac{y_1 + y_2}{2} \right)$$

The **distance** between two points, (x_1, y_1) and (x_2, y_2), is given by the **Pythagorean formula**:

$$\sqrt{(x_2 - x_1)^2 + (y_2 - y_1)^2}$$

To find the perpendicular distance between a line $Ax + By = C$ and a point (x_1, y_1) not on the line, we need to use the formula:

$$\frac{|Ax_1 + By_1 + C|}{\sqrt{A^2 + B^2}}$$

Functions

A **function** is defined as a relationship between inputs and outputs where there is only one output value for a given input. The input is called the **independent variable**. If the variable is set equal to the output, as in $y = f(x)$, then this is called the **dependent variable**. To indicate the dependent value a function, y, gives for a specific independent variable, x, the notation $y = f(x)$ is used.

As an example, the following function is in function notation:

$$f(x) = 3x - 4$$

The $f(x)$ represents the output value for an input of x. If $x = 2$, the equation becomes:

$$f(2) = 3(2) - 4 = 6 - 4 = 2$$

The **input** of 2 yields an **output** of 2, forming the ordered pair $(2, 2)$. The following set of ordered pairs corresponds to the given function:

$$(2, 2), (0, -4), (-2, -10)$$

The set of all possible inputs of a function is its **domain**, and all possible outputs is called the **range**. By definition, each member of the domain is paired with only one member of the range.

Functions can also be defined recursively. In this form, they are not defined explicitly in terms of variables. Instead, they are defined using previously-evaluated function outputs, starting with either $f(0)$ or $f(1)$. An example of a recursively-defined function is:

$$f(1) = 2, f(n) = 2f(n - 1) + 2n, n > 1$$

The domain of this function is the set of all integers.

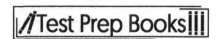
The domain and range of a function can be found visually by its plot on the coordinate plane. In the function:

$$f(x) = x^2 - 3$$

for example, the domain is all real numbers because the parabola stretches as far left and as far right as it can go, with no restrictions. This means that any input value from the real number system will yield an answer in the real number system. For the range, the inequality $y \geq -3$ would be used to describe the possible output values because the parabola has a minimum at $y = -3$. This means there will not be any real output values less than -3 because -3 is the lowest value it reaches on the y-axis.

These same answers for domain and range can be found by observing a table. The table below shows that from input values $x = -1$ to $x = 1$, the output results in a minimum of -3. On each side of $x = 0$, the numbers increase, showing that the range is all real numbers greater than or equal to -3.

x (domain/input)	y (range/output)
-2	1
-1	-2
0	-3
-1	-2
2	1

Different types of functions behave in different ways. A function is defined to be increasing over a subset of its domain if for all $x_1 \geq x_2$ in that interval $f(x_1) \geq f(x_2)$.

Also, a function is decreasing over an interval if for all $x_1 \geq x_2$ in that interval $f(x_1) \leq f(x_2)$.

A point in which a function changes from increasing to decreasing can also be labeled as the **maximum value** of a function if it is the largest point the graph reaches on the y-axis. A point in which a function changes from decreasing to increasing can be labeled as the **minimum value** of a function if it is the smallest point the graph reaches on the y-axis. Maximum values are also known as **extreme values**. The graph of a **continuous function** does not have any breaks or jumps in the graph. This description is not true of all functions. A **radical function**, for example $f(x) = \sqrt{x}$, has a restriction for the domain and range because there are no real negative inputs or outputs for this function. The domain can be stated as $x \geq 0$, and the range is $y \geq 0$.

A **piecewise-defined function** also has a different appearance on the graph. In the following function, there are three equations defined over different intervals. It is a function because there is only one y-value for each x-value, passing the **Vertical Line Test**. The domain is all real numbers less than or equal to 6. The range is all real numbers greater than zero. From left to right, the graph decreases to zero, then increases to almost 4, and then jumps to 6.

From input values greater than 2, the input decreases just below 8 to 4, and then stops.

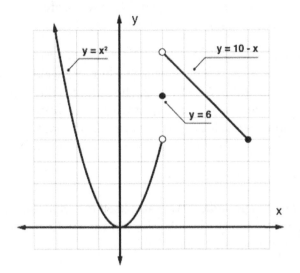

Logarithmic and **exponential functions** also have different behavior than other functions. These two types of functions are inverses of each other. The **inverse** of a function can be found by switching the place of x and y, and solving for y. When this is done for the exponential equation, $y = 2^x$, the function $y = \log_2 x$ is found. The general form of a logarithmic function is $y = \log_b x$, which says b raised to the y power equals x.

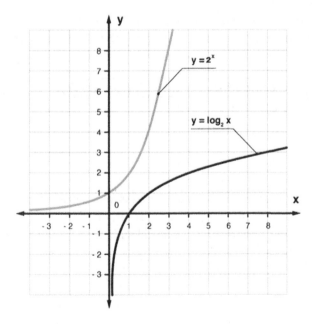

The black line on the graph above represents the logarithmic function $y = \log_2 x$. This curve passes through the point $(1, 0)$, just as all log functions do, because any value $b^0 = 1$. The graph of this logarithmic function starts very close to zero, but does not touch the y-axis. The output value will never be zero by the definition of logarithms. The lighter gray line seen above represents the exponential function $y = 2^x$. The behavior of this function is opposite the logarithmic function because the graph of an inverse function is the graph of the original function flipped over the line $y = x$. The curve passes through the point $(0, 1)$ because any number raised to the zero power is one. This curve also gets very

83

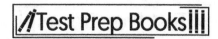

close to the x-axis but never touches it because an exponential expression never has an output of zero. The x-axis on this graph is called a horizontal asymptote. An **asymptote** is a line that represents a boundary for a function. It shows a value that the function will get close to, but never reach.

Functions can also be described as being even, odd, or neither. If $f(-x) = f(x)$ the function is **even**. For example, the function $f(x) = x^2 - 2$ is even. Plugging in $x = 2$ yields an output of $y = 2$. After changing the input to $x = -2$, the output is still $y = 2$. The output is the same for opposite inputs. Another way to observe an even function is by the symmetry of the graph. If the graph is symmetrical about the axis, then the function is even. If the graph is symmetric about the origin, then the function is **odd**.

Algebraically, if $f(-x) = -f(x)$, the function is odd.

Also, a function can be described as **periodic** if it repeats itself in regular intervals. Common periodic functions are trigonometric functions. For example, $y = \sin x$ is a periodic function with period 2π because it repeats itself every 2π units along the x-axis.

Building Functions

Functions can be built out of the context of a situation. For example, the relationship between the money paid for a gym membership and the months that someone has been a member can be described through a function. If the one-time membership fee is $40 and the monthly fee is $30, then the function can be written:

$$f(x) = 30x + 40$$

The x-value represents the number of months the person has been part of the gym, while the output is the total money paid for the membership. The table below shows this relationship. It is a representation of the function because the initial cost is $40 and the cost increases each month by $30.

x (months)	y (money paid to gym)
0	40
1	70
2	100
3	130

Functions can also be built from existing functions. For example, a given function $f(x)$ can be transformed by adding a constant, multiplying by a constant, or changing the input value by a constant. The new function $g(x) = f(x) + k$ represents a vertical shift of the original function. In $f(x) = 3x - 2$ a vertical shift 4 units up would be:

$$g(x) = 3x - 2 + 4$$

$$3x + 2$$

Multiplying the function times a constant k represents a vertical stretch, based on whether the constant is greater than or less than 1. The following function represents a stretch:

$$g(x) = kf(x)$$

$$4(3x - 2)$$

$$12x - 8$$

Changing the input x by a constant forms the function:

$$g(x) = f(x + k)$$

$$3(x + 4) - 2$$

$$3x + 12 - 2$$

$$3x + 10$$

This represents a horizontal shift to the left 4 units. If $(x - 4)$ was plugged into the function, it would represent a horizontal shift.

Common Functions

Three common functions used to model different relationships between quantities are linear, quadratic, and exponential functions. Linear functions are the simplest of the three, and the independent variable x has an exponent of 1. Written in the most common form:

$$y = mx + b$$

the coefficient of x indicates how fast the function grows at a constant rate, and the b-value denotes the starting point. A quadratic function has an exponent of 2 on the independent variable x. Standard form for this type of function is:

$$y = ax^2 + bx + c$$

The graph is a parabola. These type functions grow at a changing rate. An exponential function has an independent variable in the exponent $y = ab^x$. The graph of these types of functions is described as **growth** or **decay**, based on whether the base, b, is greater than or less than 1. These functions are different from quadratic functions because the base stays constant. A common base is base e.

The following three functions model a linear, quadratic, and exponential function respectively:

$$y = 2x, y = x^2, \text{ and } y = 2^x$$

Their graphs are shown below. The first graph, modeling the linear function, shows that the growth is constant over each interval. With a horizontal change of 1, the vertical change is 2. It models constant positive growth. The second graph shows the quadratic function, which is a curve that is symmetric across the y-axis. The growth is not constant, but the change is mirrored over the axis. The last graph models the exponential function, where the horizontal change of 1 yields a vertical change that increases more and more with each iteration of horizontal change. The exponential graph gets very

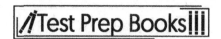

close to the x-axis, but never touches it, meaning there is an asymptote there. The y-value can never be zero because the base of 2 can never be raised to an input value that yields an output of zero.

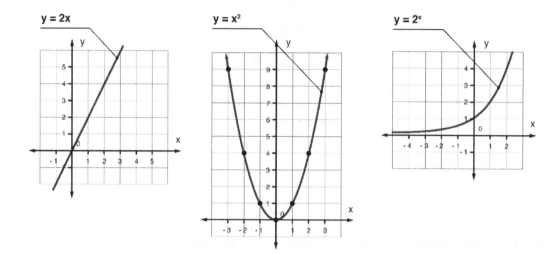

The three tables below show specific values for three types of functions. The third column in each table shows the change in the y-values for each interval. The first table shows a constant change of 2 for each equal interval, which matches the slope in the equation $y = 2x$. The second table shows an increasing change, but it also has a pattern. The increase is changing by 2 more each time, so the change is quadratic. The third table shows the change as factors of the base, 2. It shows a continuing pattern of factors of the base.

$y = 2x$		
x	y	Δy
1	2	
2	4	2
3	6	2
4	8	2
5	10	2

$y = x^2$		
x	y	Δy
1	1	
2	4	3
3	9	5
4	16	7
5	25	9

$y = 2^x$		
x	y	Δy
1	2	
2	4	2
3	8	4
4	16	8
5	32	16

Given a table of values, the type of function can be determined by observing the change in y over equal intervals. For example, the tables below model two functions. The changes in interval for the x-values is 1 for both tables. For the first table, the y-values increase by 5 for each interval. Since the change is constant, the situation can be described as a linear function. The equation would be:

$$y = 5x + 3$$

For the second table, the change for y is 20, 100, and 500, respectively. The increases are multiples of 5, meaning the situation can be modeled by an exponential function. The equation below models this situation:

$$y = 5^x + 3$$

$y = 5x + 3$	
x	y
1	8
2	13
3	18
4	23

$y = 5^x + 3$	
x	y
1	8
2	28
3	128
4	628

Quadratic equations can be used to model real-world area problems. For example, a farmer may have a rectangular field that he needs to sow with seed. The field has length $x + 8$ and width $2x$. The formula for area should be used: $A = lw$. Therefore:

$$A = (x + 8) \times 2x = 2x^2 + 16x$$

The possible values for the length and width can be shown in a table, with input x and output A. If the equation was graphed, the possible area values can be seen on the y-axis for given x-values.

Exponential growth and decay can be found in real-world situations. For example, if a piece of notebook paper is folded 25 times, the thickness of the paper can be found. To model this situation, a table can be used. The initial point is one-fold, which yields a thickness of 2 papers. For the second fold, the thickness is 4. Since the thickness doubles each time, the table below shows the thickness for the next few folds. Notice the thickness changes by the same factor each time. Since this change for a constant interval of folds is a factor of 2, the function is exponential. The equation for this is $y = 2^x$. For twenty-five folds, the thickness would be 33,554,432 papers.

x (folds)	y (paper thickness)
0	1
1	2
2	4
3	8
4	16
5	32

Conjectures, Predictions, or Generalizations Based on Patterns

An arithmetic or geometric sequence can be written as a formula and used to determine unknown steps without writing out the entire sequence. An arithmetic sequence progresses by a **common difference**. To determine the common difference, any step is subtracted by the step that precedes it. In the sequence 4, 9, 14, 19... the common difference, or d, is 5. By expressing each step as a_1, a_2, a_3, etc., a

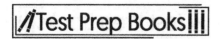

formula can be written to represent the sequence. a_1 is the first step. To produce step two, step 1 (a_1) is added to the common difference (d):

$$a_2 = a_1 + d$$

To produce step three, the common difference (d) is added twice to a_1:

$$a_3 = a_1 + 2d$$

To produce step four, the common difference (d) is added three times to a_1:

$$a_4 = a_1 + 3d$$

Following this pattern allows a general rule for arithmetic sequences to be written. For any term of the sequence (a_n), the first step (a_1) is added to the product of the common difference (d) and one less than the step of the term ($n - 1$):

$$a_n = a_1 + (n - 1)d$$

Suppose the 8th term (a_8) is to be found in the previous sequence. By knowing the first step (a_1) is 4 and the common difference (d) is 5, the formula can be used:

$$a_n = a_1 + (n - 1)d$$

$$a_8 = 4 + (7)5$$

$$a_8 = 39$$

In a geometric sequence, each step is produced by multiplying or dividing the previous step by the same number. The **common ratio,** or (r), can be determined by dividing any step by the previous step. In the sequence 1, 3, 9, 27… the common ratio (r) is:

$$3(\frac{3}{1} = 3 \text{ or } \frac{9}{3} = 3 \text{ or } \frac{27}{9} = 3)$$

Each successive step can be expressed as a product of the first step (a_1) and the common ratio (r) to some power. For example,

$$a_2 = a_1 \times r$$

$$a_3 = a_1 \times r \times r \text{ or } a_3 = a_1 \times r^2$$

$$a_4 = a_1 \times r \times r \times r \text{ or } a_4 = a\_1 \times r^3$$

Following this pattern, a general rule for geometric sequences can be written. For any term of the sequence (a_n), the first step (a_1) is multiplied by the common ratio (r) raised to the power one less than the step of the term ($n - 1$):

$$a_n = a_1 \times r^{(n-1)}$$

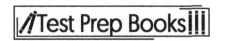

Suppose for the previous sequence, the 7th term (a_7) is to be found. Knowing the first step (a_1) is one, and the common ratio (r) is 3, the formula can be used:

$$a_n = a_1 \times r^{(n-1)}$$

$$a_7 = (1) \times 3^6$$

$$a_7 = 729$$

Corresponding Terms of Two Numerical Patterns

When given two numerical patterns, the corresponding terms should be examined to determine if a relationship exists between them. Corresponding terms between patterns are the pairs of numbers that appear in the same step of the two sequences. Consider the following patterns 1, 2, 3, 4... and 3, 6, 9, 12... The corresponding terms are: 1 and 3; 2 and 6; 3 and 9; and 4 and 12. To identify the relationship, each pair of corresponding terms is examined and the possibilities of performing an operation (+, −, ×, ÷) to the term from the first sequence to produce the corresponding term in the second sequence are determined. In this case:

$$1 + 2 = 3 \qquad \text{or} \qquad 1 \times 3 = 3$$

$$2 + 4 = 6 \qquad \text{or} \qquad 2 \times 3 = 6$$

$$3 + 6 = 9 \qquad \text{or} \qquad 3 \times 3 = 9$$

$$4 + 8 = 12 \qquad \text{or} \qquad 4 \times 3 = 12$$

The consistent pattern is that the number from the first sequence multiplied by 3 equals its corresponding term in the second sequence. By assigning each sequence a label (input and output) or variable (x and y), the relationship can be written as an equation. If the first sequence represents the inputs, or x, and the second sequence represents the outputs, or y, the relationship can be expressed as: $y = 3x$.

Consider the following sets of numbers:

a	2	4	6	8
b	6	8	10	12

To write a rule for the relationship between the values for a and the values for b, the corresponding terms (2 and 6; 4 and 8; 6 and 10; 8 and 12) are examined. The possibilities for producing b from a are:

$$2 + 4 = 6 \qquad \text{or} \qquad 2 \times 3 = 6$$

$$4 + 4 = 8 \qquad \text{or} \qquad 4 \times 2 = 8$$

$$6 + 4 = 10$$

$$8 + 4 = 12 \qquad \text{or} \qquad 8 \times 1.5 = 12$$

The consistent pattern is that adding 4 to the value of a produces the value of b. The relationship can be written as the equation $a + 4 = b$.

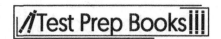

Geometry/Measurement

Geometry deals with shapes and their properties. It is also similar to measurement and number operations. The basis of geometry involves being able to label and describe shapes and their properties. That knowledge will lead to working with formulas such as area, perimeter, and volume. This knowledge will help to solve word problems involving shapes.

Flat or two-dimensional shapes include circles, triangles, hexagons, and rectangles, among others. Three-dimensional solid shapes, such as spheres and cubes, are also used in geometry. A shape can be classified based on whether it is open like the letter U or closed like the letter O. Further classifications involve counting the number of sides and **vertices** (corners) on the shapes. This will help differentiate shapes.

Polygons can be drawn by sketching a fixed number of line segments that meet to create a closed shape. In addition, **triangles** can be drawn by sketching a closed space using only three-line segments. **Quadrilaterals** are closed shapes with four-line segments. Note that a triangle has three vertices, and a quadrilateral has four vertices.

To draw circles, one curved line segment must be drawn that has only one endpoint. This creates a closed shape. Given such direction, every point on the line would be the same distance away from its center. The **radius** of a circle goes from an endpoint on the center of the circle to an endpoint on the circle. The **diameter** is the line segment created by placing an endpoint on the circle, drawing through the radius, and placing the other endpoint on the circle. A compass can be used to draw circles of a more precise size and shape.

Perimeter and Area

Perimeter is the measurement of a distance around something or the sum of all sides of a polygon. Think of perimeter as the length of the boundary, like a fence. In contrast, **area** is the space occupied by a defined enclosure, like the size of a field enclosed by a fence.

When thinking about perimeter, think about walking around the outside of something. When thinking about area, think about the amount of space or **surface area** something takes up.

Squares
The perimeter of a square is measured by adding together all of the sides. Since a square has four equal sides, its perimeter can be calculated by multiplying the length of one side by 4. Thus, the formula is:

$$P = 4 \times s$$

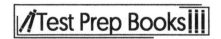
s equals one side. For example, the following square has side lengths of 5 meters:

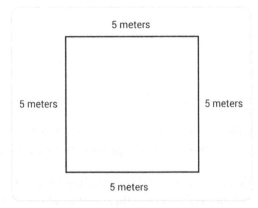

The perimeter is 20 meters because 4 times 5 is 20.

The area of a square is the length of a side squared. For example, if a side of a square is 7 centimeters, then the area is 49 square centimeters. The formula for this example is:

$$A = s^2 = 7^2 = 49 \text{ square centimeters}$$

Rectangles

Like a square, a rectangle's perimeter is measured by adding together all of the sides. But as the sides are unequal, the formula is different. A rectangle has equal values for its lengths (long sides) and equal values for its widths (short sides), so the perimeter formula for a rectangle is:

$$P = l + l + w + w$$

$$2l + 2w$$

l equals length.
w equals width.

For example, if the length of a rectangle is 10 inches and the width 8 inches, then the perimeter is 36 inches because:

$$P = 2l + 2w$$

$$2(10) + 2(8)$$

$$20 + 16 = 36 \text{ inches}$$

The area is found by multiplying the length by the width, so the formula is $A = l \times w$.

An example is if the rectangle has a length of 6 inches and a width of 7 inches, then the area is 42 square inches:

$$A = lw = 6(7) = 42 \text{ square inches}$$

Triangles

A triangle's perimeter is measured by adding together the three sides, so the formula is:

$$P = a + b + c$$

91

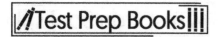
a, b, and c are the values of the three sides. The area is the product of one-half the base and height so the formula is:

$$A = \frac{1}{2} \times b \times h$$

It can be simplified to:

$$A = \frac{bh}{2}$$

The base is the bottom of the triangle, and the height is the distance from the base to the peak. If a problem asks to calculate the area of a triangle, it will provide the base and height.

For example, if the base of the triangle is 2 feet and the height 4 feet, then the area is 4 square feet. The following equation shows the formula used to calculate the area of the triangle:

$$A = \frac{1}{2}bh = \frac{1}{2}(2)(4) = 4 \text{ square feet}$$

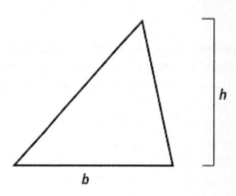

Circles

A circle's perimeter—also known as its **circumference**—is measured by multiplying the diameter by π.

Diameter is the straight line measured from a point on one side of the circle to a point directly across on the opposite side of the circle.

π is referred to as pi and is equal to 3.14 (with rounding).

So, the formula is $\pi \times d$.

This is sometimes expressed by the formula $C = 2 \times \pi \times r$, where r is the radius of the circle. These formulas are equivalent, as the radius equals half of the diameter.

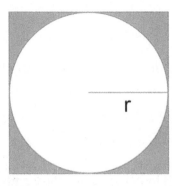

The area of a circle is calculated through the formula

$$A = \pi \times r^2$$

The test will indicate either to leave the answer with π attached or to calculate to the nearest decimal place, which means multiplying by 3.14 for π.

Parallelograms

Similar to triangles, the height of the parallelogram is measured from one base to the other at a 90° angle (or perpendicular).

Area = bh

Perimeter = 2(a + b)

Trapezoid

The area of a trapezoid can be calculated using the formula:

$$A = \frac{1}{2} \times h(b_1 + b_2)$$

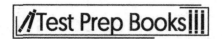

h is the height and b_1 and b_2 are the parallel bases of the trapezoid.

Irregular Shapes

The perimeter of an irregular polygon is found by adding the lengths of all of the sides. In cases where all of the sides are given, this will be very straightforward, as it will simply involve finding the sum of the provided lengths. Other times, a side length may be missing and must be determined before the perimeter can be calculated. Consider the example below:

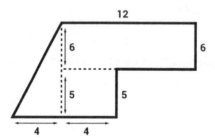

All of the side lengths are provided except for the angled side on the left. Test takers should notice that this is the hypotenuse of a right triangle. The other two sides of the triangle are provided (the base is 4 and the height is $6 + 5 = 11$). The Pythagorean Theorem can be used to find the length of the hypotenuse, remembering that $a^2 + b^2 = c^2$.

Substituting the side values provided yields:

$$(4)^2 + (11)^2 = c^2$$

Therefore,

$$c = \sqrt{16 + 121} = 11.7$$

Finally, the perimeter can be found by adding this new side length with the other provided lengths to get the total length around the figure:

$$4 + 4 + 5 + 8 + 6 + 12 + 11.7 = 50.7$$

Although units are not provided in this figure, remember that reporting units with a measurement is important.

The area of irregular polygons is found by decomposing, or breaking apart, the figure into smaller shapes. When the area of the smaller shapes is determined, the area of the smaller shapes will produce the area of the original figure when added together.

Consider the earlier example:

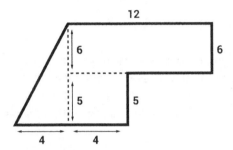

The irregular polygon is decomposed into two rectangles and a triangle. The area of the large rectangle ($A = l \times w \rightarrow A = 12 \times 6$) is 72 square units. The area of the small rectangle is 20 square units:

$$A = 4 \times 5$$

The area of the triangle:

$$A = \frac{1}{2} \times b \times h$$

$$A = \frac{1}{2} \times 4 \times 11 = 22 \text{ square units}$$

The sum of the areas of these figures produces the total area of the original polygon:

$$A = 72 + 20 + 22 \rightarrow A = 114 \text{ square units}$$

Here's another example:

This irregular polygon is decomposed into two rectangles. The area of the large rectangle:

$$A = l \times w$$

$$A = 8 \times 4 = 32 \text{ square units}$$

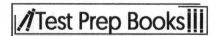
The area of the small rectangle is 20 square units ($A = 4 \times 5$). The sum of the areas of these figures produces the total area of the original polygon:

$$A = 32 + 20$$

$$A = 52 \text{ square units}$$

Surface Area and Volume

Geometry in three dimensions is similar to geometry in two dimensions. The main new feature is that three points now define a unique **plane** that passes through each of them. Three dimensional objects can be made by putting together two-dimensional figures in different surfaces. Below, some of the possible three-dimensional figures will be provided, along with formulas for their volumes and surface areas.

A **rectangular prism** is a box whose sides are all rectangles meeting at 90° angles. Such a box has three dimensions: length, width, and height. If the length is x, the width is y, and the height is z, then the **volume** is given by $V = xyz$.

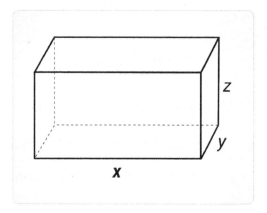

The **surface area** will be given by computing the surface area of each rectangle and adding them together. There are a total of six rectangles. Two of them have sides of length x and y, two have sides of length y and z, and two have sides of length x and z. Therefore, the total surface area will be given by:

$$SA = 2xy + 2yz + 2xz$$

A **cube** is a special type of rectangular solid in which its length, width, and height are the same. If this length is s, then the formula for the volume of a cube is $V = s \times s \times s$. The surface area of a cube is $SA = 6s^2$.

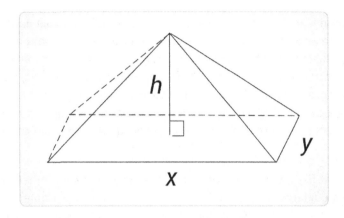

A **rectangular pyramid** is a figure with a rectangular base and four triangular sides that meet at a single vertex. If the rectangle has sides of length x and y, then the volume will be given by $V = \frac{1}{3}xyh$.

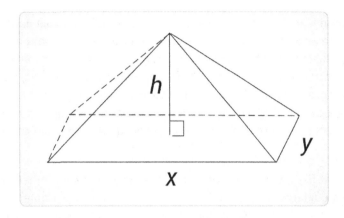

To find the surface area, the dimensions of each triangle need to be known. However, these dimensions can differ depending on the problem in question. Therefore, there is no general formula for calculating total surface area.

A **sphere** is a set of points all of which are equidistant from some central point. It is like a circle, but in three dimensions. The volume of a sphere of radius r is given by:

$$V = \frac{4}{3}\pi r^3$$

The surface area is given by:

$$A = 4\pi r^2$$

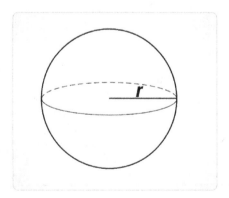

Lines and Angles

In geometry, a **line** connects two points, has no thickness, and extends indefinitely in both directions beyond the points. If it does end at two points, it is known as a **line segment**. It is important to distinguish between a line and a line segment.

An **angle** can be visualized as a corner. It is defined as the formation of two rays connecting at a vertex that extend indefinitely. Angles are usually measured in degrees. Their measurement is a measure of rotation. A full rotation equals 360 degrees and represents a circle. Half of a rotation equals 180 degrees

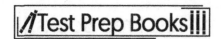
and represents a half-circle. Subsequently, 90 degrees represents a quarter-circle. Similar to the hands on a clock, an angle begins at the center point, and two lines extend indefinitely from that point in two different directions.

A clock can be useful when learning how to measure angles. At 3:00, the big hand is on the 12 and the small hand is on the 3. The angle formed is 90 degrees and is known as a **right angle**. Any angle less than 90 degrees, such as the one formed at 2:00, is known as an **acute angle**. Any angle greater than 90 degrees is known as an **obtuse angle**. The entire clock represents 360 degrees, and each clockwise increment on the clock represents an addition of 30 degrees. Therefore, 6:00 represents 180 degrees, 7:00 represents 210 degrees, etc. Angle measurement is additive. An angle can be broken into two non-overlapping angles. The total measure of the larger angle is equal to the sum of the measurements of the two smaller angles.

A **ray** is a straight path that has an endpoint on one end and extends indefinitely in the other direction. Lines are known as being **coplanar** if they are located in the same plane. Coplanar lines exist within the same two-dimensional surface. Two lines are **parallel** if they are coplanar, extend in the same direction, and never cross. They are known as being **equidistant** because they are always the same distance from each other. If lines do cross, they are known as **intersecting lines**. As discussed previously, angles are utilized throughout geometry, and their measurement can be seen through the use of an analog clock. An angle is formed when two rays begin at the same endpoint. **Adjacent angles** can be formed by forming two angles out of one shared ray. They are two side-by-side angles that also share an endpoint.

Perpendicular lines are coplanar lines that form a right angle at their point of intersection. A triangle that contains a right angle is known as a **right triangle**. The sum of the angles within any triangle is always 180 degrees. Therefore, in a right triangle, the sum of the two angles that are not right angles is 90 degrees. Any two angles that sum up to 90 degrees are known as **complementary angles**. A triangle that contains an obtuse angle is known as an **obtuse triangle**. A triangle that contains three acute angles is known as an **acute triangle**. Here is an example of a 180-degree angle, split up into an acute and obtuse angle:

98

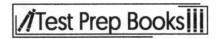

Relationships between Angles

Supplementary angles add up to 180 degrees. **Vertical angles** are two nonadjacent angles formed by two intersecting lines. For example, in the following picture, angles 4 and 2 are vertical angles and so are angles 1 and 3:

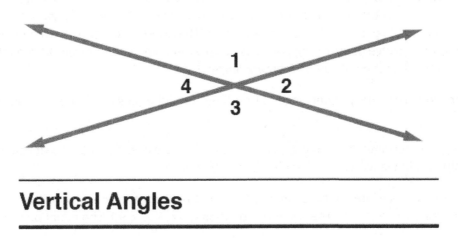

Vertical Angles

Angles that add up to 90 degrees are **complementary**. **Corresponding angles** are two angles in the same position whenever a straight line (known as a **transversal**) crosses two others. If the two lines are parallel, the corresponding angles are equal. In the following diagram, angles 1 and 3 are corresponding angles but aren't equal to each other:

Corresponding Angles

99

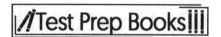

Alternate interior angles are also a pair of angles formed when two lines are crossed by a transversal. They are opposite angles that exist inside of the two lines. In the corresponding angles diagram above, angles 2 and 7 are alternate interior angles, as well as angles 6 and 3. **Alternate exterior angles** are opposite angles formed by a transversal but, in contrast to interior angles, exterior angles exist outside the two original lines. Therefore, angles 1 and 8 are alternate exterior angles and so are angles 5 and 4. Finally, **consecutive interior angles** are pairs of angles formed by a transversal. These angles are located on the same side of the transversal and inside the two original lines. Therefore, angles 2 and 3 are a pair of consecutive interior angles, and so are angles 6 and 7. These definitions are instrumental in solving many problems that involve determining relationships between angles. For example, the following problem utilizes the definition of complementary angles.

Two angles are complementary. If one angle is four times the other angle, what is the measure of each angle?

The first step is to determine the unknown, which is the measure of the first angle. (It could be the measure of either, but we will choose to solve for the first angle.)

The second step is to translate the problem into the equation using the known statement: the sum of two complementary angles is 90°. The resulting equation is $4x + x = 90$. The equation can be solved as follows:

$$5x = 90 \quad \text{Combine like terms on the left side of the equation}$$
$$x = 18 \quad \text{Divide both sides of the equation by 5}$$

The first angle is 18° and the second angle is 4 times the unknown, which is 4 times 18, or 72°.

Similarity and Congruence

Two figures are **congruent** if they have the same shape and same size. The two figures could have been rotated, reflected, or translated. Two figures are similar if they have been rotated, reflected, translated, and resized. Angle measure is preserved in similar figures. Both angle and side length are preserved in congruent figures.

In **similar figures**, if the ratio of two corresponding sides is known, then that ratio—or **scale factor**—holds true for all of the dimensions of the new figure.

Here is an example of applying this principle. Suppose that Lara is 5 feet tall and is standing 30 feet from the base of a light pole, and her shadow is 6 feet long. How high is the light on the pole? To figure this, it helps to make a sketch of the situation:

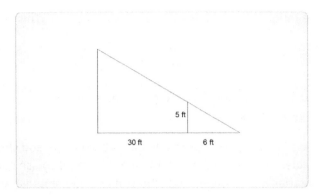

The light pole is the left side of the triangle. Lara is the 5-foot vertical line. Notice that there are two right triangles here, and that they have all the same angles as one another. Therefore, they form similar triangles and there is a ratio of proportionality between them.

The bases of these triangles are known. The small triangle, formed by Lara and her shadow, has a base of 6 feet. The large triangle formed by the light pole along with the line from the base of the pole out to the end of Lara's shadow is $30 + 6 = 36$ feet long. So, the ratio of the big triangle to the little triangle will be $\frac{36}{6} = 6$. The height of the little triangle is 5 feet. Therefore, the height of the big triangle will be $6 \times 5 = 30$ feet, meaning that the light is 30 feet up the pole.

Notice that the perimeter of a figure changes by the ratio of proportionality between two similar figures, but the area changes by the square of the ratio. This is because if the length of one side is doubled, the area is quadrupled.

As an example, suppose two rectangles are similar, but the edges of the second rectangle are three times longer than the edges of the first rectangle. The area of the first rectangle is 10 square inches. How much more area does the second rectangle have than the first?

To answer this, note that the area of the second rectangle is $3^2 = 9$ times the area of the first rectangle, which is 10 square inches. Therefore, the area of the second rectangle is going to be $9 \times 10 = 90$ square inches. This means it has $90 - 10 = 80$ square inches more area than the first rectangle.

As a second example, suppose X and Y are similar right triangles. The hypotenuse of X is 4 inches. The area of Y is $\frac{1}{4}$ the area of X. What is the hypotenuse of Y?

First, realize the area has changed by a factor of $\frac{1}{4}$. The area changes by a factor that is the **square of the ratio** of changes in lengths, so the ratio of the lengths is the square root of the ratio of areas. That means that the ratio of lengths must be is $\sqrt{\frac{1}{4}} = \frac{1}{2}$ and the hypotenuse of Y must be $\frac{1}{2} \times 4 = 2$ inches.

Volumes between similar solids change like the cube of the change in the lengths of their edges. Likewise, if the ratio of the volumes between similar solids is known, the ratio between their lengths is calculated by finding the cube root of the ratio of their volumes.

101

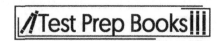
For example, suppose there are two similar rectangular pyramids X and Y. The base of X is 1 inch by 2 inches, and the volume of X is 8 inches. The volume of Y is 64 inches. What are the dimensions of the base of Y?

To answer this, first find the ratio of the volume of Y to the volume of X. This will be given by:

$$\frac{64}{8} = 8$$

Now the ratio of lengths is the cube root of the ratio of volumes, or $\sqrt[3]{8} = 2$. So, the dimensions of the base of Y must be 2 inches by 4 inches.

The criteria needed to prove triangles are congruent involves both angle and side congruence. Both pairs of related angles and sides need to be of the same measurement to use congruence in a proof. The criteria to prove similarity in triangles involves proportionality of side lengths. Angles must be congruent in similar triangles; however, corresponding side lengths only need to be a constant multiple of each other. Once similarity is established, it can be used in proofs as well. Relationships in geometric figures other than triangles can be proven using triangle congruence and similarity. If a similar or congruent triangle can be found within another type of geometric figure, their criteria can be used to prove a relationship about a given formula. For instance, a rectangle can be broken up into two congruent triangles.

If two angles of one triangle are congruent with two angles of a second triangle, the triangles are similar. This is because, within any triangle, the sum of the angle measurements is 180 degrees. Therefore, if two are congruent, the third angle must also be congruent because their measurements are equal. Three congruent pairs of angles mean that the triangles are similar.

There are five theorems to show that triangles are congruent when it's unknown whether each pair of angles and sides are congruent. Each theorem is a shortcut that involves different combinations of sides and angles that must be the same for the two triangles to be congruent. For example, **side-side-side (SSS)** states that if all sides are equal, the triangles are congruent. **Side-angle-side (SAS)** states that if two pairs of sides are equal and the included angles are congruent, then the triangles are congruent. Similarly, **angle-side-angle (ASA)** states that if two pairs of angles are congruent and the included side lengths are equal, the triangles are congruent.

Angle-angle-side (AAS) states that two triangles are congruent if they have two pairs of congruent angles and a pair of corresponding equal side lengths that aren't included. Finally, **hypotenuse-leg (HL)** states that if two right triangles have equal hypotenuses and an equal pair of shorter sides, then the triangles are congruent. An important item to note is that **angle-angle-angle (AAA)** is not enough information to have congruence. It's important to understand why these rules work by using rigid motions to show congruence between the triangles with the given properties. For example, three reflections are needed to show why *SAS* follows from the definition of congruence.

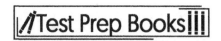

Measuring Lengths of Objects

The length of an object can be measured using standard tools such as rulers, yard sticks, meter sticks, and measuring tapes. The following image depicts a yardstick:

Choosing the right tool to perform the measurement requires determining whether United States customary units or metric units are desired, and having a grasp of the approximate length of each unit and the approximate length of each tool. The measurement can still be performed by trial and error without the knowledge of the approximate size of the tool.

For example, if you were asked to determine the length of a room in feet, a United States customary unit, you could theoretically use a few different tools for this task. These include a ruler (typically 12 inches/1 foot long), a yardstick (3 feet/1 yard long), or a tape measure displaying feet (typically either 25 feet or 50 feet). Because the length of a room is much larger than the length of a ruler or a yardstick, a tape measure should be used to perform the measurement.

When the correct measuring tool is selected, the measurement is performed by first placing the tool directly above or below the object (if making a horizontal measurement) or directly next to the object (if making a vertical measurement). The next step is aligning the tool so that one end of the object is at the mark for zero units, then recording the unit of the mark at the other end of the object. To give the length of a paperclip in metric units, a ruler displaying centimeters is aligned with one end of the paper clip to the mark for zero centimeters.

Directly down from the other end of the paperclip is the mark that measures its length. In this case, that mark is two small dashes past the 3 centimeter mark. Each small dash is 1 millimeter (or .1 centimeters). Therefore, the length of the paper clip is 3.2 centimeters.

To compare the lengths of objects, each length must be expressed with the same units. If possible, the objects should be measured with the same tool or with tools utilizing the same units.

For example, a ruler and a yardstick can both measure length in inches. If the lengths of the objects are expressed in different units, these different units must be converted to the same unit before comparing them. If two lengths are expressed in the same unit, the lengths may be compared by subtracting the

103

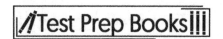

smaller value from the larger value. For example, suppose the lengths of two gardens are to be compared.

Garden A has a length of 4 feet, and garden B has a length of 2 yards. 2 yards is converted to 6 feet so that the measurements have similar units. Then, the smaller length (4 feet) is subtracted from the larger length (6 ft): 6 ft − 4 ft = 2 ft. Therefore, garden B is 2 feet larger than garden A.

Relative Sizes of United States Customary Units and Metric Units

The United States customary system and the metric system each consist of distinct units to measure lengths and volume of liquids. The U.S. customary units for length, from smallest to largest, are: inch (in), foot (ft), yard (yd), and mile (mi). The metric units for length, from smallest to largest, are: millimeter (mm), centimeter (cm), decimeter (dm), meter (m), and kilometer (km). The relative size of each unit of length is shown below.

U.S. Customary	Metric	Conversion
12 in = 1 ft	10 mm = 1 cm	1 in = 2.54 cm
36 in = 3 ft = 1 yd	10 cm = 1 dm(decimeter)	1 m ≈ 3.28 ft ≈ 1.09 yd
5,280 ft = 1,760 yd = 1 mi	100 cm = 10 dm = 1 m	1 mi ≈ 1.6 km
	1,000 m = 1 km	

The U.S. customary units for volume of liquids, from smallest to largest, are: fluid ounces (fl oz), cup (c), pint (pt), quart (qt), and gallon (gal). The metric units for volume of liquids, from smallest to largest, are: milliliter (mL), centiliter (cL), deciliter (dL), liter (L), and kiloliter (kL).

The relative size of each unit of liquid volume is shown below:

U.S. Customary	Metric	Conversion
8 fl oz = 1 c	10 mL = 1 cL	1pt ≈ 0.473L
2 c = 1 pt	10 cL = 1 dL	1L ≈ 1.057qt
4 c = 2 pt = 1 qt	1,000 mL = 100 cL = 10 dL = 1 L	1gal ≈ 3.785L
4 qt = 1 gal	1,000 L = 1 kL	

The U.S. customary system measures weight (how strongly Earth is pulling on an object) in the following units, from least to greatest: ounce (oz), pound (lb), and ton. The metric system measures mass (the quantity of matter within an object) in the following units, from least to greatest: milligram (mg), centigram (cg), gram (g), kilogram (kg), and metric ton (MT). The relative sizes of each unit of weight and mass are shown below.

U.S. Measures of Weight	Metric Measures of Mass
16 oz = 1 lb	10 mg = 1 cg
2,000 lb = 1 ton	100 cg = 1 g
	1,000 g = 1 kg
	1,000 kg = 1 MT

Note that weight and mass DO NOT measure the same thing.

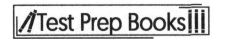

Time is measured in the following units, from shortest to longest: second (sec), minute (min), hour (h), day (d), week (wk), month (mo), year (yr), decade, century, millennium. The relative sizes of each unit of time is shown below.

- $60 \text{ sec} = 1 \text{ min}$
- $60 \text{ min} = 1 \text{ h}$
- $24 \text{ hr} = 1 \text{ d}$
- $7 \text{ d} = 1 \text{ wk}$
- $52 \text{ wk} = 1 \text{ yr}$
- $12 \text{ mo} = 1 \text{ yr}$
- $10 \text{ yr} = 1 \text{ decade}$
- $100 \text{ yrs} = 1 \text{ century}$
- $1,000 \text{ yrs} = 1 \text{ millennium}$

Conversion of Units

When working with different systems of measurement, conversion from one unit to another may be necessary. The conversion rate must be known to convert units. One method for converting units is to write and solve a proportion. The arrangement of values in a proportion is extremely important. Suppose that a problem requires converting 20 fluid ounces to cups. To do so, a proportion can be written using the conversion rate of $8 \text{ fl oz} = 1 \text{ c}$ with x representing the missing value.

The proportion can be written in any of the following ways:

$$\frac{1}{8} = \frac{x}{20} \left(\frac{c \text{ for conversion}}{fl \text{ oz for conversion}} = \frac{unknown \ c}{fl \text{ oz given}} \right)$$

$$\frac{8}{1} = \frac{20}{x} \left(\frac{fl \text{ oz for conversion}}{c \text{ for conversion}} = \frac{fl \text{ oz given}}{unknown \ c} \right)$$

$$\frac{1}{x} = \frac{8}{20} \left(\frac{c \text{ for conversion}}{unknown \ c} = \frac{fl \text{ oz for conversion}}{fl \text{ oz given}} \right)$$

$$\frac{x}{1} = \frac{20}{8} \left(\frac{unknown \ c}{c \text{ for conversion}} = \frac{fl \text{ oz given}}{fl \text{ oz for conversion}} \right)$$

To solve a proportion, the ratios are cross-multiplied and the resulting equation is solved. When cross-multiplying, all four proportions above will produce the same equation:

$$(8)(x) = (20)(1) \rightarrow 8x = 20$$

Divide by 8 to isolate the variable x, the result is $x = 2.5$. The variable x represented the unknown number of cups. Therefore, the conclusion is that 20 fluid ounces converts (is equal) to 2.5 cups.

Sometimes converting units requires writing and solving more than one proportion. Suppose an exam question asks to determine how many hours are in 2 weeks. Without knowing the conversion rate between hours and weeks, this can be determined knowing the conversion rates between weeks and days, and between days and hours. First, weeks are converted to days, then days are converted to hours.

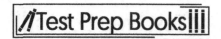
To convert from weeks to days, the following proportion can be written:

$$\frac{7}{1} = \frac{x}{2} \left(\frac{days\ conversion}{weeks\ conversion} = \frac{days\ unknown}{weeks\ given} \right)$$

Cross-multiplying produces:

$$(7)(2) = (x)(1)$$

$$14 = x$$

Therefore, 2 weeks is equal to 14 days. Next, a proportion is written to convert 14 days to hours:

$$\frac{24}{1} = \frac{x}{14} \left(\frac{conversion\ hours}{conversion\ days} = \frac{unknown\ hours}{given\ days} \right)$$

Cross-multiplying produces:

$$(24)(14) = (x)(1) \rightarrow 336 = x$$

Therefore, the answer is that there are 336 hours in 2 weeks.

Data Analysis/Probability

Graphical Representation of Data

Various graphs can be used to visually represent a given set of data. Each type of graph requires a different method of arranging data points and different calculations of the data. To construct a **histogram**, the range of the data points is divided into equal intervals. The frequency for each interval is then determined, which reveals how many points fall into each interval. A **graph** is constructed with the vertical axis representing the frequency and the horizontal axis representing the intervals. The lower value of each interval should be labeled along the horizontal axis. Finally, for each interval, a bar is drawn from the lower value of each interval to the lower value of the next interval with a height equal to the frequency of the interval. Because of the intervals, histograms do not have any gaps between bars along the horizontal axis.

To construct a **box** (or **box-and-whisker**) **plot**, the five number summary for the data set is calculated as follows: the second quartile (Q_2) is the median of the set. The first quartile (Q_1) is the median of the values below Q_2. The third quartile (Q_3) is the median of the values above Q_2. The upper extreme is the highest value in the data set if it is not an outlier (greater than 1.5 times the interquartile range $Q_3 - Q_1$). The lower extreme is the least value in the data set if it is not an outlier (more than 1.5 times lower than the interquartile range). To construct the box-and-whisker plot, each value is plotted on a number line, along with any outliers. The **box** consists of Q_1 and Q_3 as its top and bottom and Q_2 as the dividing

106

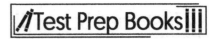

line inside the box. The **whiskers** extend from the lower extreme to Q_1 and from Q_3 to the upper extreme.

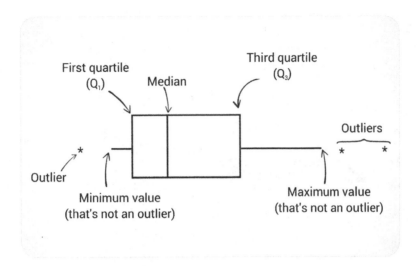

A scatter plot displays the relationship between two variables. Values for the independent variable, typically denoted by x, are paired with values for the dependent variable, typically denoted by y. Each set of corresponding values are written as an ordered pair (x, y). To construct the graph, a coordinate grid is labeled with the x-axis representing the independent variable and the y-axis representing the dependent variable. Each ordered pair is graphed.

Like a scatter plot, a **line graph** compares variables that change continuously, typically over time. Paired data values (ordered pairs) are plotted on a coordinate grid with the x- and y-axis representing the

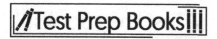

variables. A line is drawn from each point to the next, going from left to right. The line graph below displays cell phone use for given years (two variables) for men, women, and both sexes (three data sets).

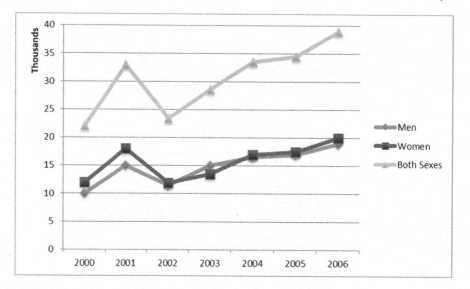

A **line plot**, also called **dot plot**, displays the frequency of data (numerical values) on a number line. To construct a line plot, a number line is used that includes all unique data values. It is marked with x's or dots above the value the number of times that the value occurs in the data set.

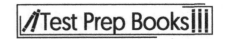

A **bar graph** is a diagram in which the quantity of items within a specific classification is represented by the height of a rectangle. Each type of classification is represented by a rectangle of equal width.

Here is an example of a bar graph:

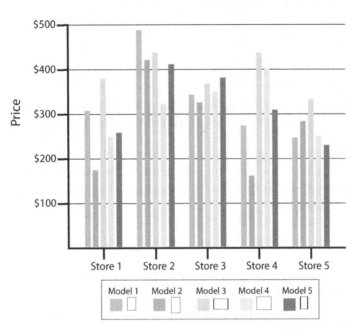

A **circle graph**, also called a **pie chart**, shows categorical data with each category representing a percentage of the whole data set. To make a circle graph, the percent of the data set for each category must be determined. To do so, the frequency of the category is divided by the total number of data points and converted to a percent. For example, if 80 people were asked what their favorite sport is and 20 responded basketball, basketball makes up 25% of the data ($\frac{20}{80} = 0.25 = 25\%$). Each category in a data set is represented by a slice of the circle proportionate to its percentage of the whole.

109

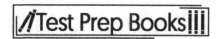
Choice of Graphs to Display Data

Choosing the appropriate graph to display a data set depends on what type of data is included in the set and what information must be displayed. Histograms and box plots can be used for data sets consisting of individual values across a wide range. Examples include test scores and incomes. Histograms and box plots will indicate the center, spread, range, and outliers of a data set. A histogram will show the shape of the data set, while a box plot will divide the set into quartiles (25% increments), allowing for comparison between a given value and the entire set.

Scatter plots and line graphs can be used to display data consisting of two variables. Examples include height and weight, or distance and time. A correlation between the variables is determined by examining the points on the graph. Line graphs are used if each value for one variable pairs with a distinct value for the other variable. Line graphs show relationships between variables.

Line plots, bar graphs, and circle graphs are all used to display categorical data, such as surveys. Line plots and bar graphs both indicate the frequency of each category within the data set. A line plot is used when the categories consist of numerical values. For example, the number of hours of TV watched by individuals is displayed on a line plot.

A bar graph is used when the categories consist of words. For example, the favorite ice cream of individuals is displayed with a bar graph. A circle graph can be used to display either type of categorical data. However, unlike line plots and bar graphs, a circle graph does not indicate the frequency of each category. Instead, the circle graph represents each category as its percentage of the whole data set.

Measures of Center and Range

The center of a set of data (statistical values) can be represented by its mean, median, or mode. These are sometimes referred to as measures of central tendency. The **mean** is the average of the data set. The mean can be calculated by adding the data values and dividing by the sample size (the number of data points). Suppose a student has test scores of 93, 84, 88, 72, 91, and 77. To find the mean, or average, the scores are added and the sum is divided by 6 because there are 6 test scores:

$$\frac{93 + 84 + 88 + 72 + 91 + 77}{6} = \frac{505}{6} = 84.17$$

Given the mean of a data set and the sum of the data points, the sample size can be determined by dividing the sum by the mean. Suppose you are told that Kate averaged 12 points per game and scored a total of 156 points for the season. The number of games that she played (the sample size or the number of data points) can be determined by dividing the total points (sum of data points) by her average (mean of data points): $\frac{156}{12} = 13$. Therefore, Kate played in 13 games this season.

If given the mean of a data set and the sample size, the sum of the data points can be determined by multiplying the mean and sample size. Suppose you are told that Tom worked 6 days last week for an average of 5.5 hours per day. The total number of hours worked for the week (sum of data points) can be determined by multiplying his daily average (mean of data points) by the number of days worked (sample size):

$$5.5 \times 6 = 33$$

Therefore, Tom worked a total of 33 hours last week.

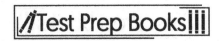

The **median** of a data set is the value of the data point in the middle when the sample is arranged in numerical order. To find the median of a data set, the values are written in order from least to greatest. The lowest and highest values are simultaneously eliminated, repeating until the value in the middle remains. Suppose the salaries of math teachers are:

$$\$35,000; \ \$38,500; \ \$41,000; \ \$42,000; \ \$42,000; \ \$44,500; \ \$49,000$$

The values are listed from least to greatest to find the median. The lowest and highest values are eliminated until only the middle value remains. Repeating this step three times reveals a median salary of $42,000. If the sample set has an even number of data points, two values will remain after all others are eliminated. In this case, the mean of the two middle values is the median. Consider the following data set: 7, 9, 10, 13, 14, 14. Eliminating the lowest and highest values twice leaves two values, 10 and 13, in the middle. The mean of these values $\left(\frac{10+13}{2}\right)$ is the median. Therefore, the set has a median of 11.5.

The **mode** of a data set is the value that appears most often. A data set may have a single mode, multiple modes, or no mode. If different values repeat equally as often, multiple modes exist. If no value repeats, no mode exists. Consider the following data sets:

- A: 7, 9, 10, 13, 14, 14
- B: 37, 44, 33, 37, 49, 44, 51, 34, 37, 33, 44
- C: 173, 154, 151, 168, 155

Set A has a mode of 14. Set B has modes of 37 and 44. Set C has no mode.

The **range** of a data set is the difference between the highest and the lowest values in the set. The range can be considered to be the span of the data set. To determine the range, the smallest value in the set is subtracted from the largest value. The ranges for the data sets A, B, and C above are calculated as follows:

$$A: 14 - 7 = 7$$
$$B: 51 - 33 = 18$$
$$C: 173 - 151 = 22$$

Best Description of a Set of Data

Measures of central tendency, namely mean, median, and mode, describe characteristics of a set of data. Specifically, they are intended to represent a *typical* value in the set by identifying a central position of the set. Depending on the characteristics of a specific set of data, different measures of central tendency are more indicative of a typical value in the set.

When a data set is grouped closely together with a relatively small range and the data is spread out somewhat evenly, the mean is an effective indicator of a typical value in the set. Consider the following data set representing the height of sixth grade boys in inches: 61 inches, 54 inches, 58 inches, 63 inches, 58 inches. The mean of the set is 58.8 inches. The data set is grouped closely (the range is only 9 inches) and the values are spread relatively evenly (three values below the mean and two values above the mean). Therefore, the mean value of 58.8 inches is an effective measure of central tendency in this case.

When a data set contains a small number of values, with one either extremely large or extremely small when compared to the other values, the mean is not an effective measure of central tendency. Consider

111

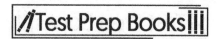
the following data set representing annual incomes of homeowners on a given street: $71,000; $74,000; $75,000; $77,000; $340,000. The mean of this set is $127,400. This figure does not indicate a typical value in the set, which contains four out of five values between $71,000 and $77,000. The median is a much more effective measure of central tendency for data sets such as these. Finding the middle value diminishes the influence of outliers, or numbers that may appear out of place, like the $340,000 annual income. The median for this set is $75,000 which is much more typical of a value in the set.

The mode of a data set is a useful measure of central tendency for categorical data when each piece of data is an option from a category. Consider a survey of 31 commuters asking how they get to work with results summarized below.

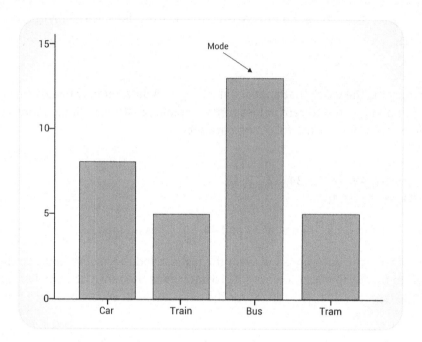

The mode for this set represents the value, or option, of the data that repeats most often. This indicates that the bus is the most popular method of transportation for the commuters.

Effects of Changes in Data

Changing all values of a data set in a consistent way produces predictable changes in the measures of the center and range of the set. A linear transformation changes the original value into the new value by either adding a given number to each value, multiplying each value by a given number, or both. Adding (or subtracting) a given value to each data point will increase (or decrease) the mean, median, and any modes by the same value. However, the range will remain the same due to the way that range is calculated. Multiplying (or dividing) a given value by each data point will increase (or decrease) the mean, median, and any modes, and the range by the same factor.

Consider the following data set, call it set P, representing the price of different cases of soda at a grocery store: $4.25, $4.40, $4.75, $4.95, $4.95, $5.15. The mean of set P is $4.74. The median is $4.85. The mode of the set is $4.95. The range is $0.90. Suppose the state passes a new tax of $0.25 on every case of soda sold. The new data set, set T, is calculated by adding $0.25 to each data point from set P. Therefore, set T consists of the following values: $4.50, $4.65, $5.00, $5.20, $5.20, $5.40. The mean of set T is $4.99. The median is $5.10. The mode of the set is $5.20. The range is $.90. The mean, median

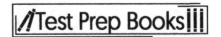
and mode of set T is equal to $0.25 added to the mean, median, and mode of set P. The range stays the same.

Now suppose, due to inflation, the store raises the cost of every item by 10 percent. Raising costs by 10 percent is calculated by multiplying each value by 1.1. The new data set, set I, is calculated by multiplying each data point from set T by 1.1. Therefore, set I consists of the following values: $4.95, $5.12, $5.50, $5.72, $5.72, $5.94. The mean of set I is $5.49. The median is $5.61. The mode of the set is $5.72. The range is $0.99. The mean, median, mode, and range of set I is equal to 1.1 multiplied by the mean, median, mode, and range of set T because each increased by a factor of 10 percent.

Describing a Set of Data

A set of data can be described in terms of its center, spread, shape and any unusual features. The center of a data set can be measured by its mean, median, or mode. The spread of a data set refers to how far the data points are from the center (mean or median). The spread can be measured by the range or by the quartiles and interquartile range. A data set with all its data points clustered around the center will have a small spread. A data set covering a wide range of values will have a large spread.

When a data set is displayed as a **histogram** or frequency distribution plot, the shape indicates if a sample is normally distributed, symmetrical, or has measures of skewness or kurtosis. When graphed, a data set with a **normal distribution** will resemble a bell curve.

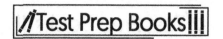
If the data set is symmetrical, each half of the graph when divided at the center is a mirror image of the other. If the graph has fewer data points to the right, the data is **skewed right**. If it has fewer data points to the left, the data is **skewed left**.

Right-Skewed   Symmetric   Left-Skewed

Kurtosis is a measure of whether the data is heavy-tailed with a high number of outliers, or light-tailed with a low number of outliers.

A description of a data set should include any unusual features such as gaps or outliers. A **gap** is a span within the range of the data set containing no data points. An **outlier** is a data point with a value either extremely large or extremely small when compared to the other values in the set.

Interpreting Displays of Data

A set of data can be visually displayed in various forms allowing for quick identification of characteristics of the set. Histograms, such as the one shown below, display the number of data points (vertical axis) that fall into given intervals (horizontal axis) across the range of the set. Suppose the histogram below displays IQ scores of students. Histograms can display the center, spread, shape, and any unusual characteristics of a data set.

Histogram

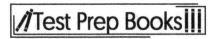

As mentioned, a box plot, also called a box-and-whisker plot, divides the data points into four groups and displays the five-number summary for the set as well as any outliers. The five-number summary consists of:

- The lower extreme: the lowest value that is not an outlier
- The higher extreme: the highest value that is not an outlier
- The median of the set: also referred to as the second quartile or Q_2
- The first quartile or Q_1: the median of values below Q_2
- The third quartile or Q_3: the median of values above Q_2

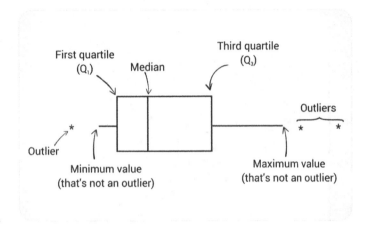

Suppose the box plot displays IQ scores for 12th grade students at a given school. The five number summary of the data consists of: lower extreme (67); upper extreme (127); Q_2 or median (100); Q_1 (91); Q_3 (108); and outliers (135 and 140). Although all data points are not known from the plot, the points are divided into four quartiles each, including 25% of the data points. Therefore, 25% of students scored between 67 and 91, 25% scored between 91 and 100, 25% scored between 100 and 108, and 25% scored between 108 and 127. These percentages include the normal values for the set and exclude the outliers. This information is useful when comparing a given score with the rest of the scores in the set.

A scatter plot is a mathematical diagram that visually displays the relationship or connection between two variables. The independent variable is placed on the x-axis (the horizontal axis), and the dependent variable is placed on the y-axis (the vertical axis). When visually examining the points on the graph, if the points model a linear relationship, or if a line of best-fit can be drawn through the points with the points relatively close on either side, then a correlation exists. If the line of best-fit has a positive slope (rises from left to right), then the variables have a positive correlation. If, like the image below, the line of best-fit has a negative slope (falls from left to right), then the variables have a negative correlation. If a line of best-fit cannot be drawn, then no correlation exists. A positive or negative correlation can be categorized as strong or weak, depending on how closely the points are graphed around the line of best-fit.

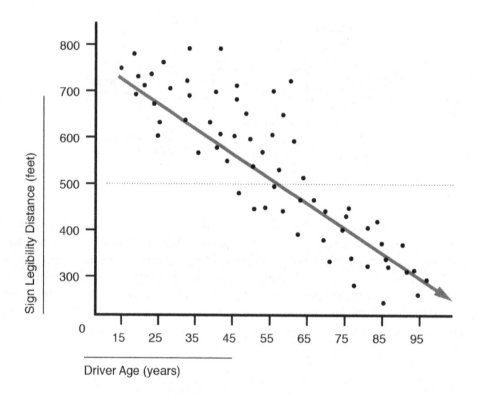

Probabilities Relative to Likelihood of Occurrence

Probability is a measure of how likely an event is to occur. Probability is written as a fraction or decimal between zero and one. If an event has a probability of zero, the event will never occur. If an event has a probability of one, the event will definitely occur. If the probability of an event is closer to zero, the event is unlikely to occur. If the probability of an event is closer to one, the event is more likely to occur. For example, a probability of $\frac{1}{2}$ means that the event is equally as likely to occur as it is to not occur. An example of this is tossing a coin. The probability of an event can be calculated by dividing the number of favorable outcomes by the number of total outcomes. For example, suppose you have 2 raffle tickets out of 20 total tickets sold. The probability that you win the raffle is calculated:

$$\frac{number\ of\ favorable\ outcomes}{total\ number\ of\ outcomes} = \frac{2}{20} = \frac{1}{10}\ \text{(always reduce fractions)}$$

116

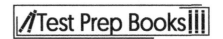

Therefore, the probability of winning the raffle is $\frac{1}{10}$ or 0.1.

Chance is the measure of how likely an event is to occur, written as a percent. If an event will never occur, the event has a 0% chance. If an event will certainly occur, the event has a 100% chance. If an event will sometimes occur, the event has a chance somewhere between 0% and 100%. To calculate chance, probability is calculated and the fraction or decimal is converted to a percent.

The probability of multiple events occurring can be determined by multiplying the probability of each event. For example, suppose you flip a coin with heads and tails, and roll a six-sided die numbered one through six. To find the probability that you will flip heads AND roll a two, the probability of each event is determined, and those fractions are multiplied. The probability of flipping heads is $\frac{1}{2}\left(\frac{1 \text{ side with heads}}{2 \text{ sides total}}\right)$, and the probability of rolling a two is $\frac{1}{6}\left(\frac{1 \text{ side with a 2}}{6 \text{ total sides}}\right)$. The probability of flipping heads AND rolling a 2 is:

$$\frac{1}{2} \times \frac{1}{6} = \frac{1}{12}$$

The above scenario with flipping a coin and rolling a die is an example of independent events. **Independent events** are circumstances in which the outcome of one event does not affect the outcome of the other event. Conversely, **dependent events** are ones in which the outcome of one event affects the outcome of the second event. Consider the following scenario: a bag contains 5 black marbles and 5 white marbles. What is the probability of picking 2 black marbles without replacing the marble after the first pick?

The probability of picking a black marble on the first pick is:

$$\frac{5}{10}\left(\frac{5 \text{ black marbles}}{10 \text{ total marbles}}\right)$$

Assuming that a black marble was picked, there are now 4 black marbles and 5 white marbles for the second pick. Therefore, the probability of picking a black marble on the second pick is:

$$\frac{4}{9}\left(\frac{4 \text{ black marbles}}{9 \text{ total marbles}}\right)$$

To find the probability of picking two black marbles, the probability of each is multiplied:

$$\frac{5}{10} \times \frac{4}{9} = \frac{20}{90} = \frac{2}{9}$$

Practice Quiz

1. At the beginning of the day, Xavier has 20 apples. At lunch, he meets his sister Emma and gives her half of his apples. After lunch, he stops by his neighbor Jim's house and gives him six of his apples. He then uses $\frac{3}{4}$ of his remaining apples to make an apple pie for dessert at dinner. At the end of the day, how many apples does Xavier have left?
   a. 4
   b. 6
   c. 2
   d. 1
   e. 3

2. If $\frac{5}{2} \div \frac{1}{3} = n$, then n is between which of the following?
   a. 5 and 7
   b. 7 and 9
   c. 9 and 11
   d. 3 and 5
   e. 11 and 13

3. Apples cost $2 each, while bananas cost $3 each. Maria purchased a total of 10 pieces of fruit and spent $22. How many apples did she buy?
   a. 4
   b. 5
   c. 6
   d. 7
   e. 8

4. A rectangle has a length that is 5 feet longer than 3 times its width. If the perimeter is 90 feet, what is the length in feet?
   a. 10
   b. 20
   c. 25
   d. 30
   e. 35

5. Five of six numbers have a sum of 25. The average of all six numbers is 6. What is the sixth number?
   a. 8
   b. 10
   c. 13
   d. 12
   e. 11

See answers on the next page.

118

Answer Explanations

1. D: This problem can be solved using basic arithmetic. Xavier starts with 20 apples, then gives his sister half, which is 20 divided by 2.

$$\frac{20 - 20}{2} = 20 - 10 = 10$$

He then gives his neighbor 6 apples, so 6 is subtracted from 10.

$$10 - 6 = 4$$

Finally, he uses 3/4 of his remaining apples to make a pie. Since $\frac{3}{4}$ of 4 is 3, he uses 3 apples, so 3 is subtracted from 4.

$$4 - 3 = 1$$

Finally, he uses $\frac{3}{4}$ of his apples to make a pie, which means he has $\frac{1}{4}$ left:

$$\frac{1}{4} \times 4 = 1$$

2. B: $\frac{5}{2} \div \frac{1}{3} = \frac{5}{2} \times \frac{3}{1} = \frac{15}{2} = 7.5$.

3. E: Let a be the number of apples, and let b represent the number of bananas. The total number of fruits is $a + b = 10$, and the total cost is $2a + 3b = 22$. To solve this pair of equations, we can multiply the first equation by –3:

$$-3(a + b) = -3(10)$$

$$-3a - 3b = -30$$

Now we can add this to the other equation, and the b terms cancel out:

$$(-3a - 3b = -30)$$

$$+(2a + 3b = 22)$$

$$= (-a = -8)$$

This simplifies to $a = 8$.

4. E: Denote the width as w and the length as l. Then, $l = 3w + 5$. The perimeter is:

$$2w + 2l = 90$$

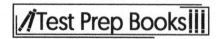
Substituting the first expression for l into the second equation yields:

$$2(3w + 5) + 2w = 90$$

$$6w + 10 + 2w = 90$$

$$8w = 80$$

$$w = 10$$

Putting this into the first equation, it yields:

$$l = 3(10) + 5 = 35$$

5. E: The average is calculated by adding all six numbers, then dividing by 6. The first five numbers have a sum of 25. This scenario can be expressed by the equation $\frac{(25+n)}{6} = 6$, where n is the unknown number. After multiplying both sides by 6, we get $25 + n = 36$, which means $n = 11$.

Reading Comprehension

In the Reading section, test takers will encounter passages that are roughly 250 to 350 words long, and each passage is followed by several multiple-choice questions. Test takers are given 40 questions and 40 minutes to complete the section. The passages may be poetry, fiction, and nonfiction texts from a variety of disciplines such as the humanities, sciences, social studies, and literary fiction. The questions ask students to locate information in the text and to demonstrate literal, inferential, and evaluative comprehension. Definitions of words, identifying main ideas and supporting details, and literal from nonliteral language may be addressed.

Recognizing the Main Idea

Typically, in a piece of narrative writing there are only a couple of ideas that the author is trying to convey to the reader. Be careful to understand the difference between a topic and a main idea. A topic might be "horses," but the main idea should be a complete sentence such as, "Racehorses run faster when they have a good relationship with the jockey." Here are some guidelines, tips, and tricks to follow that will help identify the main idea:

Identifying the Main Idea
The most important part of the text
Text title and pictures may reveal clues
Opening sentences and final sentences may reveal clues
Key vocabulary words that are repeatedly used may reveal clues

Topic versus the Main Idea

It is very important to know the difference between the topic and the main idea of the text. Even though these two are similar because they both present the central point of a text, they have distinctive differences. A **topic** is the subject of the text; This can usually be described in a concise one- to two-word phrase. On the other hand, the **main idea** is more detailed and provides the author's central point of the text. It can be expressed through a complete sentence and is often found in the beginning, the middle, or at the end of a paragraph. In most nonfiction books, the first sentence of the passage usually (but not always) states the main idea. Take a look at the passage below to review the topic versus the main idea:

Cheetahs

Cheetahs are one of the fastest mammals on the land, reaching up to 70 miles an hour over short distances. Even though cheetahs can run as fast as 70 miles an hour, they usually only have to run half that speed to catch up with their choice of prey. Cheetahs cannot maintain a fast pace over long periods of time because they will overheat their bodies. After a chase, cheetahs need to rest for approximately 30 minutes prior to eating or returning to any other activity.

In the example above, the topic of the passage is "Cheetahs" simply because that is the subject of the text. The main idea of the text is "Cheetahs are one of the fastest mammals on the land but can only maintain a fast pace for shorter distances." While it covers the topic, it is more detailed and refers to the text in its entirety. The text continues to provide additional details called **supporting details**, which will be discussed in the next section.

Identifying Theme or Central Message

The **theme** is the central message of a fictional work, whether that work is structured as prose, drama, or poetry. It is the heart of what an author is trying to say to readers through the writing, and theme is largely conveyed through literary elements and techniques.

In literature, a theme can often be determined by considering the overarching narrative conflict within the work. Though there are several types of conflicts and several potential themes within them, the following are the most common:

- Individual against the self—relevant to themes of self-awareness, internal struggles, pride, coming of age, facing reality, fate, free will, vanity, loss of innocence, loneliness, isolation, fulfillment, failure, and disillusionment

- Individual against nature— relevant to themes of knowledge vs. ignorance, nature as beauty, quest for discovery, self-preservation, chaos and order, circle of life, death, and destruction of beauty

- Individual against society— relevant to themes of power, beauty, good, evil, war, class struggle, totalitarianism, role of men/women, wealth, corruption, change vs. tradition, capitalism, destruction, heroism, injustice, and racism

- Individual against another individual— relevant to themes of hope, loss of love or hope, sacrifice, power, revenge, betrayal, and honor

For example, in Hawthorne's *The Scarlet Letter*, one possible narrative conflict could be the individual against the self, with a relevant theme of internal struggles. This theme is alluded to through characterization—Dimmesdale's moral struggle with his love for Hester and Hester's internal struggles with the truth and her daughter, Pearl. It's also alluded to through plot—Dimmesdale's suicide and Hester helping the very townspeople who initially condemned her.

Sometimes, a text can convey a **message** or **universal lesson**—a truth or insight that the reader infers from the text, based on analysis of the literary and/or poetic elements. This message is often presented as a statement. For example, a potential message in Shakespeare's *Hamlet* could be "Revenge is what ultimately drives the human soul." This message can be immediately determined through plot and characterization in numerous ways, but it can also be determined through the setting of Norway, which is bordering on war.

Authors employ a variety of techniques to present a theme. They may compare or contrast characters, events, places, ideas, or historical or invented settings to speak thematically. They may use analogies, metaphors, similes, allusions, or other literary devices to convey the theme. An author's use of diction, syntax, and tone can also help convey the theme. Authors will often develop themes through the development of characters, use of the setting, repetition of ideas, use of symbols, and through

122

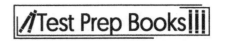

contrasting value systems. Authors of both fiction and nonfiction genres will use a variety of these techniques to develop one or more themes.

Regardless of the literary genre, there are commonalities in how authors, playwrights, and poets develop themes or central ideas.

Authors often do research, the results of which contribute to theme. In prose fiction and drama, this research may include real historical information about the setting the author has chosen or include elements that make fictional characters, settings, and plots seem realistic to the reader. In nonfiction, research is critical since information contained within this literature must be accurate.

In fiction, authors present a narrative conflict that will contribute to the overall theme. This conflict, in fiction texts, may involve the storyline itself and some trouble within characters that needs resolution. In nonfiction, this conflict may be an explanation or commentary on factual people and events.

Authors will sometimes use character motivation to convey theme, such as in the example from *Hamlet* regarding revenge. In fiction, the characters an author creates will think, speak, and act in ways that effectively convey the theme to readers. In nonfiction, the characters are factual, as in a biography, but authors pay particular attention to presenting those motivations to make them clear to readers.

Authors also use literary devices as a means of conveying theme. For example, the use of moon symbolism in Mary Shelley's *Frankenstein* is significant as its phases can be compared to the phases that the Creature undergoes as he struggles with his identity.

The selected point of view can also contribute to a work's theme. The use of first-person point of view in a fiction or nonfiction work engages the reader's response differently than third person point of view. The central idea or theme from a first-person narrative may differ from a third-person limited text.

In literary nonfiction, authors usually identify the purpose of their writing, which differs from fiction, where the general purpose is to entertain. The purpose of nonfiction is usually to inform, persuade, or entertain the audience. The stated purpose of a non-fiction text will drive how the central message or theme, if applicable, is presented.

Authors identify an audience for their writing, which is critical in shaping the theme of the work. For example, the audience for J.K. Rowling's *Harry Potter* series would be different than the audience for a biography of George Washington. The audience an author chooses to address is closely tied to the purpose of the work. The choice of an audience also drives the choice of language and level of diction an author uses. Ultimately, the intended audience determines the level to which that subject matter is presented and the complexity of the theme.

Locating Details

Supporting details of texts are defined as those elements of a text that help readers make sense of the main idea. They either qualitatively and/or quantitatively describe the main idea, strengthening the reader's understanding.

Supporting details answer questions like *who, what, where, when, why,* and *how.* Different types of supporting details include examples, facts and statistics, anecdotes, and sensory details.

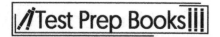

Persuasive and informative texts often use supporting details. In persuasive texts, authors attempt to make readers agree with their points of view, and supporting details are often used as "selling points." If authors make a statement, they need to support the statement with evidence in order to adequately persuade readers. Informative texts use supporting details such as examples, facts, and details to inform readers. Take a look at the "Cheetahs" example again below to find examples of supporting details.

Cheetahs

Cheetahs are one of the fastest mammals on the land, reaching up to 70 miles an hour over short distances. Even though cheetahs can run as fast as 70 miles an hour, they usually only have to run half that speed to catch up with their choice of prey. Cheetahs cannot maintain a fast pace over long periods of time because they will overheat their bodies. After a chase, cheetahs need to rest for approximately 30 minutes prior to eating or returning to any other activity.

In the example above, supporting details include:

- Cheetahs reach up to 70 miles per hour over short distances.
- They usually only have to run half that speed to catch up with their prey.
- Cheetahs will overheat their bodies if they exert a high speed over longer distances.
- They need to rest for 30 minutes after a chase.

Look at the diagram below (applying the cheetah example) to help determine the hierarchy of topic, main idea, and supporting details.

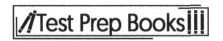

Making Inferences

Simply put, an inference is an educated guess drawn from evidence, logic, and reasoning. The key to making inferences is identifying clues within a passage, and then using common sense to arrive at a reasonable conclusion. Consider it "reading between the lines."

One way to make an inference is to look for main topics. When doing so, readers should pay particular attention to any titles, headlines, or opening statements made by the author. Topic sentences or repetitive ideas can be clues in gleaning inferred ideas. For example, if a passage contains the phrase *While some consider DNA testing to be infallible, it is an inherently flawed technique*, the test taker can infer the rest of the passage will contain information that points to problems with DNA testing.

The test taker may be asked to make an inference based on prior knowledge but may also be asked to make predictions based on new ideas. For example, the test taker may have no prior knowledge of DNA other than its genetic property to replicate. However, if the reader is given passages on the flaws of DNA testing with enough factual evidence, the test taker may arrive at the inferred conclusion that the author does not support the infallibility of DNA testing in all identification cases.

When making inferences, it is important to remember that the critical thinking process involved must be fluid and open to change. While a reader may infer an idea from a main topic, general statement, or other clues, he or she must be open to receiving new information within a particular passage. New ideas presented by an author may require the test taker to alter an inference. Similarly, when asked questions that require making an inference, it's important to read the entire test passage and all of the answer options. Often, a test taker will need to refine a general inference based on new ideas that may be presented within the test itself.

Inferences also refer to the ability to make logical assumptions based on clues from the text. People make inferences about the world around them on a daily basis but may not be aware of what they are doing. For example, a young boy may infer that it is likely cold outside if he wakes up and his bedroom is chilly or the floor is cold. While being driven somewhere on the highway and a girl notices a person at the side of the road with a parked car, that girl will likely infer that the individual is having car problems and is awaiting some assistance. Both of these are example of how inferences are used every day and the same skill can be applied to different stories and texts.

In a way, making inferences is similar to detective work by collecting evidence. Sometimes, clues can be found in the pictures or visual aids (like diagrams) that accompany a story or text. For example, a story may show a picture of a school in which all children are gathered in the parking lot. Upon closer examination, careful readers might spot a fire truck parked at the side of the road and may infer that the school had a fire drill or an actual fire.

Synthesis

Synthesis also requires a reader to make inferences while reading. Inference has been addressed earlier in this guide. Review the section and take note of the required skills in making inferences.

In order to achieve synthesis and full reading comprehension, a reader must take their prior knowledge, the knowledge or main ideas an author presents, and fill in the gaps to reach a logical conclusion. In a testing situation, a test taker may be asked to infer ideas from a given passage, asked to choose from a set of inferences that best express a summary of what the author hints at, or arrive at a logical conclusion based on their inferences. This is not an easy task, but it is approachable.

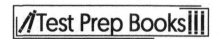
While inference requires a reader to make educated guesses based on stated information, it's important that the reader does not assume too much. It's important the reader does not insert information into a passage that's not there. It's important to make an inference based solely on the presented information and to make predictions using a logical thought process.

After reviewing the earlier section on making inferences, keep the following in mind:

- Do not jump to conclusions early in the passage. Read the full text before trying to infer meaning.
- Rely on asking questions (see the above section). What is the author stating? More important, what is the author not saying? What information is missing? What conclusions can be made about that missing information, if any?
- Make an inference then apply it back to the text passage. Does the inference make sense? Is it likely an idea with which the author would agree?
- What inferences can be made from any data presented? Are these inferences sound, logical, and do they hold water?

While this is not an exhaustive list of questions related to making inferences, it should help the reader with the skill of synthesis in achieving full reading comprehension.

Deriving the Meaning of a Word or Phrase from its Context

It's common to find words that aren't familiar in writing. When you don't know a word, there are some "tricks" that can be used to find out its meaning. **Context clues** are words or phrases in a sentence or paragraph that provide hints about a word and what it means. For example, if an unknown word is attached to a noun with other surrounding words as clues, these can help you figure out the word's meaning. Consider the following example:

> After the treatment, Grandma's natural rosy cheeks looked *wan* and ghostlike.

The word we don't know is *wan.* The first clue to its meaning is in the phrase *After the treatment,* which tells us that something happened after a procedure (possibly medical). A second clue is the word *rosy,* which describes Grandma's natural cheek color that changed after the treatment. Finally, the word *ghostlike* infers that Grandma's cheeks now look white. By using the context clues in the sentence, we can figure out that the meaning of the word *wan* means *pale.*

Contrasts

Look for context clues that **contrast** the unknown word. When reading a sentence with a word we don't know, look for an opposite word or idea. Here's an example:

> Since Mary didn't cite her research sources, she lost significant points for *plagiarizing* the content of her report.

In this sentence, *plagiarizing* is the word we don't know. Notice that when Mary *didn't cite her research sources,* it resulted in her losing points for *plagiarizing the content of her report.* These contrasting ideas tell us that Mary did something wrong with the content. This makes sense because the definition of *plagiarizing* is "taking the work of someone else and passing it off as your own."

Contrasts often use words like *but, however, although,* or phrases like *on the other hand.* For example:

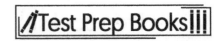

The *gargantuan* television won't fit in my car, but it will cover the entire wall in the den.

The word we don't know is *gargantuan*. Notice that the television is too big to fit in a car, *but it will cover the entire wall in the den*. This tells us that the television is extremely large. The word *gargantuan* means *enormous*.

Synonyms
Another way to find out a word you don't know is to think of synonyms for that word. **Synonyms** are words with the same meaning. To do this, replace synonyms one at a time. Then read the sentence after each synonym to see if the meaning is clear. By replacing a word we don't know with a word we do know, it's easier to uncover its meaning. For example:

Gary's clothes were *saturated* after he fell into the swimming pool.

In this sentence, we don't know the word *saturated*. To brainstorm synonyms for *saturated*, think about what happens to Gary's clothes after falling into the swimming pool. They'd be *soaked* or *wet*. These both turn out to be good synonyms to try. The actual meaning of *saturated* is "thoroughly soaked."

Antonyms
Sometimes sentences contain words or phrases that oppose each other. Opposite words are known as **antonyms**. An example of an antonym is *hot* and *cold*. For example:

Although Mark seemed *tranquil*, you could tell he was actually nervous as he paced up and down the hall.

The word we don't know is *tranquil*. The sentence says that Mark was in fact not *tranquil*. He was *actually nervous*. The opposite of the word *nervous* is *calm*. *Calm* is the meaning of the word *tranquil*.

Explanations or Descriptions
Explanations or descriptions of other things in the sentence can also provide clues to an unfamiliar word. Take the following example:

Golden Retrievers, Great Danes, and Pugs are the top three *breeds* competing in the dog show.

We don't know the word *breeds*. Look at the sentence for a clue. The subjects (*Golden Retrievers, Great Danes,* and *Pugs*) describe different types of dogs. This description helps uncover the meaning of the word *breeds*. The word *breeds* means "a particular type of animal."

Inferences
Inferences are clues to an unknown word that tell us its meaning. These inferences can be found within the sentence where the word appears. Or, they can be found in a sentence before the word or after the word. Look at the following example:

The *wretched* old lady was kicked out of the restaurant. She was so mean and nasty to the waiter!

Here, we don't know the word *wretched*. The first sentence says that the *old lady was kicked out of the restaurant*, but it doesn't say why. The sentence after tells us why: *She was so mean and nasty to the waiter!* This infers that the old lady was *kicked out* because she was *so mean and nasty* or, in other words, *wretched*.

127

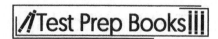

When you prepare for a vocabulary test, try reading harder materials to learn new words. If you don't know a word on the test, look for prefixes and suffixes to find out what the word means and get rid of wrong answers. If two answers both seem right, see if there are any differences between them. Then select the word that best fits. Context clues in the sentence or paragraph can also help you find the meaning of a word you don't know. By learning new words, a person can expand their knowledge. They can also improve the quality of their writing.

Determining the Author's Purpose

Authors want to capture the interest of the reader. An effective reader is attentive to an author's **position**. Authors write with intent, whether implicit or explicit. An author may hold a bias or use emotional language, which in turn creates a very clear position. Finding an author's **purpose** is usually easier than figuring out their position. An author's purpose of a text may be to persuade, inform, entertain, or be descriptive. Most narratives are written with the intent to entertain the reader, although some may also be informative or persuasive. When an author tries to persuade a reader, the reader must be cautious of the intent or argument. Therefore, the author keeps the persuasion lighthearted and friendly to maintain the entertainment value in narrative texts even though he or she is still trying to convince the reader of something.

An author's purpose will influence their writing style. As mentioned previously, the purpose can inform, entertain, or persuade a reader. If an author writes an informative text, their purpose is to educate the reader about a certain topic. Informative texts are usually nonfiction, and the author rarely states their opinion. The purpose of an informative text is also indicated by the outline of the text itself. In some cases, an informative text may have headings, subtitles, and bold key words. The purpose for this type of text is to educate the reader.

Entertaining texts, whether fiction or nonfiction, are meant to captivate readers' attention. Entertaining texts are usually stories that describe real or fictional people, places, or things. These narratives often use expressive language, emotions, imagery, and figurative language to captivate the readers. If readers do not want to put the entertaining text down, the author has fulfilled their purpose for this type of text.

Descriptive texts use adjectives and adverbs to describe people, places, or things to provide a clear image to the reader throughout the story. If an author fails to provide detailed descriptions, readers may find texts boring or confusing. Descriptive texts are almost always informative but can also be persuasive or entertaining pending the author's purpose.

Determining the Author's Attitude and Tone

Tone refers to the writer's attitude toward the subject matter. Tone conveys how the writer feels about characters, situations, events, ideas, etc. Nonfiction writing is sometimes thought to have no tone at all, but this is incorrect.

A lot of nonfiction writing has a neutral tone, which is an extremely important tone for the writer to take. A neutral tone demonstrates that the writer is presenting a topic impartially and letting the information speak for itself. On the other hand, nonfiction writing can be just as effective and appropriate if the tone isn't neutral. For instance, take the previous examples involving seat belt use. In them, the writer mostly chooses to retain a neutral tone when presenting information. If the writer would instead include their own personal experience of losing a friend or family member in a car accident, the tone would change dramatically. The tone would no longer be neutral. Now it would show

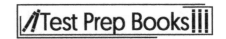

that the writer has a personal stake in the content, allowing them to interpret the information in a different way. When analyzing tone, consider what the writer is trying to achieve in the passage, and how they *create* the tone using style.

Understanding and Evaluating Opinions/Arguments

A **fact** is information that is true. If information can be disproven, it is not a fact. For example, water freezes at or below thirty-two degrees Fahrenheit. An argument stating that water freezes at seventy degrees Fahrenheit cannot be supported by data and is therefore not a fact. Facts tend to be associated with science, mathematics, and statistics.

Opinions are information open for debate. Opinions are often tied to subjective concepts like feelings, desires, or manners. They can also be controversial.

Stereotypes and biases are viewpoints based in opinion and held despite evidence that they are incorrect. A **stereotype** is a widely held belief projected onto a group, while a **bias** is an individual's belief. Biased people ignore evidence that contradicts their position while offering as proof any evidence that supports it. Those who stereotype tend to make assumptions based on what others have told them and usually have little firsthand experience with the group or item in question.

Readers should always identify the author's position or stance in a text. No matter how objective a text may seem, assume the author has preconceived beliefs. Reduce the likelihood of accepting an invalid argument, by looking for multiple articles on the topic, including those with varying opinions. If several opinions point in the same direction, and are backed by reputable peer-reviewed sources, it's more likely the author has a valid argument. Positions that run contrary to widely held beliefs and existing data should invite scrutiny. There are exceptions to the rule, so be a careful consumer of information.

Making Predictions Based on Information in the Passage

An active reader uses prior knowledge while reading to make accurate predictions. Prior knowledge is best utilized when readers make links between the current text, previously read texts, and life experiences. Some texts use suspense and foreshadowing to captivate readers. For example, an intriguing aspect of murder mysteries is that the reader is never sure of the culprit until the author reveals the individual's identity. Authors often build suspense, and add depth and meaning to a work by leaving clues to provide hints or predict future events in the story; this is called **foreshadowing**. While some instances of foreshadowing are subtle, others are quite obvious.

Another way to read actively is to identify examples of inference within text. Authors employ literary devices such as tone, characterization, and theme to engage the audience by showing details of the story instead of merely telling them. For example, if an author said *Bob is selfish*, there's little left to infer. If the author said, *Bob cheated on his test, ignored his mom's calls, and parked illegally*, the reader can infer Bob is selfish. Authors also make implications through character dialogue, thoughts, effects on others, actions, and looks. Like in life, readers must assemble all the clues to form a complete picture.

Active readers should also draw conclusions. A conclusion should be based only on the text details, not personal experiences. This means the reader should first determine the author's intent. Identify the author's viewpoint and connect relevant evidence to support it. Readers may then move to the most important step: deciding whether to agree and whether they are correct. Always read cautiously and critically. Interact with text and record reactions in the margins. These active reading skills help determine not only what the author thinks, but what the reader thinks.

Practice Quiz

Questions 1-4 refer to the following passage, titled "Education is Essential to Civilization."

Early in my career, a master teacher shared this thought with me: "Education is the last bastion of civility." While I did not completely understand the scope of those words at the time, I have since come to realize the depth, breadth, truth, and significance of what he said. Education provides society with a vehicle for raising its children to be civil, decent human beings with something valuable to contribute to the world. It is really what makes us human and what distinguishes us as civilized creatures.

Being "civilized" humans means being "whole" humans. Education must address the minds, bodies, and souls of students. It would be detrimental to society if our schools were myopic in their focus, only meeting the needs of the mind. As humans, we are multidimensional, multifaceted beings who need more than head knowledge to survive. The human heart and psyche have to be fed in order for the mind to develop properly, and the body must be maintained and exercised to help fuel brain functioning.

Education is a basic human right, and it allows us to sustain a democratic society in which participation is fundamental to its success. It should inspire students to seek better solutions to world problems and to dream of a more equitable society. Education should never discriminate on any basis, and it should create individuals who are self-sufficient, patriotic, and tolerant of other's ideas.

All children can learn, although not all children learn in the same manner. All children learn best, however, when their basic physical needs are met, and they feel safe, secure, and loved. Students are much more responsive to a teacher who values them and shows them respect as individual people. Teachers must model at all times the way they expect students to treat them and their peers. If teachers set high expectations for their students, the students will rise to that high level. Teachers must make the well-being of their students their primary focus and must not be afraid to let their students learn from their own mistakes.

In the modern age of technology, a teacher's focus is no longer the "what" of the content, but more importantly, the "why." Students are bombarded with information and have access to any information they need right at their fingertips. Teachers have to work harder than ever before to help students identify salient information and to think critically about the information they encounter. Students have to read between the lines, identify bias, and determine who they can trust in the milieu of ads, data, and texts presented to them.

Schools must work in concert with families in this important mission. While children spend most of their time in school, they are dramatically and indelibly shaped by the influences of their family and culture. Teachers must respect this fact, strive to include parents in the education of their children, and work to keep parents informed of progress and problems. Communication between the classroom and home is essential for a child's success.

Humans have always aspired to be more, to do more, and to better ourselves and our communities. This is where education lies, right at the heart of humanity's desire to be all that we can be. Education helps us strive for higher goals and better treatment of ourselves and others. I shudder to think what would become of us if education ceased to be the "last bastion of civility." We must be unapologetic about expecting excellence from our students—our very existence depends upon it.

1. Which of the following best summarizes the author's main point?
   a. Education as we know it is overvalued in modern society, and we should find alternative solutions.
   b. The survival of the human race depends on the educational system, and it is worth fighting for to make it better.
   c. The government should do away with all public schools and require parents to home school their children instead.
   d. While education is important, some children simply are not capable of succeeding in a traditional classroom.
   e. Students are learning new ways to learn while teachers are learning to adapt to their needs.

2. Based on this passage, which of the following can be inferred about the author?
   a. The author feels passionately about education.
   b. The author does not feel strongly about their point.
   c. The author is angry at the educational system.
   d. The author is unsure about the importance of education.
   e. The author does not trust the government.

3. Based on this passage, which of the following conclusions could be drawn about the author?
   a. The author would not support raising taxes to help fund much-needed reforms in education.
   b. The author would support raising taxes to help fund much-needed reforms in education, as long as those reforms were implemented in higher socio-economic areas first.
   c. The author would support raising taxes to help fund much-needed reforms in education for all children in all schools.
   d. The author would support raising taxes only in certain states to help fund much-needed reforms in education.
   e. The author would not support raising taxes unless the people in the communities agreed to it.

4. According to the passage, which of the following is NOT mentioned as an important factor in education today?
   a. Parent involvement
   b. Communication between parents and teachers
   c. Impact of technology
   d. Cost of textbooks
   e. Safe and healthy children

Question 5 refers to the following paragraph:

The Brookside area is an older part of Kansas City, developed mainly in the 1920s and '30s, and is considered one of the nation's first "planned" communities with shops, restaurants, parks, and churches all within a quick walk. A stroll down any street reveals charming two-story Tudor and Colonial homes with smaller bungalows sprinkled throughout the beautiful tree-lined streets. It is common to see lemonade stands on the corners and baseball games in the numerous "pocket" parks tucked neatly behind rows of well-manicured houses. The Brookside shops on 63rd street between Wornall Road and Oak Street are a hub of commerce and

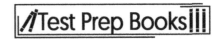

entertainment where residents freely shop and dine with their pets (and children) in tow. This is also a common "hangout" spot for younger teenagers because it is easily accessible by bike for most. In short, it is an idyllic neighborhood just minutes from downtown Kansas City.

5. Which of the following states the main idea of this paragraph?
   a. The Brookside shops are a popular hangout for teenagers.
   b. There are a number of pocket parks in the Brookside neighborhood.
   c. Brookside is a great place to live.
   d. Brookside has a high crime rate.
   e. Everyone should move to Brookside.

See answers on the next page.

Answer Explanations

1. B: The author clearly states that education is crucial to the survival of the human race, and it can be easily inferred that if this is true, then improvements to our educational system are certainly worth fighting for. Choices *A* and *C* are incorrect because there is nothing in the passage that relates to these statements. Choice *D* is incorrect because it directly contradicts what the author states about all children's ability to learn. Choice *E* is mentioned in the passage, but it is not the main point.

2. A: Clearly, this author feels passionately about the importance of education. This is evident especially in the word choices. For this reason, all the other answer choices are incorrect.

3. C: Based on the author's passionate stance about the importance of education for all children, Choice *C* makes the most sense. For this reason, all the other answer choices are incorrect.

4. D: The author mentions the importance of parent involvement and communication between the school and home. He also devotes one full paragraph to the impact of technology on education. Nowhere in the passage does the author mention the cost of textbooks, so Choice *D* is correct.

5. C: All the details in this paragraph suggest that Brookside is a great place to live, plus the last sentence states that it is an *idyllic neighborhood*, meaning it is perfect, happy, and blissful. Choices *A* and *B* are incorrect, because although they do contain specific details from the paragraph that support the main idea, they are not the main idea. Choice *D* is incorrect because there is no reference in the paragraph to the crime rate in Brookside. Choice *E* is incorrect; the author does think Brookside is a great place, but they don't try and convince the audience to move there.

134

Verbal

Test takers encounter two parts in the verbal section of the Upper Level SSAT. In the first part, the vocabulary section, questions address the test taker's understanding of language and the meanings of different words. The second part is the analogy section, which assesses the test taker's ability to logically relate words to one another.

The vocabulary words are pulled from all areas of study and are of age-appropriate difficulty. Words may include those encountered specifically in science class, technology-related, social studies, mathematics, and language arts. Successful test takers should think about the parts of a word and the structure of the English language, including things like:

- Word origins
- Root words
- Prefixes
- Suffixes
- Words with multiple meanings

Synonyms

This portion of the exam is specifically constructed to test vocabulary skills and the ability to discern the best answer that matches the provided word. Unlike verbal analogies, which will test communication skills and problem-solving abilities along with vocabulary, these questions chiefly test vocabulary knowledge by asking test takers to select the best synonym for the provided word. While logic and reasoning come into play in this section, they are not as heavily emphasized as with the analogies. A prior knowledge of what the words mean is helpful in order to answer correctly. If the meaning of the words is unknown, that's fine, too. Strategies should be used to rule out false answers and choose the correct ones. Here are some study strategies for an optimum performance.

Format of the Questions

The synonyms questions are very simple in construction. Instead of a comparison of words with an underlying connection, like the verbal analogies, the prompt is just a single word. There are no special directions, alternate meanings, or analogies to work with. The objective is to analyze the given word and then choose the answer that means the same thing or is closest in meaning to the given word. Note the example below:

Blustery
    a. Hard
    b. Windy
    c. Mythical
    d. Stoney
    e. Corresponding

All of the questions on the Synonyms portion will appear exactly like the above sample. This is generally the standard layout throughout other exams, so some test-takers may already be familiar with the structure. The principle remains the same. At the top of the section, clear directions will be given to

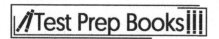

choose the answer that most precisely defines the given word. In this case, the answer is windy (B), since windy and blustery are synonymous.

Preparation

In truth, there is no set way to prepare for this portion of the exam that will guarantee a perfect score. This is simply because the words used on the test are unpredictable. There is no set list provided to study from. The definition of the provided word needs to be determined on the spot. This sounds challenging, but there are still ways to prepare mentally for the test. It may help to expand your vocabulary a little each day. Several resources are available, in books and online, that collect words and definitions that tend to show up frequently on standardized tests. Knowledge of words can increase the strength of your vocabulary.

Mindset is key. The meanings of challenging words can often be found by relying on the past experiences of the test-taker to help deduce the correct answer. How? Well, test-takers have been talking their entire lives—knowing words and how words work. It helps to have a positive mindset from the start. It's unlikely that all definitions of words will be known immediately, but the answer can still be found. There are aspects of words that are recognizable to help discern the correct answers and eliminate the incorrect ones. Here are some of the factors that contribute to word meanings!

Word Origins and Roots

Studying a foreign language in school, particularly Latin or any of the romance languages (Latin-influenced), is advantageous. English is a language highly influenced by Latin and Greek words. The roots of much of the English vocabulary have Latin origins; these roots can bind many words together and often allude to a shared definition. Here's an example:

Fervent
  a. Lame
  b. Joyful
  c. Thorough
  d. Boiling
  e. Cunning

Fervent descends from the Latin word, *fervere*, which means "to boil or glow" and figuratively means "impassioned." The Latin root present in the word is *ferv*, which is what gives fervent the definition: showing great warmth and spirit or spirited, hot, glowing. This provides a link to boiling (D) just by root word association, but there's more to analyze. Among the other choices, none relate to fervent. The word lame (A) means crippled, disabled, weak, or inadequate. None of these match with fervent.

While being fervent can reflect joy, joyful (B) directly describes "a great state of happiness," while fervent is simply expressing the idea of having very strong feelings—not necessarily joy. Thorough (C) means complete, perfect, painstaking, or with mastery; while something can be done thoroughly and fervently, none of these words match fervent as closely as boiling does. Cunning (E) means crafty, deceiving or with ingenuity or dexterity. Doing something fervently does not necessarily mean it is done with dexterity. Not only does boiling connect in a linguistic way, but also in the way it is used in our language. While boiling can express being physically hot and undergoing a change, boiling is also used to reflect emotional states. People say they are "boiling over" when in heightened emotional states;

136

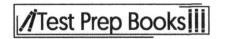

"boiling mad" is another expression. Boiling, like fervent, also embodies a sense of heightened intensity. This makes boiling the best choice!

The Latin root *ferv* is seen in other words such as fervor, fervid, and even ferment. All of them are connected to and can be described by boil or glow, whether it is in a physical sense or in a metaphorical one. Such a pattern can be seen in other word sets! Here's another example:

Gracious
>   a. Fruitful
>   b. Angry
>   c. Grateful
>   d. Understood
>   e. Overheard

This one's a little easier; the answer is grateful (*C*) because both words mean thankful! Even if the meanings of both words are known, there's a connection found by looking at the beginnings of both words: *gra/grat*. Once again, there is a root that stretches back to classical language. Both terms come from the Latin, *gratis*, which literally means "thanks."

Understanding root words can help identify the meaning in a lot of word choices, and help the test-taker grasp the nature of the given word. Many dictionaries, both in book form and online, offer information on the origins of words, which highlight these roots. When studying for the test, it helps to look up an unfamiliar word for its definition and then check to see if it has a root that can be connected to any of the other terms.

Pay Attention to Prefixes

The prefix of a word can actually reveal a lot about its definition. Many prefixes are actually Greco-Roman roots as well—but these are more familiar and a lot easier to recognize! When encountering any unfamiliar words, try looking at prefixes to discern the definition and then compare that with the choices. The prefix should be determined to help find the word's meaning. Here's an example question:

Premeditate
>   a. Sporadic
>   b. Calculated
>   c. Interfere
>   d. Determined
>   e. Noble

With premeditate, there's the common prefix *pre*. This helps draw connections to other words like prepare or preassemble. *Pre* refers to "before, already being, or having already." Meditate means to think or plan. Premeditate means to think or plan beforehand with intent. Therefore, a term that deals with thinking or planning should be found, but also something done in preparation. Among the word choices, noble (E) and determined (D) are both adjectives with no hint of being related to something done before or in preparation. These choices are incorrect. Sporadic (A) refers to events happening in irregular patterns, so this is quite the opposite of premeditated. Interfere (C) also has nothing to do with premeditate; it goes counter to premeditate in a way similar to sporadic. Calculated (B), however, fits! A route and the cost of starting a plan can be calculated. Calculated refers to acting with a full awareness of consequences, so inherently planning is involved. In fact, calculated is synonymous with

137

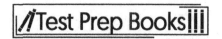

premeditated, thus making it the correct choice. Just by paying attention to a prefix, the doors to a meaning can open to help easily figure out which word would be the best choice. Here's another example.

Regain
    a. Erupt
    b. Ponder
    c. Seek
    d. Recoup
    e. Enamor

Recoup (D) is the right answer. The prefix *re* often appears in front of words to give them the meaning of occurring again. Regain means to repossess something that was lost. Recoup, which also has the *re* prefix, literally means to regain. In this example, both the given word and the answer share the *re* prefix, which makes the pair easy to connect. However, don't rely only on prefixes to choose an answer. Make sure to analyze all options before marking an answer. Going through the other words in this sample, none of them come close to meaning regain except recoup. After checking to make sure that recoup is the best matching word, then mark it!

Positive Versus Negative Sounding Words

Another tool for the mental toolbox is simply distinguishing whether a word has a positive or negative connotation. Like electrical wires, words carry energy; they are crafted to draw certain attention and to have certain strength to them. Words can be described as positive and uplifting (a stronger word) or they can be negative and scathing (a stronger word). Sometimes they are neutral—having no particular connotation. Distinguishing how a word is supposed to be interpreted will not only help learn its definition, but also draw parallels with word choices. While it's true that words must usually be taken in the context of how they are used, word definitions have inherent meanings as well. So, they have a distinct vibe to pick up on. Here is an example.

Excellent
    a. Fair
    b. Optimum
    c. Reasonable
    d. Negative
    e. Agitation

As you know, excellent is a very positive word. It refers to something being better than good, above average. In this sample, negative (D) and agitation (E) can easily be eliminated because these are both words with negative connotations. Reasonable (C) is more or less a neutral word: it's not bad but it doesn't communicate the higher quality that excellent represents. It's just, well, reasonable. This leaves the possible choices of fair (A) and optimum (B). Or does it? Fair *is* a positive word; it's used to describe things that are good, even beautiful. But in the modern context, fair is defined as good, but somewhat average or just decent: "You did a fairly good job." or, "That was fair." On the other hand, optimum is positive and is a stronger word. Optimum describes the most favorable outcome. This makes optimum the best word choice that matches excellent in both strength and connotation. Not only are the two words positive, but they also express the same level of positivity! Here's another example:

Repulse
   a. Draw
   b. Encumber
   c. Force
   d. Disgust
   e. Magnify

Repulse sounds negative when said. It is commonly used in the context of something being repulsive, disgusting, or that which is distasteful. It's also defined as an attack that drives people away. This tells us we need a word that also carries a negative meaning. Magnify (E) is positive, while draw (A) and force (C) are both neutral. Encumber (B) and disgust (D) are negative. Disgust is a stronger negative than encumber. Of all the words given, only disgust directly defines a feeling of distaste and aversion that is synonymous with repulse, and matches in both negativity and strength.

Parts of Speech

It is often very helpful to determine the part of speech of a word. Is it an adjective, adverb, noun, or verb, etc.? Often the correct answer will also be the same part of speech as the given word. Isolate the part of speech and what it describes and look for an answer choice that also describes the same part of speech. For example: if the given word is an adverb describing an action word, then look for another adverb describing an action word.

Swiftly
   a. Fast
   b. Quietly
   c. Angry
   d. Sudden
   e. Quickly

Swiftly is an adverb that describes the speed of an action. Angry (C), fast (A), and sudden (D) can be eliminated because they are not adverbs, and quietly (B) can be eliminated because it does not describe speed. This leaves quickly (E), which is the correct answer. Fast and sudden may throw off some test-takers because they both describe speed, but quickly matches more closely because it is an adverb, and swiftly is also an adverb.

Place the Word in a Sentence

Often it is easier to discern the meaning of a word if it is used in a sentence. If the given word can be used in a sentence, then try replacing it with some of the answer choices to see which words seem to make sense in the same sentence. Here's an example:

Remarkable
   a. Often
   b. Capable
   c. Outstanding
   d. Shining
   e. Excluding

139

A sentence can be formed with the word remarkable. "My grade point average is remarkable." None of the examples make sense when replacing the word remarkable in the sentence other than the word outstanding (C), so outstanding is the obvious answer. Shining (D) is also a word with a positive connotation, but outstanding fits better in the sentence.

Pick the Closest Answer

As the answer choices are reviewed, two scenarios might stand out. An exact definition match might not be found for the given word among the choices, or there are several word choices that can be considered synonymous to the given word. This is intentionally done to test the ability to draw parallels between the words to produce an answer that best fits the prompt word. Again, the closest fitting word will be the answer. Even when facing these two circumstances, finding the one word that fits best is the proper strategy. Here's an example:

Insubordination
    a. Cooperative
    b. Disciplined
    c. Rebel
    d. Contagious
    e. Wild

Insubordination refers to a defiance or utter refusal of authority. Looking over the choices, none of these terms provide definite matches to insubordination like insolence, mutiny, or misconduct would. This is fine; the answer doesn't have to be a perfect synonym. The choices don't reflect insubordination in any way, except rebel (C). After all, when rebel is used as a verb, it means to act against authority. It's also used as a noun: someone who goes against authority. Therefore, rebel is the best choice.

As with the verbal analogies section, being a detective is a good course to take. Two or even three choices might be encountered that could be the answer. However, the answer that most perfectly fits the prompt word's meaning is the best answer. Choices should be narrowed one word at a time. The least-connected word should be eliminated first and then proceed until one word is left that is the closest synonym.

Sequence
    a. List
    b. Range
    c. Series
    d. Replicate
    e. Iconic

A sequence reflects a particular order in which events or objects follow. The two closest options are list (A) and series (C). Both involve grouping things together, but which fits better? Consider each word more carefully. A list is comprised of items that fit in the same category, but that's really it. A list doesn't have to follow any particular order; it's just a list. On the other hand, a series is defined by events happening in a set order. A series relies on sequence, and a sequence can be described as a series. Thus, series is the correct answer!

For both portions of the Verbal Section in the Upper Level SSAT, the following information about English language usage can provide helpful background knowledge to successfully answer questions. While

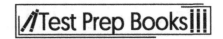

some of this information has previously been touched upon, test takers can benefit from further explanation for several of these concepts.

Verbal Analogies

What are Verbal Analogies?

Analogies compare two different things that have a relationship or some similarity. For example, a basic analogy is apple is to fruit as cucumber is to vegetable. This analogy points out the category under which each item falls. On the SSAT, the final term (vegetable, in this case) will be blank and must be filled in from the multiple choices, selecting the word that best demonstrates the relationship in the first pair of words. Other analogies include words that are *synonyms,* which are words that share similar meanings to one another. For example, big and large are synonyms and tired and sleepy are also synonyms. Verbal analogy questions can be difficult because they require the test taker to demonstrate an understanding of small differences and similarities in both word meanings and word relationships.

Layout of the Questions

Verbal analogy sections are on other standardized tests such as the SAT. The format on the SSAT remains basically the same. First, two words are paired together that provide a frame for the analogy. Then, you are given a third word. You must find the relationship between the first two words, and then choose the fourth word to match the relationship to the third word. It may help to think of it like this: A is to B as C is to D. Examine the breakdown below:

Apple (A) is to fruit (B) as carrot (C) is to vegetable (D).

As shown above, there are four words: the first three are given and the fourth word is the answer that must be found. The first two words are given to set up the kind of analogy that is to be replicated for the next pair. We see that apple is paired with fruit. In the first pair, a specific food item, apple, is paired to the food group category it corresponds with, which is fruit. When presented with the third word in the verbal analogy, carrot, a word must be found that best matches carrot in the way that fruit matched with apple. Again, carrot is a specific food item, so a match should be found with the appropriate food group: vegetable! Here's a sample prompt:

Morbid is to dead as jovial is to
   a. Hate.
   b. Fear.
   c. Disgust.
   d. Happiness.
   e. Desperation.

As with the apple and carrot example, here is an analogy frame in the first two words: morbid and dead. Again, this will dictate how the next two words will correlate with one another. The word morbid can be defined as having a disturbing interest in unpleasant subjects, such as death and disease. In other words, morbid can mean ghastly or death-like, which is why the word dead is paired with it. Dead relates to morbid because it describes morbid. With this in mind, jovial becomes the focus. Jovial means joyful, so out of all the choices given, the closest answer describing jovial is happiness (D).

141

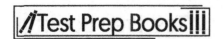

Prompts on the exam will be structured just like the one above. "A is to B as C is to ?" will be given, where the answer completes the second pair. Or sometimes, "A is to B as ? is to ?" is given, where the second pair of words must be found that replicate the relationship between the first pair. The only things that will change are the words and the relationships between the words provided.

Discerning the Correct Answer

While it wouldn't hurt in test preparation to expand vocabulary, verbal analogies are all about delving into the words themselves and finding the right connection, the right word that will fit an analogy. People preparing for the test shouldn't think of themselves as human dictionaries, but rather as detectives. Remember that the first two words that are connected dictates the second pair. From there, picking the correct answer or simply eliminating the ones that aren't correct is the best strategy.

Just like a detective, a test-taker needs to carefully examine the first two words of the analogy for clues. It's good to get in the habit of asking the questions: What do the two words have in common? What makes them related or unrelated? How can a similar relationship be replicated with the word I'm given and the answer choices? Here's another example:

Pillage is to steal as meander is to
    a. Stroll.
    b. Burgle.
    c. Cascade.
    d. Accelerate.
    e. Pinnacle.

Why is pillage paired with steal? In this example, pillage and steal are synonymous: they both refer to the act of stealing. This means that the answer is a word that means the same as meander, which is stroll. In this case, the defining relationship in the whole analogy was a similar definition.

What if test-takers don't know what stroll or meander mean, though? Using logic helps to eliminate choices and pick the correct answer. Looking closer into the contexts of the words pillage and steal, here are a few facts: these are things that humans do; and while they are actions, these are not necessarily types of movement. Again, pick a word that will not only match the given word, but best completes the relationship.

It wouldn't make sense that burgle (B) would be the correct choice because meander doesn't have anything to do with stealing, so that eliminates burgle. Pinnacle (E) also can be eliminated because this is not an action at all but a position or point of reference. Cascade (C) refers to pouring or falling, usually in the context of a waterfall and not in reference to people, which means we can eliminate cascade as well. While people do accelerate when they move, they usually do so under additional circumstances: they accelerate while running or driving a car. All three of the words we see in the analogy are actions that can be done independently of other factors. Therefore, accelerate (D) can be eliminated, and stroll (A) should be chosen. Stroll and meander both refer to walking or wandering, so this fits perfectly.

The process of elimination will help rule out wrong answers. However, the best way to find the correct answer is simply to differentiate the correct answer from the other choices. For this, test-takers should go back to asking questions, starting with the chief question: What's the connection? There are actually many ways that connections can be found between words. The trick is to look for the answer that is

142

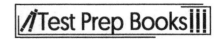

consistent with the relationship between the words given. What is the prevailing connection? Here are a few different ways verbal analogies can be formed.

Finding Connections in Word Analogies

Categories

One of the easiest ways to choose the correct answer in word analogies is simply to group the words. Ask if the words can be compartmentalized into distinct categories. Here are some examples:

Terrier is to dog as mystery is to

    a. Thriller.
    b. Murder.
    c. Detective.
    d. Novel.
    e. Investigation.

This one might have been a little confusing, but when looking at the first two words in the analogy, this is clearly one in which a category is the prevailing theme. Think about it: a terrier is a type of dog. While there are several breeds of dogs that can be categorized as a terrier, in the end, all terriers are still dogs. Therefore, mystery needs to be grouped into a category. Murders, detectives, and investigations can all be involved in a mystery plot, but a murder (B), a detective (C), or an investigation (E) is not necessarily a mystery. A thriller (A) is a purely fictional concept, a kind of story or film, just like a mystery. A thriller can describe a mystery, but the same issue appears as the other choices. What about novel (D)? For one thing, it's distinct from all the other terms. A novel isn't a component of a mystery, but a mystery can be a type of novel. The relationship fits: a terrier is a type of dog, just like a mystery is a type of novel.

Synonym/Antonym

Some analogies are based on words meaning the same thing or expressing the same idea. Sometimes it's the complete opposite!

Marauder is to brigand as

    a. King is to peasant.
    b. Juice is to orange.
    c. Soldier is to warrior.
    d. Engine is to engineer.
    e. Paper is to photocopier.

Here, soldier is to warrior (C) is the correct answer. Marauders and brigands are both thieves. They are synonyms. The only pair of words that fits this analogy is soldier and warrior because both terms describe combatants who fight.

Cap is to shoe as jacket is to

    a. Ring.
    b. T-shirt.
    c. Vest.
    d. Glasses.
    e. Pants.

Opposites are at play here because a cap is worn on the head/top of the person, while a shoe is worn on the foot/bottom. A jacket is worn on top of the body too, so the opposite of jacket would be pants (E) because these are worn on the bottom. Often the prompts on the test provide a synonym or antonym relationship. Just consider if the sets in the prompt reflect similarity or stark difference.

Parts of a Whole

Another thing to consider when first looking at an analogy prompt is whether the words presented come together in some way. Do they express parts of the same item? Does one word complete the other? Are they connected by process or function?

Tire is to car as
    a. Wing is to bird.
    b. Oar is to boat.
    c. Box is to shelf.
    d. Hat is to head.
    e. Knife is to sheath.

We know that the tire fits onto the car's wheels and this is what enables the car to drive on roads. The tire is part of the car. This is the same relationship as oar is to boat (B). The oars are attached onto a boat and enable a person to move and navigate the boat on water. At first glance, wing is to bird (A) seems to fit too, since a wing is a part of a bird that enables it to move through the air. However, since a tire and car are not alive and transport people, oar and boat fit better because they are also not alive, and they transport people. Subtle differences between answer choices should be found.

Other Relationships

There are a number of other relationships to look for when solving verbal analogies. Some relationships focus on one word being a *characteristic/NOT a characteristic* of the other word. Sometimes the first word is the *source/comprised of* the second word. Still, other words are related by their *location*. Some analogies have *sequential* relationships, and some are *cause/effect* relationships. There are analogies that show *creator/provider* relationships with the *creation/provision*. Another relationship might compare an *object* with its *function* or a *user* with their *tool*. An analogy may focus on a *change of grammar* or a *translation of language*. Finally, one word of an analogy may have a relationship to the other word in its *intensity*.

The type of relationship between the first two words of the analogy should be determined before continuing to analyze the second set of words. One effective method of determining a relationship between two words is to form a comprehensible sentence using both words. Then plug the answer choices into the same sentence. For example in the analogy: *Bicycle is to handlebars as car is to steering wheel*, a sentence could be formed that says: A bicycle navigates using its handlebars; therefore, a car navigates using its steering wheel. If the second sentence makes sense, then the correct relationship likely is found. A sentence may be more complex depending on the relationship between the first two words in the analogy. An example of this may be: *food is to dishwasher as dirt is to carwash*. The formed sentence may be: A dishwasher cleans food off of dishes in the same way that a carwash cleans dirt off of a car.

Dealing with Multiple Connections

There are many other ways to draw connections between word sets. Several word choices might form an analogy that would fit the word set in your prompt. This is when an analogy from multiple angles

144

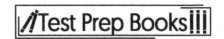

needs to be explored. Several words might even fit in a relationship. If so, which one is an even closer match than the others? The framing word pair is another important point to consider. Can one or both words be interpreted as actions or ideas, or are they purely objects? Here's a question where words could have alternate meanings:

Hammer is to nail as saw is to
   a. Electric.
   b. Hack.
   c. Cut.
   d. Machete.
   e. Groove.

Looking at the question above, it becomes clear that the topic of the analogy involves construction tools. Hammers and nails are used in concert since the hammer is used to pound the nail. The logical first thing to do is to look for an object that a saw would be used on. Seeing that there is no such object among the answer choices, a test-taker might begin to worry. After all, that seems to be the choice that would complete the analogy—but that doesn't mean it's the only choice that may fit. Encountering questions like this tests the ability to see multiple connections between words. Don't get stuck thinking that words have to be connected in a single way. The first two words given can be verbs instead of just objects. To hammer means to hit or beat; oftentimes it refers to beating something into place. This is also what nail means when it is used as a verb. Here are the word choices that reveal the answer.

First, it's known that a saw, well, saws. It uses a steady motion to cut an object, and indeed to saw means to cut! Cut (C) is one of our answer choices, but the other options should be reviewed. While some tools are electric (a), the use of power in the tools listed in the analogy isn't a factor. Again, it's been established that these word choices are not tools in this context. Therefore, machete (D) is also ruled out because machete is also not a verb. Another important thing to consider is that while a machete is a tool that accomplishes a similar purpose as a saw, the machete is used in a slicing motion rather than a sawing/cutting motion. The verb that describes machete is hack (B), another choice that can be ruled out. A machete is used to hack at foliage. However, a saw does not hack. Groove (E) is just a term that has nothing to do with the other words, so this choice can be eliminated easily. This leaves cut (C), which confirms that this is the word needed to complete the analogy!

Vocabulary

Defining Words and English Origins

A **word** is a group of letters joined to form a single meaning. On their own, letters represent single sounds, but when placed together in a certain order, letters represent a specific image in the reader's mind in a way that provides meaning. Words can be nouns, verbs, adjectives, and adverbs, among others. Words also represent a verb tense of past, present, or future. Words allow for effective communication for commerce, social progress, technical advances, and much more. Simply put, words allow people to understand one another and create meaning in a complex world.

Throughout history, English words were shaped by other cultures and languages, such as Greek, Latin, French, Spanish, German, and others. They were borne from inventions, discoveries, and literary works, such as plays or science fiction novels. Others formed by shortening words that were already in existence. Some words evolved from the use of acronyms, such as *radar* (Radio Detection and Ranging)

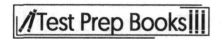

and *scuba* (Self-Contained Underwater Breathing Apparatus). The English language will continue to evolve as the needs and values of its speakers evolve.

Word Formation

How do English words form? They can be single root words, such as *love, hate, boy*, or *girl*. A **root word** is a word in its most basic form that carries a clear and distinct meaning. Complex English words combine affixes with root words. Some words have no root word, but are instead formed by combining various affixes, such as reject: *re-* is defined as repeating an action or actions, and *-ject* means throw or thrown. Therefore, **reject** is defined as the act of being thrown back. Words consisting of affixes alone are not the norm. Most words consist of either root words on their own or with the addition of affixes. To **affix** is to attach to something. Therefore, affixes in linguistic study are groups of letters that attach themselves to the beginning, middle, or end of root words to enhance or alter the word's meaning. Affixes added to verbs can change the word's tense, and affixes added to nouns can change the word's part of speech from noun to adjective, verb, or adverb.

Roots and Root Words
Words that exist on their own, without affixes, are root words. **Root words** are words written in their most basic form, and they carry a clear and distinct meaning. Consider the word *safe*. The root word, *safe*, acts as both a noun and adjective, and stands on its own, carrying a clear and distinct meaning.

The root of a word however, is not necessarily a part of the word that can stand on its own, although it does carry meaning. Since many English words come from Latin and Greek roots, it's helpful to have a general understanding of roots. Here is a list of common Greek and Latin roots used in the English language:

Root	Definition	Example
ami	Love	Amiable
ethno	Race	Ethnological
infra	Beneath or Below	Infrastructure
lun	Moon	Lunar
max	Greatest	Maximum
pent/penta	Five	Pentagon
sol	Sun	Solar
vac	Empty	Vacant

Affixes
Affixes are groups of letters that when added to the beginning or ending of root words, or are attachments within a root or root word itself, can:

- Intensify the word's meaning
- Create a new meaning
- Somewhat alter the existing meaning

146

- Change the verb tense
- Change the part of speech

There are three types of affixes: prefixes, suffixes, and infixes.

Prefixes

Prefixes are groups of letters attached to the beginning of a root word. *Pre-* refers to coming before, and *fix* refers to attaching to something. Consider the example of the root word *freeze*:

- Freeze: verb – to change from a liquid to solid by lowering the temperature to a freezing state.

- *Anti*freeze: noun – a liquid substance that prevents freezing when added to water, as in a vehicle's radiator.

By adding the prefix *anti-* to the root word *freeze*, the part of speech changed from verb to noun, and completely altered the meaning. *Anti-* as a prefix always creates the opposite in meaning, or the word's antonym.

By having a basic understanding of how prefixes work and what their functions are in a word's meaning, English speakers strengthen their fluency. Here is a list of some common prefixes in the English language, accompanied by their meanings:

Prefix	Definition	Example
ante-	before	antecedent
ex-	out/from	expel
inter-	between/among	intergalactic
multi-	much/many	multitude
post-	after	postscript
sub-	under	submarine
trans-	move between/across	transport
uni-	single/one	universe

Suffixes

Suffixes are groups of letters attached to the ending of a root or root word. Like prefixes, suffixes can:

- Intensify the word's meaning
- Create a new meaning
- Somewhat alter the existing meaning
- Change the verb tense
- Change the part of speech

Consider the example of the root word *fish* when suffixes are added:

- Fish: noun – a cold-blooded animal that lives completely in water and possesses fins and gills.
- Fishing: noun – I love the sport of fishing.
- Fishing: verb – Are you fishing today?

With the addition of the suffix *-ing*, the meaning of root word *fish* is altered, as is the part of speech.

A verb tense shift is made with the addition of the suffix *-ed*:

- Jump: present tense of to jump as in "I jump."
- Jumped: past tense of to jump as in "I jumped."
- Climb: present tense of to climb as in "We climb."
- Climbed: past tense of to climb as in "We climbed."

Here are a few common suffixes in the English language, along with their meanings:

Suffix	Meaning	Example
-ed	past tense	cooked
-ing	materials, present action	clothing
-ly	in a specific manner	lovely
-ness	a state or quality	brightness
-ment	action	enjoyment
-script	to write	transcript
-ee	receiver/performer	nominee
-ation/-ion	action or process	obligation

Infixes

Infixes are letters that attach themselves inside the root or root words. They generally appear in the middle of the word and are rare in the English language. Easily recognizable infixes include parent*s*-in-law, passer*s*-by, or cup*s*ful. Notice the *-s* is added inside the root word, making the word plural.

Special types of infixes, called **tmesis** words, are made from inserting an existing word into the middle of another word or between a compound word, creating a new word. Tmesis words are generally used in casual dialogue and slang speech. They add emphasis to the word's overall meaning and to evoke emotion on the part of the reader. Examples are fan-*bloody*-tastic and un-*freaking*-believable.

Tmesis words have been in existence since Shakespeare's time, as in this phrase from *Romeo and Juliet*, "...he is some *other*where." Shakespeare split up the compound word *somewhere* by inserting the word *other* between the two root words.

Compound Words

A **compound word** is created with the combination of two shorter words. To be a true compound word, two shorter words are combined, and the meaning of the longer word retains the meaning of the two

148

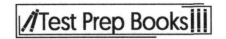

shorter words. Compound words enhance the overall meaning, giving a broader description. There are three types of compound words: closed, hyphenated, and open.

Closed Compound Words

There was a time when closed compound words were not considered legitimate words. Over time and with continued, persistent use, they found a place in the English language. A **closed compound word** refers to a word that shows no separation between the two shorter words from which it is composed. Some examples of closed compound words are:

Closed Compound Word	Individual Words	Meaning
bookshelf	book/shelf	a shelf that holds books
doorstop	door/stop	an object to hold a door open
bedroom	bed/room	a room where one sleeps
bathroom	bath/room	a room where one bathes
backyard	back/yard	a yard in the back of a building
nightstand	night/stand	a small table beside one's bed

Hyphenated Compound Words

As the name suggests, **hyphenated compound words** include a hyphen that separates the two shorter words within the longer word. Some examples of hyphenated compound words are:

Hyphenated Compound Words	Individual Words	Meaning
self-service	self/serve	the act of serving one's self
color-blind	color/blind	incapable of accurately distinguishing colors
check-in	check/in	the act of registering as in attendance
year-round	year/round	any affair that takes place throughout the year
toll-free	toll/free	no application of toll/no charge
sugar-coated	sugar/coated	anything sweetened or coated with sugar

Open Compound Words

Open compound words appear as individual words but are they dependent on their partners to form the complete meaning of the compound word. Individually, the words may have meanings that are different than that of the pair together (the open compound word). For example, in *real estate*, *real* and *estate* have their own meanings that are different than the unique meaning of the compound word. Open compound words are separated from each other by a single space and do not require a hyphen. Some examples of open compound words are:

Open Compound Words	Meaning
polka dot	a repeated circular dot that forms a pattern
sleeping bag	a special bag used to sleep in (usually when camping)
solar system	the collection of planets that orbit around the Sun
tape recorder	magnetic tape used to record sound
middle class	social group that is considered above lower class and below upper class
family room	a specific room for relaxation and entertainment used by all family members

Parts of Speech

Also referred to as word classes, **parts of speech** refer to the various categories in which words are placed. Words can be placed in any one or a combination of the following categories:

- Nouns
- Determiners
- Pronouns
- Verbs
- Adjectives
- Adverbs
- Prepositions
- Conjunctions

Understanding the various parts of speech used in the English language helps readers to better understand the written language.

Nouns

A **noun** is defined as any word that represents a person, place, animal, object, or idea. Nouns can identify a person's title or name, a person's gender, and a person's nationality, such as banker, commander-in-chief, female, male, or an American.

150

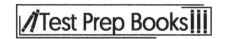

With animals, nouns identify the kingdom, phylum, class, etc. For example: the animal is an *elephant*, the phylum is *chordata*, and the class is *Mammalia*. It should be noted that the words *animal, phylum,* and *class* in the previous sentence are also nouns.

When identifying places, nouns refer to a physical location, a general vicinity, or the proper name of a city, state, or country. Some examples include the *desert*, the *East*, *Phoenix*, the *bathroom*, *Arizona*, an *office*, or the *United States*.

There are eight types of nouns: common, proper, countable, uncountable, concrete, abstract, compound, and collective.

Common nouns are used in general terms, without specific identification. Examples include *girl, boy, country,* or *school*. Proper nouns refer to the specific proper name given to people, places, animals, or entities, such as *Melissa, Martin, Italy,* or *Harvard*.

Countable nouns can be counted: *one car, two cars,* or *three cars*. **Uncountable nouns** cannot be counted, such as *air, liquid,* or *gas*.

To be abstract is to exist, but only in thought or as an idea. An **abstract noun** cannot be physically touched, seen, smelled, heard, or tasted. Examples include *chivalry, day, fear, thought, truth, friendship,* or *freedom*.

To be **concrete** is to be seen, touched, tasted, heard, and/or smelled. Examples include *pie, snow, tree, bird, desk, hair,* or *dog*.

A **compound noun** is another term for an open compound word. Any noun that is written as two nouns that together form a specific meaning is a compound noun. For example, *post office, ice cream,* or *swimming pool*.

A **collective noun** refers to groups or collection of things that together form the whole. The members of the group are often people or individuals. Examples include *orchestra, squad, committee,* or the *majority*. It should be noted that the nouns in these examples are singular, but the word itself refers to a group containing more than one individual.

Determiners

Determiners modify a noun and usually refer to something specific. Determiners fall into one of four categories: *articles, demonstratives, quantifiers,* or *possessive determiners*.

Articles can be both definite articles, as in *the*, and indefinite as in *a, an, some,* or *any*:

> *The* man with *the* red hat.

> *A* flower growing in *the* yard.

> *Any* person who visits *the* store.

There are four different types of demonstratives: *this, that, these,* and *those*.

True demonstrative words will not directly precede the noun of the sentence but will be the noun. Some examples:

> *This* is the one.

> *That* is the place.

> *Those* are the files.

Once a demonstrative is placed directly in front of the noun, it becomes a demonstrative pronoun:

> *This* one is perfect.

> *That* place is lovely.

> *Those* boys are annoying.

Quantifiers proceed nouns to give additional information to the noun about how much or how many is referred to. They can be used with countable and uncountable nouns:

> She bought *plenty* of apples.

> *Few* visitors came.

> I got a *little* change.

Possessive determiners, sometimes called **possessive adjectives**, indicate possession. They are the possessive forms of personal pronouns, such as *for my, your, hers, his, its, their*, or *our*:

> That is *my* car.

> Tom rode *his* bike today.

> Those papers are *hers*.

Pronouns

Pronouns are words that stand in place of nouns. There are three different types of pronouns: **subjective pronouns** (*I, you, he, she, it, we, they*), **objective pronouns** (*me, you, him, her it, us, them*), and **possessive pronouns** (*mine, yours, his, hers, ours, theirs*).

Note that some words are found in more than one pronoun category. See examples and clarifications are below:

> *You* are going to the movies.

In the previous sentence, *you* is a subjective pronoun; it is the subject of the sentence and is performing the action.

> I threw the ball to *you*.

Here, *you* is an objective pronoun; it is receiving the action and is the object of the sentence.

> We saw *her* at the movies.

152

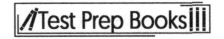

Her is an objective pronoun; it is receiving the action and is the object of the sentence.

> The house across the street from the park is *hers.*

In this example, *hers* is a possessive pronoun; it shows possession of the house.

Verbs

Verbs are words in a sentence that show action or state. A sentence must contain a subject and a verb. Without a verb, a sentence is incomplete. Verbs may be in the present, past, or future tenses. To form auxiliary, or helping, verbs are required for some tenses in the future and in the past.

> I *see* the neighbors across the street.

See is an action.

> We *were eating* at the picnic.

Eating is the main action, and the verb *were* is the past tense of the verb *to be*, and is the helping or auxiliary verb that places the sentence in the past tense.

> You *will turn* 20 years of age next month.

Turn is the main verb, but *will* is the helping verb to show future tense of the verb *to be.*

Adjectives

Adjectives are a special group of words used to modify, describe, or provide more information about a noun. For example:

> The boy went to school. (There is no adjective.)

Rewriting the sentence, adding an adjective to further describe the boy and/or the school yields:

> The *young* boy went to the *old* school. (The adjective *young* describes the boy, and the adjective *old* describes the school.)

Adverbs

Adverb can play one of two roles: to modify the adjective or to modify the verb. For example:

> The young boy went to the old school.

We can further describe the adjectives *young* and *old* with adverbs placed directly in front of the adjectives:

> The *very* young boy went to the *very* old school. (The adverb *very* further describes the adjectives *young* and *old*.)

Other examples of using adverbs to further describe verbs include:

> The boy *slowly* went to school.

> The boy *happily* went to school.

153

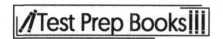

The adverbs *slowly* and *happily* further modify the verbs.

Prepositions

Prepositions are special words that generally precede a noun. Prepositions clarify the relationship between the subject and another word or element in the sentence. They clarify time, place, and the positioning of the subjects and objects in a sentence. Common prepositions in the English language include: *near, far, under, over, on, in, between, beside, of, at, until, behind, across, after, before, for, from, to, by,* and *with*.

Conjunctions

Conjunctions are a group of unique words that connect clauses or sentences. They also work to coordinate words in the same clause. It is important to choose an appropriate conjunction based on the meaning of the sentence. Consider these sentences:

I really like the flowers, *however* the smell is atrocious.

I really like the flowers, *besides* the smell is atrocious.

The conjunctions *however* and *besides* act as conjunctions, connecting the two ideas: *I really like the flowers,* and, *the smell is atrocious*. In the second sentence, the conjunction *besides* makes no sense and would confuse the reader. Conjunctions must be chosen that clearly state the intended message without ambiguity.

Some conjunctions introduce an opposing opinion, thought, or fact. They can also reinforce an opinion, introduce an explanation, reinforce cause and effect, or indicate time. For example:

Opposition: She wishes to go to the movies, *but* she doesn't have the money.

Cause and effect: The professor became ill, *so* the class was postponed.

Time: They visited Europe *before* winter came.

Each conjunction serves a specific purpose in uniting two separate ideas. Below are common conjunctions in the English language:

Opposition	Cause & Effect	Reinforcement	Time	Explanation
however	Therefore	besides	afterward	for example
nevertheless	as a result	anyway	before	in other words
but	because of this	after all	firstly	for instance
although	Consequently	furthermore	next	such as

Synonyms

Recall that **synonyms** are words that mean the same or nearly the same thing in the same language. When presented with several words and asked to choose the synonym, more than one word may be similar to the original. However, one word is generally the strongest match. Synonyms should always share the same part of speech. For instance, *shy* and *timid* are both adjectives and hold similar

154

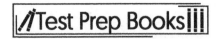

meanings. The words *shy* and *loner* are similar, but *shy* is an adjective while *loner* is a noun. Another way to test for the best synonym is to reread the sentence with each possible word and determine which one makes the most sense. Consider the following sentence: *He will love you forever.*

Now consider the words: *adore, sweet, kind*, and *nice*. They seem similar, but when used in the following applications with the initial sentence, not all of them are synonyms for *love.*

He will *adore* you forever.

He will *sweet* you forever.

He will *kind* you forever.

He will *nice* you forever.

In the first sentence, the word *love* is used as a verb. The best synonym from the list that shares the same part of speech is *adore*. *Adore* is a verb, and when substituted in the sentence, it is the only substitution that makes grammatical and semantic sense.

Synonyms can be found for nouns, adjectives, verbs, adverbs, and prepositions. Here are some examples of synonyms from different parts of speech:

- **Nouns**: clothes, wardrobe, attire, apparel
- **Verbs**: run, sprint, dash
- **Adjectives**: fast, quick, rapid, swift
- **Adverbs**: slowly, nonchalantly, leisurely
- **Prepositions**: near, proximal, neighboring, close

Here are several more examples of synonyms in the English language:

Word	Synonym	Meaning
smart	intelligent	having or showing a high level of intelligence
exact	specific	clearly identified
almost	nearly	not quite but very close
to annoy	to bother	to irritate
to answer	to reply	to form a written or verbal response
building	edifice	a structure that stands on its own with a roof and four walls
business	commerce	the act of purchasing, negotiating, trading, and selling
defective	faulty	when a device is not working or not working well

Antonyms

Antonyms are words that are complete opposites. As with synonyms, there may be several words that represent the opposite meaning of the word in question. When choosing an antonym, one should choose the word that represents as close to the exact opposite in meaning as the given word, and ensure it shares the same part of speech.

Here are some examples of antonyms:

- Nouns: predator – prey
- Verbs: love – hate
- Adjectives: good – bad
- Adverbs: slowly – swiftly
- Prepositions: above – below

Homonyms

Homonyms are words that sound alike but carry different meanings. There are two different types of homonyms: homophones and homographs.

Homophones

Homophones are words that sound alike but carry different meanings and spellings. In the English language, there are several examples of homophones. Consider the following list:

Word	Meaning	Homophone	Meaning
I'll	I + will	aisle	a specific lane between seats
Allowed	past tense of the verb, 'to allow'	aloud	to utter a sound out loud
Eye	a part of the body used for seeing	I	first-person singular
Ate	the past tense of the verb, 'to eat'	eight	the number preceding the number nine
Peace	the opposite of war	piece	part of a whole
Seas	large bodies of natural water	seize	to take ahold of/to capture

Homographs

Homographs are words that share the same spelling but carry different meanings and different pronunciations. Consider the following list:

Word	Meaning	Homograph	Meaning
bass	fish	bass	musical instrument
bow	a weapon used to fire arrows	bow	to bend
Polish	of or from Poland	polish	a type of shine (n); to shine (v)
desert	dry, arid land	desert	to abandon

157

Practice Quiz

Synonyms

1. DEDUCE
    a. Explain
    b. Win
    c. Reason
    d. Gamble
    e. Undo

2. ELUCIDATE
    a. Learn
    b. Enlighten
    c. Plan
    d. Corroborate
    e. Conscious

3. VERIFY
    a. Criticize
    b. Change
    c. Teach
    d. Substantiate
    e. Resolve

4. BREVITY
    a. Dullness
    b. Dangerous
    c. Brief
    d. Ancient
    e. Calamity

5. PERCEIVE
    a. Sustain
    b. Collect
    c. Prove
    d. Lead
    e. Comprehend

Verbal Analogies

1. *Sand* is to *glass* as
    a. Protons are to atoms.
    b. Ice is to snow.
    c. Seeds are to plants.
    d. Water is to steam.
    e. Air is to wind.

158

2. *Design* is to *create* as *allocate* is to
   a. Finish.
   b. Manage.
   c. Multiply.
   d. Find.
   e. Distribute.

3. *Cool* is to *frigid* as *warm* is to
   a. Toasty.
   b. Summer.
   c. Sweltering.
   d. Hot.
   e. Mild.

4. *Arid* is to *damp* as *anxious* is to
   a. Happy.
   b. Petrified.
   c. Ireful.
   d. Confident.
   e. Sorrowful.

5. *Validate* is to *verify* as *conquer* is to
   a. Withdraw.
   b. Subjugate.
   c. Expand.
   d. Surrender.
   e. Expose.

See answers on the next page.

Answer Explanations

Synonyms

1. C: To deduce something is to figure it out using reasoning. While you can explain something you've deduced, explain is not a synonym for deduce.

2. B: To elucidate is to figuratively shine a light on a previously unknown or confusing subject. This Latin root, "lux" meaning "light," prominently figures into the solution. *Enlighten* means to educate or bring to light.

3. D: Looking at the Latin word "veritas," meaning "truth," will yield a clue as to the meaning of verify. To verify is the act of finding or assessing the truthfulness of something. This usually means amassing evidence to substantiate a claim. *Substantiate,* of course, means to provide evidence to prove a point.

4. C: *Brevity* literally means brief or concise. Note the similar beginnings of brevity and brief—from the Latin "brevis," meaning brief.

5. E: All the connotations of *perceive* involve the concept of seeing. Whether figuratively or literally, perceiving implies the act of understanding what is presented. Comprehending is synonymous with this understanding.

Verbal Analogies

1. D: This is a source/comprised of analogy. The common thread is addition of fire. Protons contribute to atoms and seeds grow into plants, but these are simple matters of building and growing without necessarily involving fire. Choices *B* and *E* relate objects that already have similar properties.

2. E: This is a synonym analogy. The determining factor is synonymous definition. Design and create are synonyms, as are allocate and distribute. One could argue that an item could be found and then allocated or that management sometimes requires allocation of items. However, allocate is not a synonym for find or manage like it is for distribute. Allocation generally refers to the division of commodities instead of multiplication.

3. C: This is an intensity analogy. The common thread is degree of severity. While *A, D,* and *E* can all describe warmth, they don't convey the harshness of sweltering. Choice *B* simply describes a time when people may be more likely to think of warmth.

4. D: This is an antonym analogy. The prevailing connection is opposite meanings. While happy can be an opposite of anxious, it's also possible for someone to experience both emotions at once. Choices *B, C,* and *E* are also concurrent with anxious, not opposite.

5. B: This is a synonym analogy, which relies on matching terms that are most closely connected. Validate and verify both mean to confirm that something is accurate or true. Therefore, finding the term that best fits conquer is a good strategy. While nations have conquered others to expand their territory, they are ultimately subjugating those lands and people to their will. Therefore, subjugate is the best-fitting answer.

Practice Test #1

Practice Writing Sample

Select one of the following two-story starters and write a creative story in the space provided. Make sure that your story has a beginning, middle, and end and is interesting for readers.

- The wind whipped through the trees, and the windows began to rattle.

- Karen raced home from the bus stop, flung open the door, and yelled, "Mom!"

Quantitative Reasoning 1

1. Which of the following is equivalent to the value of the digit 3 in the number 792.134?
   a. 3×10
   b. 3×100
   c. $\frac{3}{10}$
   d. $\frac{3}{100}$
   e. $100 \div 3$

2. Simplify:

$$\frac{4a^{-1}b^3}{a^4b^{-2}} \times \frac{3a}{b}$$

   a. $12a^3b^5$
   b. $12\frac{b^4}{a^4}$
   c. $\frac{12}{a^4}$
   d. $7\frac{b^4}{a}$
   e. $4\frac{7b}{a}$

3. How would the number 847.89632 be written if rounded to the nearest hundredth?
   a. 850
   b. 900
   c. 847.89
   d. 847.896
   e. 847.90

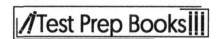

4. What is the sum of $\frac{1}{3}$ and $\frac{2}{5}$?

    a. $\frac{3}{8}$

    b. $\frac{11}{15}$

    c. $\frac{11}{30}$

    d. $\frac{4}{5}$

    e. $\frac{2}{8}$

5. What is the value of the expression: $7^2 - 3 \times (4 + 2) + 15 \div 5$?

    a. 12.2
    b. 40.2
    c. 34
    d. 58.2
    e. 193

6. How will $\frac{4}{5}$ be written as a percent?

    a. 40%
    b. 125%
    c. 50%
    d. 80%
    e. 90%

7. If Danny takes 48 minutes to walk 3 miles, how long should it take him to walk 5 miles maintaining the same speed?

    a. 32 min
    b. 64 min
    c. 80 min
    d. 96 min
    e. 78 min

8. What are all the factors of 12?

    a. 12, 24, 36
    b. 1, 2, 4, 6, 12
    c. 12, 24, 36, 48
    d. 1, 2, 3, 4, 6, 12
    e. 0, 1, 12

9. A construction company is building a new housing development with the property of each house measuring 30 feet wide. If the length of the street is zoned off at 345 feet, how many houses can be built on the street?

    a. 10 houses
    b. 11 houses
    c. 115 houses
    d. 11.5 houses
    e. 12 houses

10. Simplify: $(5x^2 - 3x + 4) - (2x^2 - 7)$

    a. x^5

    b. $3x^2 - 3x + 11$

    c. $3x^2 - 3x - 3$

    d. $x - 3$

    e. $7x^2 - 3x - 3$

11. Kassidy drove for 3 hours at a speed of 60 miles per hour. Using the distance formula, $d = r \times t$ ($distance = rate \times time$), calculate how far Kassidy traveled.

    a. 20 miles

    b. 90 miles

    c. 65 miles

    d. 120 miles

    e. 180 miles

12. If $-3(x + 4) \geq x + 8$, what is the value of x?

    a. $x = 4$

    b. $x \geq 2$

    c. $x \geq -5$

    d. $x \leq -5$

    e. $x \leq 10$

13. Karen gets paid a weekly salary and a commission for every sale that she makes. The table below shows the number of sales and her pay for different weeks.

Sales	2	7	4	8
Pay	$380	$580	$460	$620

Which of the following equations represents Karen's weekly pay?

    a. $y = 90x + 200$

    b. $y = 90x - 200$

    c. $y = 40x + 300$

    d. $y = 40x - 300$

    e. $y = 40x + 200$

14. Which inequality represents the values displayed on the number line?

    a. $x < 1$

    b. $x \leq 1$

    c. $x > 1$

    d. $x \geq 1$

    e. $x \geq 5$

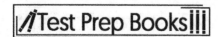
15. What is the 42nd item in the pattern: ▲○○□▲○○□▲ ...?

    a. ○

    b. ▲

    c. □

    d. ○○

    e. None of the above

16. Which of the following statements is true about the two lines below?

    a. The two lines are parallel but not perpendicular.

    b. The two lines are perpendicular but not parallel.

    c. The two lines are both parallel and perpendicular.

    d. The two lines are neither parallel nor perpendicular.

    e. There is not enough information to determine their relationship.

17. Which of the following shows the correct result of simplifying the following expression?

$$(7n + 3n^3 + 3) + (8n + 5n^3 + 2n^4)$$

    a. $9n^4 + 15n - 2$

    b. $2n^4 + 5n^3 + 15n - 2$

    c. $9n^4 + 8n^3 + 15n$

    d. $2n^4 + 8n^3 + 15n + 3$

    e. $3n^4 + 4n^3 + 15n - 4$

18. What is the product of the following expression?

$$(4x - 8)(5x^2 + x + 6)$$

    a. $20x^3 - 36x^2 + 16x - 48$

    b. $6x^3 - 41x^2 + 12x + 15$

    c. $20x^4 + 11x^2 - 37x - 12$

    d. $2x^3 - 11x^2 - 32x + 20$

    e. $10x^3 + 2x^2 - 8x + 48$

19. How do you solve $V = lwh$ for h?

    a. $lwV = h$

    b. $h = \dfrac{V}{lw}$

    c. $h = \dfrac{Vl}{w}$

    d. $h = \dfrac{Vw}{l}$

    e. $h = \dfrac{wl}{V}$

20. What are the coordinates of the point plotted on the grid?

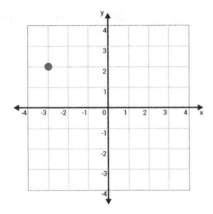

    a. (-3, 2)
    b. (2, -3)
    c. (-3, -2)
    d. (2, 3)
    e. (3, 2)

21. The phone bill is calculated each month using the equation $c = 50g + 75$. The cost of the phone bill per month is represented by c, and g represents the gigabytes of data used that month. What is the value and interpretation of the slope of this equation?

    a. 75 dollars per day
    b. 75 gigabytes per day
    c. 50 dollars per day
    d. 50 dollars per gigabyte
    e. 25 dollars per day

165

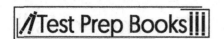

22. Katie works at a clothing company and sold 192 shirts over the weekend. One-third of the shirts were patterned and the rest were solid. Which mathematical expression would calculate the number of solid shirts Katie sold over the weekend?

   a. $192 \times \frac{1}{3}$

   b. $192 \div \frac{1}{3}$

   c. $192 \times (1 - \frac{1}{3})$

   d. $192 \div 3$

   e. $192 \div (1 - \frac{1}{3})$

23. Which measure for the center of a small sample set is most affected by outliers?
   a. Mean
   b. Median
   c. Mode
   d. Range
   d. None of the above

24. Given the value of a particular stock at monthly intervals, which graph should be used to best represent the trend of the stock?
   a. Box plot
   b. Line plot
   c. Scatter plot
   d. Circle graph
   e. Line graph

25. Before a race of 4 horses, you make a random guess of which horse will get first place and which will get second place. What is the probability that both your guesses will be correct?

   a. $\frac{1}{4}$

   b. $\frac{1}{2}$

   c. $\frac{1}{16}$

   d. $\frac{1}{12}$

   e. $\frac{1}{3}$

Reading Comprehension

Questions 1–5 are based on the following passage.

George Washington emerged out of the American Revolution as an unlikely champion of liberty. On June 14, 1775, the Second Continental Congress created the Continental Army, and John Adams, serving in the Congress, nominated Washington to be its first commander. Washington had fought under the British during the French and Indian War, and his experience and prestige proved instrumental to the American war effort.

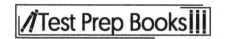

Washington provided invaluable leadership, training, and strategy during the Revolutionary War. He emerged from the war as the embodiment of liberty and freedom from tyranny.

After vanquishing the heavily favored British forces, Washington could have pronounced himself the autocratic leader of the former colonies without any opposition, but he famously refused and returned to his Mount Vernon plantation. His restraint proved his commitment to the fledgling state's republicanism. Washington was later unanimously elected as the first American president. But it is Washington's farewell address that cemented his legacy as a visionary worthy of study.

In 1796, President Washington issued his farewell address by public letter. Washington enlisted his good friend, Alexander Hamilton, in drafting his most famous address. The letter expressed Washington's faith in the Constitution and rule of law. He encouraged his fellow Americans to put aside partisan differences and establish a national union. Washington warned Americans against meddling in foreign affairs and entering military alliances. Additionally, he stated his opposition to national political parties, which he considered partisan and counterproductive.

Americans would be wise to remember Washington's farewell, especially during presidential elections, when politics hit a fever pitch. They might want to question the political institutions that were not planned by the Founding Fathers, such as the nomination process and political parties themselves.

1. Which of the following statements is based on the information in the passage above?
   a. George Washington's background as a wealthy landholder directly led to his faith in equality, liberty, and democracy.
   b. George Washington would have opposed America's involvement in the Second World War.
   c. George Washington would not have been able to write as great a farewell address without the assistance of Alexander Hamilton.
   d. George Washington would probably not approve of modern political parties.
   e. George Washington would likely befriend former President Barack Obama.

2. What is the purpose of this passage?
   a. To caution American voters about being too political during election times because George Washington would not have agreed with holding elections
   b. To introduce George Washington to readers as a historical figure worthy of study
   c. To note that George Washington was more than a famous military hero
   d. To convince readers that George Washington is a hero of republicanism and liberty
   e. To inform American voters about a Founding Father's sage advice on a contemporary issue and explain its applicability to modern times

3. What is the tone of the passage?
   a. Informative
   b. Excited
   c. Bitter
   d. Comic
   e. Somber

167

4. What does the word *meddling* mean in paragraph 3?
    a. Supporting
    b. Speaking against
    c. Interfering
    d. Gathering
    e. Avoiding

5. According to the passage, what did George Washington do when he was offered a role as leader of the former colonies?
    a. He refused the offer.
    b. He accepted the offer.
    c. He became angry at the offer.
    d. He accepted the offer then regretted it later.
    e. He ignored the offer.

Questions 6–10 are based on the following passage:

Christopher Columbus is often credited with discovering America. This is incorrect. First, it is impossible to "discover" something where people already live; however, Christopher Columbus did explore places in the New World that were previously untouched by Europe, so the term "explorer" would be more accurate. Another correction must be made, as well: Christopher Columbus was not the first European explorer to reach the Americas! Rather, it was Leif Erikson who first came to the New World and contacted the natives nearly 500 years before Christopher Columbus.

Leif Erikson, the son of Erik the Red (a famous Viking outlaw and explorer in his own right), was born in either 970 or 980, depending on which historian you read. His own family, though, did not raise Leif, which was a Viking tradition. Instead, one of Erik's prisoners taught Leif reading and writing, languages, sailing, and weaponry. At age 12, Leif was considered a man and returned to his family. He killed a man during a dispute shortly after his return, and the council banished the Erikson clan to Greenland.

In 999, Leif left Greenland and traveled to Norway, where he would serve as a guard to King Olaf Tryggvason. It was there that he became a convert to Christianity. Leif later tried to return home with the intention of taking supplies and spreading Christianity to Greenland, but his ship was blown off course and he arrived in a strange new land: present-day Newfoundland, Canada.

When he finally returned to his adopted homeland of Greenland, Leif consulted with a merchant who had also seen the shores of this previously unknown land. The son of the legendary Viking explorer then gathered a crew of 35 men and set sail. Leif became the first European to set foot in the New World as he explored present-day Baffin Island and Labrador, Canada. His crew called the land Vinland since it was plentiful with grapes.

During their time in present-day Newfoundland, Leif's expedition made contact with the natives, whom they referred to as Skraelings (which translates to "wretched ones" in Norse). There are several secondhand accounts of their meetings. Some contemporaries described trade between the peoples. Other accounts describe clashes where the Skraelings defeated the Viking explorers with long spears, while still others claim the

168

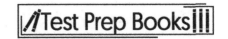

Vikings dominated the natives. Regardless of the circumstances, it seems that the Vikings made contact of some kind. This happened around the year 1000, nearly five hundred years before Columbus famously sailed the ocean blue.

Eventually, in 1003, Leif set sail for home and arrived at Greenland with a ship full of timber.

In 1020, 17 years later, the legendary Viking died. Many believe that Leif Erikson should receive more credit for his contributions in exploring the New World.

6. Which of the following best describes how the author generally presents the information?
   a. Chronological order
   b. Comparison-contrast
   c. Cause-effect
   d. Conclusion-premises
   e. Spatial order

7. Which of the following is an opinion, rather than a historical fact, expressed by the author?
   a. Leif Erikson was definitely the son of Erik the Red; however, historians debate the year of his birth.
   b. Leif Erikson's crew called the land Vinland since it was plentiful with grapes.
   c. Leif Erikson deserves more credit for his contributions in exploring the New World.
   d. Leif Erikson explored the Americas nearly 500 years before Christopher Columbus.
   e. Leif's expedition made contact with the natives, whom they referred to as Skraelings.

8. Which of the following most accurately describes the author's main conclusion?
   a. Leif Erikson is a legendary Viking explorer.
   b. Leif Erikson deserves more credit for exploring America hundreds of years before Columbus.
   c. Spreading Christianity motivated Leif Erikson's expeditions more than any other factor.
   d. Leif Erikson contacted the natives nearly five hundred years before Columbus.
   e. Leif Erikson discovered the Americas.

9. Which of the following best describes the author's intent in the passage?
   a. To entertain
   b. To inform
   c. To alert
   d. To suggest
   e. To share

10. Which of the following can be logically inferred from the passage?
    a. The Vikings disliked exploring the New World.
    b. Leif Erikson's banishment from Iceland led to his exploration of present-day Canada.
    c. Leif Erikson never shared his stories of exploration with the King of Norway.
    d. Historians have difficulty definitively pinpointing events in the Vikings' history.
    e. Christopher Columbus knew of Leif Erikson's explorations.

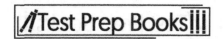
Questions 11–15 are based on the following passage:

Smoking is Terrible

Smoking tobacco products is terribly destructive. A single cigarette contains over 4,000 chemicals, including 43 known carcinogens and 400 deadly toxins. Some of the most dangerous ingredients include tar, carbon monoxide, formaldehyde, ammonia, arsenic, and DDT. Smoking can cause numerous types of cancer, including throat, mouth, nasal cavity, esophageal, gastric, pancreatic, renal, bladder, and cervical cancer.

Cigarettes contain a drug called nicotine, one of the most addictive substances known. Addiction is defined as a compulsion to seek the substance despite negative consequences. According to the National Institute on Drug Abuse, nearly 35 million smokers expressed a desire to quit smoking in 2015; however, more than 85 percent of those who struggle with addiction will not achieve their goal. Almost all smokers regret picking up that first cigarette. You would be wise to learn from their mistake if you have not yet started smoking.

According to the US Department of Health and Human Services, 16 million people in the United States presently suffer from a smoking-related condition, and nearly nine million suffer from a serious smoking-related illness. According to the Centers for Disease Control and Prevention (CDC), tobacco products cause nearly six million deaths per year. This number is projected to rise to over eight million deaths by 2030. Smokers, on average, die ten years earlier than their nonsmoking peers.

In the United States, local, state, and federal governments typically tax tobacco products, which leads to high prices. Nicotine users who struggle with addiction sometimes pay more for a pack of cigarettes than for a few gallons of gas. Additionally, smokers tend to stink. The smell of smoke is all-consuming and creates a pervasive nastiness. Smokers also risk staining their teeth and fingers with yellow residue from the tar.

Smoking is deadly, expensive, and socially unappealing. Clearly, smoking is not worth the risks.

11. Which of the following statements most accurately summarizes the passage?
    a. Almost all smokers regret picking up that first cigarette.
    b. Tobacco is deadly, expensive, and socially unappealing, and smokers would be much better off kicking the addiction.
    c. In the United States, local, state, and federal governments typically tax tobacco products, which leads to high prices.
    d. Tobacco products shorten smokers' lives by ten years and kill more than six million people per year.
    e. Tobacco is less healthy than many alternatives.

170

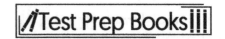

12. The author would be most likely to agree with which of the following statements?
    a. Smokers should only quit cold turkey and should avoid all nicotine cessation devices.
    b. Other substances are more addictive than tobacco.
    c. Smokers should quit for whatever reason gets them to stop smoking.
    d. People who want to continue smoking should advocate for a reduction in tobacco product taxes.
    e. Smokers don't have the desire to quit and often don't see their smoking as a bad habit.

13. Which of the following is the author's opinion?
    a. According to the Centers for Disease Control and Prevention (CDC), tobacco products cause nearly six million deaths per year.
    b. Nicotine users who struggle with addiction sometimes pay more for a pack of cigarettes than for a few gallons of gas.
    c. Smokers also risk staining their teeth and fingers with yellow residue from the tar.
    d. Additionally, smokers tend to stink. The smell of smoke is all-consuming and creates a pervasive nastiness.
    e. Smokers, on average, die ten years earlier than their nonsmoking peers.

14. What is the tone of this passage?
    a. Objective
    b. Cautionary
    c. Indifferent
    d. Admiring
    e. Philosophical

15. What does the word *pervasive* mean in paragraph 4?
    a. Pleasantly appealing
    b. A floral scent
    c. To convince someone
    d. Difficult to sense
    e. All over the place

Questions 16–20 are based on the following passage.

The Myth of Head Heat Loss

It has recently been brought to my attention that most people believe that 75% of your body heat is lost through your head. I had certainly heard this before, and I'm not going to attempt to say I didn't believe it when I first heard it. It is natural to be gullible to anything said with enough authority. But the "fact" that the majority of your body heat is lost through your head is a lie.

Let me explain. Heat loss is proportional to surface area exposed. An elephant loses a great deal more heat than an anteater because it has a much greater surface area than an anteater. Each cell has mitochondria that produce energy in the form of heat, and it takes a lot more energy to run an elephant than an anteater.

So, each part of your body loses its proportional amount of heat in accordance with its surface area. The human torso probably loses the most heat, though the legs lose a significant amount as well. Some people have asked, "Why does it feel so much warmer

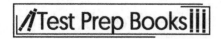

when you cover your head than when you don't?" Well, that's because your head loses a lot of heat when it is not clothed, while the clothing on the rest of your body provides insulation. If you went outside with a hat and pants but no shirt, not only would you look silly, but your heat loss would be significantly greater because so much more of you would be exposed. So, if given the choice to cover your chest or your head in the cold, choose the chest. It could save your life.

16. Why does the author compare elephants and anteaters?
    a. To express an opinion
    b. To give an example that helps clarify the main point
    c. To show the differences between the two
    d. To persuade why one is better than the other
    e. To educate about animals

17. Which of the following best describes the tone of the passage?
    a. Harsh
    b. Angry
    c. Casual
    d. Indifferent
    e. Comical

18. The author appeals to which branch of rhetoric to prove their case?
    a. Expert testimony
    b. Emotion
    c. Ethics and morals
    d. Author qualification
    e. Factual evidence

19. What does the word *gullible* mean in paragraph 1?
    a. To be angry toward
    b. To distrust something
    c. To believe something easily
    d. To be happy toward
    e. To be frightened

20. What is the main idea of the passage?
    a. To illustrate how people can easily believe anything they are told
    b. To prove that you have to have a hat to survive in the cold
    c. To persuade the audience that anteaters are better than elephants
    d. To convince the audience that heat loss comes mostly from the head
    e. To debunk the myth that heat loss comes mostly from the head

This article discusses the famous poet and playwright William Shakespeare. Read it and answer questions 21–25.

People who argue that William Shakespeare is not responsible for the plays attributed to his name are known as anti-Stratfordians (from the name of Shakespeare's birthplace, Stratford-upon-Avon). The most common anti-Stratfordian claim is that William Shakespeare simply was not educated enough or from a high enough social class to have written plays overflowing with references to such a wide range of subjects like history, the classics, religion, and international culture. William Shakespeare was the son of a glove-maker, he only had a basic grade-school education, and he never set foot outside of England—so how could he have produced plays of such sophistication and imagination? How could he have written in such detail about historical figures and events, or about different cultures and locations around Europe? According to anti-Stratfordians, the depth of knowledge contained in Shakespeare's plays suggests a well-traveled writer from a wealthy background with a university education, not a countryside writer like Shakespeare. But in fact, there is not much substance to such speculation, and most anti-Stratfordian arguments can be refuted with a little background about Shakespeare's time and upbringing.

First of all, those who doubt Shakespeare's authorship often point to his common birth and brief education as stumbling blocks to his writerly genius. Although it is true that Shakespeare did not come from a noble class, his father was a very *successful* glove-maker and his mother was from a very wealthy landowning family—so while Shakespeare may have had a country upbringing, he was certainly from a well-off family and would have been educated accordingly. Also, even though he did not attend university, grade-school education in Shakespeare's time was actually quite rigorous and exposed students to classic drama through writers like Seneca and Ovid. It is not unreasonable to believe that Shakespeare received a very solid foundation in poetry and literature from his early schooling.

Next, anti-Stratfordians tend to question how Shakespeare could write so extensively about countries and cultures he had never visited before. For instance, several of his most famous works like Romeo and Juliet and The Merchant of Venice were set in Italy, which is located on the opposite side of Europe from England. But again, this criticism does not hold up under scrutiny. For one thing, Shakespeare was living in London, a bustling metropolis of international trade, the most populous city in England, and a political and cultural hub of Europe. In the daily crowds of people, Shakespeare would certainly have been able to meet travelers from other countries and hear firsthand accounts of life in their home country. And, in addition to the influx of information from world travelers, this was also the age of the printing press. This jump in technology made it possible to print and circulate books much more easily than in the past. This also facilitated a freer flow of information across different countries, allowing people to read about life and ideas from all over Europe. One needn't travel the continent in order to learn and write about its different cultures.

21. Which sentence contains the author's thesis?
    a. People who argue that William Shakespeare is not responsible for the plays attributed to his name are known as anti-Stratfordians.
    b. First of all, those who doubt Shakespeare's authorship often point to his common birth and brief education as stumbling blocks to his writerly genius.
    c. It is not unreasonable to believe that Shakespeare received a very solid foundation in poetry and literature from his early schooling.
    d. Next, anti-Stratfordians tend to question how Shakespeare could write so extensively about countries and cultures he had never visited before.
    e. But in fact, there is not much substance to such speculation, and most anti-Stratfordian arguments can be refuted with a little background about Shakespeare's time and upbringing.

22. In the first paragraph, "How could he have written in such detail about historical figures and events, or about different cultures and locations around Europe?" is an example of which of the following?
    a. Hyperbole
    b. Onomatopoeia
    c. Rhetorical question
    d. Appeal to authority
    e. Figurative language

23. How does the author respond to the claim that Shakespeare was not well-educated because he did not attend university?
    a. By insisting upon Shakespeare's natural genius
    b. By explaining grade-school curriculum in Shakespeare's time
    c. By comparing Shakespeare with other uneducated writers of his time
    d. By pointing out that Shakespeare's wealthy parents probably paid for private tutors
    e. By discussing Shakespeare's upbringing in London which was a political and cultural hub of Europe

24. The word *bustling* in the third paragraph most nearly means which of the following?
    a. Busy
    b. Foreign
    c. Expensive
    d. Undeveloped
    e. Quiet

25. According to the passage, what did Shakespeare's father do to make a living?
    a. He was a king's guard.
    b. He acted in plays.
    c. He was a glove-maker.
    d. He was a cobbler.
    e. He was a musician.

Questions 26–30 are based on the following passage:

Do you want to vacation at a Caribbean island destination? We chose to go to St. Lucia, and it was the best vacation we ever had. We lounged in crystal blue waters, swam with dolphins, and enjoyed a family-friendly resort and activities. One of the activities we did was free diving in the ocean. We put our snorkels on, waded into the ocean, and swam

174

down to the ocean floor. The water was clear all the way down—the greens and blues were so beautiful. We saw a stingray, some conches, and a Caribbean Reef Shark. The shark was so scary, I came up to the surface after that! But the rest of the day was spent lying on the beach, getting massages, and watching other kids play with a Frisbee in front of the water.

Towards the end of our vacation, I was reluctant to go home. We started to pack our things, and then I realized I wanted to take one more walk with my mom and dad. Our resort was between the ocean and some mountains, so we decided to hike up a mountain and enjoy the view of the beach from way up high! We trekked for what seemed like miles, observing the vegetation along the way; it was so lush with reds and greens and blues. Finally, we got up to the top of the mountain and observed the wonderful ocean that stretched on for hundreds of miles. On our way back down, I felt totally at peace to be leaving the island, although I would miss it very much and would want to visit the island again soon. You should visit St. Lucia, or pick another island in the Caribbean! Every island offers a unique and dazzling vacation destination.

26. What island did the family stay on?
    a. St. Lucia
    b. Barbados
    c. Antigua
    d. Saint Kitts
    e. Aruba

27. What is/are the supporting detail(s) of this passage?
    a. Cruising to the Caribbean
    b. Local events
    c. Family activities
    d. Exotic cuisine
    e. All of the above

28. What was the last activity the speaker did?
    a. Swam with the sharks
    b. Went for a hike up a mountain
    c. Lounged on the beach
    d. Surfed in the waves
    e. Received a massage

29. Which of the following is the best definition for the word *trekked* in the second paragraph?
    a. Drove
    b. Ran
    c. Swam
    d. Sang
    e. Walked

30. Which of the following words best describes the author's attitude toward the topic?
    a. Worried
    b. Resigned
    c. Objective
    d. Enthusiastic
    e. Apathetic

Questions 31–35 are based on the following passage:

> Even though the rain can put a damper on the day, it can be helpful and fun, too. For one, the rain helps plants grow. Without rain, grass, flowers, and trees would be deprived of vital nutrients they need to develop. It's like how humans need water to survive; plants also need water to survive and flourish and keep that wonderful green color instead of turning brown.
>
> Not only does the rain help plants grow, but on days where there are brief spurts of sunshine, rainbows can appear. The rain reflects and refracts the light, creating beautiful rainbows in the sky. One time I was on a trip with my brother across the United States. Before the trip, we said that we wanted to see a rainbow in every state we went through. We ended up driving through eleven states, and guess what? We saw fifteen rainbows, at least one in each state. What an incredible trip!
>
> Finally, puddle jumping is another fun activity that can be done in or after the rain. Whenever there are heavy thunder storms, I always look forward to when the storm lifts. I usually go outside right after, because there are a lot of families in my neighborhood, and I love to watch all the children jump, skip, and splash in the puddles. The bigger kids create huge torrents of water and the smaller kids create little splashes. Thinking about all the positive things rain brings to us, I know that rain can be helpful and fun.

31. What is the *cause* in this passage?
    a. Plants growing
    b. Rainbows
    c. Puddle jumping
    d. Rain
    e. Interstate trip

32. In the following sentence, the author is using what literary device regarding the grass, flowers, and trees?

> "Without rain, grass, flowers, and trees would be deprived of vital nutrients they need to develop."

    a. Comparing
    b. Contrasting
    c. Describing
    d. Transitioning
    e. Imagery

176

33. In the same sentence from above, what is most likely the meaning of *vital?*
    a. Energetic
    b. Truthful
    c. Lively
    d. Dangerous
    e. Necessary

34. What is an *effect* in this passage?
    a. Rain
    b. Brief spurts of sunshine
    c. Rainbows
    d. Weather
    e. Thunderstorms

35. What kind of evidence does the author use most in this passage?
    a. Interviews
    b. Personal testimonies
    c. Journal articles
    d. Statistics
    e. Analogical comparison

Questions 36–40 are based on the following passage.

Sylvia's father was a beekeeper and Sylvia loved watching him take care of bees. When he was gone to work, Sylvia would stealthily try to find bees in her garden and pretend like she was her father on a magnificent mission to save all the bees she came into contact with. She really just wanted to be helpful. So, she started to pick out all the bees (she wasn't afraid of the stingers, though she had been stung several times in the past), and put them in jars in her house so that they could all be safe from harm.

One day Sylvia's mother walked into her bedroom and noticed that Sylvia had a large container that her mother had never seen before. When Sylvia's mother opened the container, a swarm of bees flew out and started to buzz around her mother's head! Sylvia's mother screamed and ran out of the room, her face scrunched in terror. Sylvia was outside playing, and when she saw her mother run out of the house, Sylvia knew immediately what had happened. Her mother found the bee jar! She quickly helped her mother swat away the bees and told her mother that she just wanted to help the bees stay safe from the outside harms that could come to them. "Sylvia," her mother said, "Do you feel afraid when you are outside?" "No," Sylvia replied. "I feel safe, and I have lots of fun out here." "Well," her mother said, "the bees are just like you! They love the sunlight, and the flowers are so important to them they fly around them all day and never get tired. Leave the bees outside, and they will thank you for it." Sylvia laughed at her own thoughts and knew that the bees would be safer outside, away from her terrified mother and into the hands of nature.

177

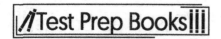

36. What does the word *stealthily* mean in the first paragraph?
    a. Hurriedly
    b. Begrudgingly
    c. Confidently
    d. Secretly
    e. Efficiently

37. What point of view is the story written in?
    a. First person
    b. Second person
    c. Third person
    d. No person
    e. None of the above

38. According to the passage, why did Sylvia want to keep the bees inside a jar?
    a. She wanted to conduct a science experiment with them.
    b. She wanted to learn how to work as a beekeeper.
    c. She wanted to bring them as a gift to her father.
    d. She wanted to use them to scare her mother.
    e. She wanted to keep them away from harm.

39. What organization does this passage use?
    a. Chronological
    b. Cause and effect
    c. Problem to solution
    d. Sequential
    e. Order of importance

40. Which of the following most closely matches the theme of the passage?
    a. Loss/Grief
    b. Friendship
    c. Freedom
    d. Suffering
    e. Growth

Verbal Section

Synonyms

1. GARISH
    a. Drab
    b. Flashy
    c. Gait
    d. Hardy
    e. Lithe

2. INANE
    a. Ratify
    b. Illicit
    c. Uncouth
    d. Senseless
    e. Wry

3. SOLACE
    a. Marred
    b. Induce
    c. Depose
    d. Inherent
    e. Comfort

4. COPIOUS
    a. Dire
    b. Adept
    c. Indignant
    d. Ample
    e. Nuance

5. SUPERCILIOUS
    a. Tenuous
    b. Waning
    c. Arrogant
    d. Placate
    e. Extol

6. LURID
    a. Gruesome
    b. Placid
    c. Irate
    d. Quell
    e. Torpor

7. VANQUISH
    a. Saturate
    b. Conquer
    c. Reproach
    d. Parch
    e. Surrender

8. TRITE
    a. Scanty
    b. Banal
    c. Polemical
    d. Indulgent
    e. Eclectic

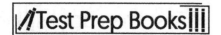

9. DIVULGE
    a. Dupe
    b. Flummox
    c. Indulgent
    d. Germinate
    e. Admit

10. INDOLENT
    a. Adamant
    b. Dour
    c. Noisome
    d. Lackadaisical
    e. Remiss

11. BOLSTER
    a. Bequeath
    b. Abate
    c. Support
    d. Palliate
    e. Tractable

12. UNWITTING
    a. Undermine
    b. Unintentional
    c. Rife
    d. Pernicious
    e. Stolid

13. UNGAINLY
    a. Clumsy
    b. Absurd
    c. Unruly
    d. Tenuous
    e. Petulant

14. PRATTLE
    a. Babble
    b. Prosaic
    c. Deluded
    d. Meddle
    e. Folly

15. PROLIFIC
    a. Devoid
    b. Elusive
    c. Laconic
    d. Productive
    e. Judicious

16. FORTITUDE
    a. Aura
    b. Disparage
    c. Finesse
    d. Cowardice
    e. Courage

17. ACUMEN
    a. Diligent
    b. Ingenuity
    c. Congenial
    d. Embroiled
    e. Reverent

18. RELEGATE
    a. Relay
    b. Temporize
    c. Demote
    d. Vigilant
    e. Spurn

19. CURTAIL
    a. Covet
    b. Abridge
    c. Foil
    d. Construe
    e. Bilk

20. CONSERVE
    a. Constrain
    b. Adjourn
    c. Stipulate
    d. Maintain
    e. Improve

21. AMBIVALENT
    a. Accosted
    b. Engrossed
    c. Impartial
    d. Conflicted
    e. Convinced

22. DISREPUTE
    a. Benevolent
    b. Condone
    c. Dishonor
    d. Emit
    e. Postulate

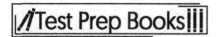

23. INSTIGATE
    a. Provoke
    b. Renounce
    c. Prescribe
    d. Modify
    e. Diminish

24. MAXIM
    a. Discord
    b. Clout
    c. Apex
    d. Temperament
    e. Adage

25. PRESAGE
    a. Tactful
    b. Viability
    c. Vow
    d. Prediction
    e. Exploit

26. ONEROUS
    a. Dubious
    b. Cultivate
    c. Arduous
    d. Squalid
    e. Emphatic

27. MUNIFICENT
    a. Candid
    b. Generous
    c. Livid
    d. Suitable
    e. Malleable

28. EXTANT
    a. Capitalize
    b. Surviving
    c. Foment
    d. Tentative
    e. Yield

29. DEFUNCT
    a. Simple
    b. Potent
    c. Geriatric
    d. Expend
    e. Extinct

30. CUPIDITY
    a. Happiness
    b. Greed
    c. Love
    d. Grief
    e. Anger

Verbal Analogies

31. Begonia is to flower as
    a. Daisy is to pollen.
    b. Cat is to catnip.
    c. Cardiologist is to doctor.
    d. Radiology is to disease.
    e. Nutrition is to reproduction.

32. Malleable is to pliable as
    a. Corroborate is to invalidate.
    b. Avenue is to city.
    c. Blacksmith is to anvil.
    d. Hostile is to hospitable.
    e. Disparage is to criticize.

33. Cerebellum is to brain as
    a. Nurse is to medication.
    b. Nucleus is to cell.
    c. Bacteria is to spores.
    d. Refraction is to light.
    e. Painting is to sculpting.

34. Whisk is to baking as
    a. Glove is to boxing.
    b. Swimming is to water.
    c. Love is to romance.
    d. Azalea is to flower.
    e. Bench is to park.

35. Umpire is to officiate as
    a. Coaching is to coach.
    b. Baseball is to pastime.
    c. Counselor is to guide.
    d. Notary is to paper.
    e. Messenger is to letter.

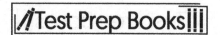

36. Chuckle is to guffaw as
    a. Snicker is to lament.
    b. Affection is to nurturing.
    c. Sensitivity is to brevity.
    d. Whisper is to bellow.
    e. Serenity is to tranquility.

37. Fire is to passion as
    a. Sultry is to ferment.
    b. Emotion is to stagnant.
    c. Heat is to happiness.
    d. Ice is to rigidity.
    e. Comfort is to travel.

38. Geriatric is to youth as
    a. Transparent is to opaque.
    b. Soldier is to war.
    c. Subtle is to sophisticated.
    d. Yellow is to happiness.
    e. Surly is to scandalous.

39. Lying is to distrust as
    a. Prohibit is to outlaw.
    b. Petulant is to children.
    c. Exploit is to gain.
    d. Imprudent is to money.
    e. Hurricane is to devastation.

40. Desolate is to barren as
    a. Defend is to prosecute.
    b. Contend is to maintain.
    c. Avid is to cheerleader.
    d. Bittersweet is to happiness.
    e. King is to ambition.

41. Chapter is to novel as
    a. Whisper is to silence.
    b. Tangle is to lengthening.
    c. Poem is to poet.
    d. Feeling is to past.
    e. Stroke is to painting.

42. Carpenter is to construction as
    a. Adaptation is to insect.
    b. Acquisition is to possession.
    c. Wizard is to magic.
    d. Baker is to bread.
    e. Microsoft is to programming.

43. Tepid is to boiling as
    a. Moon is to femininity.
    b. Cornered is to immunity.
    c. Greedy is to rapacious.
    d. Sword is to dagger.
    e. Burning is to smoke.

44. Read is to learn as
    a. Ball is to soccer.
    b. Brand is to marketing.
    c. Exercise is to health.
    d. Disease is to energy.
    e. Party is to birthday.

45. Competent is to impotent as
    a. Demur is to accept.
    b. Dispute is to argument.
    c. Brandish is to gold.
    d. Honorary is to metal.
    e. Reach is to grab.

46. Merengue is to music as
    a. Cluster is to assemblage.
    b. Tension is to headache.
    c. Fiscal is to government.
    d. Hunger is to starving.
    e. Nomadic is to tribe.

47. Car is to transport as
    a. Radio is to sound.
    b. Volume is to voice.
    c. Triangles are to circles.
    d. Fireplace is to heat.
    e. Mangos are to fruit.

48. Flower is to femininity as
    a. Sunflower is to bees.
    b. Technology is to cell phones.
    c. Envy is to relationships.
    d. Plant is to carbon dioxide.
    e. Light is to transcendence.

49. Principle is to truth as
    a. Squalid is to shabby.
    b. Frame is to picture.
    c. Static is to movement.
    d. Format is to index.
    e. Sour is to sweet.

185

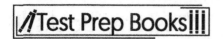

50. Careful is to fastidious as
    a. Indulge is to deprive.
    b. Fluctuate is to trapeze.
    c. Majesty is to a lion.
    d. Endow is to bestow.
    e. Grieve is to lament.

51. Mantle is to earth as
    a. Volcano is to lava.
    b. Bundle is to uniform.
    c. Bun is to hamburger.
    d. Letter is to mailman.
    e. Spider is to spiderweb.

52. Maestro is to conducting as
    a. Barista is to coffee.
    b. Acupuncturist is to healing.
    c. Professor is to essay.
    d. President is to executive branch.
    e. Agent is to housing.

53. Contentious is to agreeable as
    a. Petulant is to irritable.
    b. Vocation is to career.
    c. Serendipity is to luck.
    d. Expedient is to useful.
    e. Penurious is to generous.

54. Cumulus is to cloud as
    a. Weather is to rain.
    b. Grape is to wine.
    c. Tortellini is to pasta.
    d. Elicit is to snow.
    e. Spanish is to English.

55. Pot is to boil as
    a. Belay is to climb.
    b. Water is to faucet.
    c. Chef is to cook.
    d. Mirror is to reflection.
    e. Temper is to rage.

56. Laurel is to victory as
    a. Branch is to vine.
    b. Dove is to peace.
    c. Chair is to sit.
    d. Plumb is to apple.
    e. Curtain is to floor.

57. Transient is to ephemeral as
    a. Renounce is to acknowledge.
    b. Placate is to subversive.
    c. Relinquish is to vapid.
    d. Sanguine is to cheerful.
    e. Verbose is to scanty.

58. Diverge is to agree as
    a. Assail is to belittle.
    b. Dire is to folly.
    c. Lurid is to spartan.
    d. Antipathy is to friendliness.
    e. Waning is to recant.

59. Nitrogen is to element as
    a. Species is to canine.
    b. Valley is to river.
    c. Crayon is to elementary.
    d. Project is to brand.
    e. Calico is to cat.

60. Small is to miniscule as
    a. Chagrin is to elusive.
    b. Confined is to rotten.
    c. Unhealthy is to ailing.
    d. Tall is to short.
    e. Cough is to allergy.

Quantitative Reasoning 2

1. Which of the following numbers has the greatest value?
    a. 1.43785
    b. 1.07548
    c. 1.43592
    d. 0.89409
    e. 0.94739

2. The value of 6×12 is the same as:
    a. $2 \times 4 \times 4 \times 2$
    b. $7 \times 4 \times 3$
    c. $6 \times 6 \times 3$
    d. $3 \times 3 \times 4 \times 2$
    e. $5 \times 9 \times 8$

3. A company invests $50,000 in a building where they can produce saws. If the cost of producing one saw is $40, then which function expresses the total amount of money the company spends on producing saws? The variable y is the money paid, and x is the number of saws produced.
   a. $y = 50{,}000x + 40$
   b. $y + 40 = x - 50{,}000$
   c. $y = 40x - 50{,}000$
   d. $y = 50x - 400{,}000$
   e. $y = 40x + 50{,}000$

4. After a 20% sale discount, Frank purchased a new refrigerator for $850. How much money did he save off of the original price?
   a. $170
   b. $212.50
   c. $105.75
   d. $200
   e. $187.50

5. Four people split a bill. The first person pays for $\frac{1}{5}$, the second person pays for $\frac{1}{4}$, and the third person pays for $\frac{1}{3}$. What fraction of the bill does the fourth person pay?

   a. $\frac{13}{60}$

   b. $\frac{47}{60}$

   c. $\frac{1}{4}$

   d. $\frac{4}{15}$

   e. $\frac{1}{2}$

6. What is the value of b in this equation?

$$5b - 4 = 2b + 17$$

   a. 13
   b. 24
   c. 7
   d. 21
   e. 15

7. A school's faculty consists of 15 teachers and 20 teaching assistants. They have 200 students. What is the ratio of faculty to students?
   a. $3 : 20$
   b. $4 : 17$
   c. $11 : 54$
   d. $3 : 2$
   e. $7 : 40$

8. What is the next number in the following sequence? $1, 3, 6, 10, 15, 21, ...$
   a. 26
   b. 27
   c. 28
   d. 29
   e. 31

9. A student gets an 85% on a test with 20 questions. How many questions did the student solve correctly?
   a. 15 questions
   b. 16 questions
   c. 17 questions
   d. 18 questions
   e. 19 questions

10. If Sarah reads at an average rate of 21 pages in 4 nights, how long will it take her to read 140 pages?
    a. 6 nights
    b. 26 nights
    c. 8 nights
    d. 27 nights
    e. 21 nights

11. Alan currently weighs 200 pounds, but he wants to lose weight to get down to 175 pounds. What is this difference in kilograms? (1 pound is approximately equal to 0.45 kilograms.)
    a. 9 kg
    b. 25 kg
    c. 78.75 kg
    d. 90 kg
    e. 11.25 kg

12. Johnny earns $2,334.50 from his job each month. He pays $1,437 for monthly expenses and saves the rest. Johnny is planning a vacation in 3 months that he estimates will cost $1,750 total. How much will Johnny have left over from 3 months of saving once he pays for his vacation?
    a. $948.50
    b. $584.50
    c. $852.50
    d. $942.50
    e. $742.50

13. Solve the following:

$$4 \times 7 + (25 - 21)^2 \div 2$$

    a. 512
    b. 36
    c. 60.5
    d. 22
    e. 16

14. The variable y is directly proportional to x. If $y = 3$ when $x = 5$, then what is y when $x = 20$?
    a. 10
    b. 12
    c. 14
    d. 16
    e. 18

15. A line passes through the point $(1, 2)$ and crosses the y-axis at $y = 1$. Which of the following is an equation for this line?
    a. $y = 2x$

    b. $y = 3x$

    c. $x + y = 1$

    d. $y = \frac{x}{2} - 2$

    e. $y = x + 1$

16. Dwayne has received the following scores on his math tests: 78, 92, 83, 97. What score must Dwayne get on his next math test to have an overall average of 90?
    a. 89
    b. 98
    c. 95
    d. 94
    e. 100

17. What is the overall median of Dwayne's current scores: 78, 92, 83, 97?
    a. 80.5
    b. 85
    c. 90
    d. 87.5
    e. 86

18. Evaluate:

$$\left(\sqrt{36} \times \sqrt{16}\right) - 3^2$$

    a. 30
    b. 21
    c. 15
    d. 13
    e. 25

19. In Jim's school, there are a total of 650 students. There are three girls for every two boys. How many students are girls?
    a. 260 girls
    b. 130 girls
    c. 65 girls
    d. 390 girls
    e. 410 girls

20. What is the value of x in the following equation?

$$13 - \frac{3x}{4} = -11$$

   a. 18
   b. 24
   c. 36
   d. 32
   e. 19

21. Kimberley earns $10 an hour babysitting, and after 10 p.m., she earns $12 an hour. The time she works is rounded to the nearest hour for pay purposes. On her last job, she worked from 5:30 p.m. to 11:00 p.m. In total, how much did Kimberley earn on her last job?
   a. $45
   b. $57
   c. $62
   d. $42
   e. $53

22. What value of x would solve the following equation?

$$9x + x - 7 = 16 + 2x$$

   a. $x = -4$

   b. $x = 3$

   c. $x = \frac{9}{8}$

   d. $x = \frac{23}{8}$

   e. $x = \frac{3}{4}$

23. Arrange the following numbers from least to greatest value:

$$0.85, \frac{4}{5}, \frac{2}{3}, \frac{91}{100}$$

   a. $0.85, \frac{4}{5}, \frac{2}{3}, \frac{91}{100}$

   b. $\frac{4}{5}, 0.85, \frac{91}{100}, \frac{2}{3}$

   c. $\frac{2}{3}, \frac{4}{5}, 0.85, \frac{91}{100}$

   d. $0.85, \frac{91}{100}, \frac{4}{5}, \frac{2}{3}$

   e. $\frac{4}{5}, \frac{91}{100}, \frac{2}{3}, 0.85$

24. Keith's bakery had 252 customers go through its doors last week. This week, that number increased to 378. Express this increase as a percentage.

    a. 26%

    b. 50%

    c. 35%

    d. 12%

    e. 18%

25. If $4x - 3 = 5$, what is the value of x?

    a. 1

    b. 2

    c. 3

    d. 4

    e. 5

Answer Explanations #1

Quantitative Reasoning 1

1. D: Digits to the left of the decimal point represent the digit value times increasing multiples of 10 (first 1, then 10, 100, 1,000, and so on). Digits to the right of the decimal point represent the digit value divided by increasing multiples of 10 (first $\frac{1}{10}$, then $\frac{1}{100}$, $\frac{1}{1,000}$, and so on). So, the second digit to the right of the decimal point equals the digit value divided by 100.

2. B: The first step is to make all exponents positive by moving the terms with negative exponents to the opposite side of the fraction. This expression becomes:

$$\frac{4b^3b^2}{a^1a^4} \times \frac{3a}{b}$$

Then the rules for exponents can be used to simplify. Multiplying the same bases means the exponents can be added. Dividing the same bases means the exponents are subtracted. Thus, after multiplying the exponents in the first fraction, the expression becomes:

$$\frac{4b^5}{a^5} \times \frac{3a}{b}$$

Therefore, we can first multiply to get:

$$\frac{12ab^5}{a^5b}$$

Then, simplifying yields:

$$12\frac{b^4}{a^4}$$

3. E: The hundredths place value is located two digits to the right of the decimal point (the digit 9 in the original number). To decide whether to round up or keep the digit, examine the digit to the right, and if it is 5 or greater, round up. In this case, the digit to the right is 6, so the hundredths place is rounded up. When rounding up, if the digit to be increased is a 9, the digit to its left is increased by one and the digit in the desired place value is made a zero. Therefore, the number is rounded to 847.90.

4. B: Fractions must have like denominators to be added. The common denominator is the least common multiple (LCM) of the two original denominators. In this case, the LCM is 15, so both fractions should be changed to equivalent fractions with a denominator of 15. Multiply the bottom of each fraction by whatever number is needed to produce 15, and multiply the top of each fraction by that same number:

$$\frac{1 \times 5}{3 \times 5} = \frac{5}{15} \text{ and } \frac{2 \times 3}{5 \times 3} = \frac{6}{15}$$

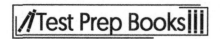
Now, add the numerators and keep the denominator the same:

$$\frac{5}{15} + \frac{6}{15} = \frac{11}{15}$$

5. C: When performing calculations consisting of more than one operation, the order of operations should be followed: parentheses, exponents, multiplication & division, addition & subtraction.

Parentheses:

$$7^2 - 3 \times (4 + 2) + 15 \div 5$$

$$7^2 - 3 \times (6) + 15 \div 5$$

Exponents:

$$49 - 3 \times 6 + 15 \div 5$$

Multiplication & division (from left to right):

$$49 - 18 + 3$$

Addition & subtraction (from left to right):

$$49 - 18 + 3 = 34$$

6. D: To convert a fraction to a percent, the fraction is first converted to a decimal. To do so, the numerator is divided by the denominator:

$$4 \div 5 = 0.8$$

To convert a decimal to a percent, the number is multiplied by 100:

$$0.8 \times 100 = 80\%$$

7. C: To solve the problem, we can write a proportion consisting of ratios comparing distance and time. One way to set up the proportion is:

$$\frac{3}{48} = \frac{5}{x}$$

To solve this proportion, we can cross-multiply: $(3)(x) = (5)(48)$, or $3x = 240$. To isolate the variable, we divide by 3 on both sides, producing $x = 80$.

8. D: To find the factors of 12, determine what whole numbers when multiplied equal 12. 1×12, 2×6, and 3×4 are all the ways to multiply to 12 using whole numbers, so the factors of 12 are: 1, 2, 3, 4, 6, 12.

9. B: To determine the number of houses that can fit on the street, we can divide the length of the street by the width of each house's property:

$$345 \div 30 = 11.5$$

194

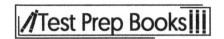

However, the construction company is not going to build half a house, so they will need to build either 11 or 12 houses. Since the width of 12 houses (360 feet) would extend past the length of the street, only 11 houses can be built.

10. B: By distributing the implied 1 in front of the first set of parentheses and the negative one in front of the second set of parentheses, the parentheses can be eliminated:

$$1(5x^2 - 3x + 4) - 1(2x^2 - 7)$$

$$5x^2 - 3x + 4 - 2x^2 + 7$$

Next, like terms are combined by adding the coefficients of the same variables with the same exponents, while keeping the variables and their powers unchanged:

$$5x^2 - 3x + 4 - 2x^2 + 7$$

$$3x^2 - 3x + 11$$

11. E: The rate, 60 miles per hour, and time, 3 hours, are given for the scenario. To determine the distance traveled, the given values for the rate (r) and time (t) are substituted into the distance formula and evaluated:

$$d = r \times t$$

$$d = \left(\frac{60 \text{ mi}}{\text{h}}\right) \times (3 \text{ h})$$

$$d = 180 \text{ mi}$$

12. D: Solve a linear inequality in a similar way to solving a linear equation. First, start by distributing the -3 on the left side of the inequality.

$$-3x - 12 \geq x + 8$$

Then, add 12 to both sides.

$$-3x \geq x + 20$$

Next, subtract x from both sides.

$$-4x \geq 20$$

Finally, divide both sides of the inequality by -4. Don't forget to flip the inequality sign because you are dividing by a negative number.

$$x \leq -5$$

13. C: In this scenario, the variables are the number of sales and Karen's weekly pay. The weekly pay depends on the number of sales. Therefore, weekly pay is the dependent variable (y), and the number of sales is the independent variable (x). All four answer choices are in slope-intercept form, $y = mx + b$, so we just need to find m (the slope) and b (the y-intercept). We can calculate both by picking any two points, for example, $(2, 380)$ and $(4, 460)$.

The slope is given by $m = \frac{y_2 - y_1}{x_2 - x_1}$, so $m = \frac{460 - 380}{4 - 2} = 40$. This gives us the equation $y = 40x + b$. Now we can plug in the x and y values from our first point to find b. Since $380 = 40(2) + b$, we find $b = 300$. This means the equation is $y = 40x + 300$.

14. D: The closed dot on 1 indicates that the value is included in the set. The arrow pointing right indicates that numbers greater than 1 (numbers get larger to the right) are included in the set. Therefore, the set includes numbers greater than or equal to 1, which can be written as $x \geq 1$.

15. A: The core of the pattern consists of 4 items: ▲○○□. Therefore, the core repeats in multiples of 4, with the pattern starting over on the next step. The highest multiple of 4 that's below 42 is 40. Step 40 is the end of the core (□), so step 41 will start the core over (▲) and step 42 is ○.

16. D: Parallel lines will never intersect. Therefore, the lines are not parallel. Perpendicular lines intersect to form a right angle (90°). Although the lines intersect, they do not form a right angle, which is usually indicated with a box at the intersection point. Therefore, the lines are not perpendicular.

17. D: The expression is simplified by collecting like terms. Terms with the same variable and exponent are like terms, and their coefficients can be added.

18. A: Finding the product means distributing one polynomial onto the other. Each term in the first polynomial must be multiplied by each term in the second polynomial. Then, like terms can be collected. Multiplying the factors yields the expression:

$$20x^3 + 4x^2 + 24x - 40x^2 - 8x - 48$$

Collecting like terms means adding the x^2 terms and adding the x terms. Then, simplify:

$$20x^3 - 36x^2 + 16x - 48$$

19. B: The formula can be manipulated by dividing both the length, l, and the width, w, on both sides. The length and width will cancel on the right, leaving height, h, by itself.

20. A: The coordinates of a point are written as an ordered pair (x, y). To determine the x-coordinate, a line is traced directly above or below the point until reaching the x-axis. This step notes the value on the x-axis. In this case, the x-coordinate is -3. To determine the y-coordinate, a line is traced directly to the right or left of the point until reaching the y-axis, which notes the value on the y-axis. In this case, the y-coordinate is 2. Therefore, the ordered pair is written $(-3, 2)$.

21. D: The slope from this equation is 50, and it is interpreted as the cost per gigabyte used. Since the g-value represents the number of gigabytes and the equation is set equal to the cost in dollars, the slope relates these two values. For every gigabyte used on the phone, the bill goes up 50 dollars.

22. C: $\frac{1}{3}$ of the shirts sold were patterned. Therefore, $1 - \frac{1}{3}$ (that is, $\frac{2}{3}$) of the shirts sold were solid. A fraction of something is calculated with multiplication, so $192 \times (1 - \frac{1}{3})$ solid shirts were sold. (We could calculate that this equals 128, but that's not necessary for this question.)

23. A: An outlier is a data value that is either far above or far below the majority of values in a sample set. The mean is the average of all the values in the set. In a small sample set, a very high or very low number could drastically change the average of the data points. Outliers will have no more of an effect

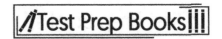

on the median (the middle value when arranged from lowest to highest) than any other value above or below the median. If the same outlier does not repeat, outliers will have no effect on the mode (value that repeats most often). The range is not a measure of the center of a data set; it merely gives the highest and lowest values. Therefore, even though the outlier will affect the range, Choice *D* is incorrect because the question asks for a measure of center.

24. E: The scenario involves data consisting of two variables: month and stock value. Box plots display data consisting of values for one variable. Therefore, a box plot is not an appropriate choice. Both line plots and circle graphs are used to display frequencies within categorical data. Neither can be used for the given scenario. Scatter plots compare the values of two variables to see if there are any patterns present. Line graphs display two numerical variables on a coordinate grid and show trends among the variables.

25. D: The probability of picking the winner of the race is $\frac{1}{4}$, or $\left(\frac{\text{number of favorable outcomes}}{\text{number of total outcomes}}\right)$. Assuming the winner was picked on the first selection, three horses remain from which to choose the runner-up (these are dependent events). Therefore, the probability of picking the runner-up is $\frac{1}{3}$. To determine the probability that multiple events all happen, multiply the probabilities of the events:

$$\frac{1}{4} \times \frac{1}{3} = \frac{1}{12}$$

Reading Comprehension

1. D: Although Washington was from a wealthy background, the passage does not say that his wealth led to his republican ideals, so Choice *A* is not supported. Choice *B* also does not follow from the passage. Washington's warning against meddling in foreign affairs does not mean that he would oppose wars of every kind, so Choice *B* is incorrect. Choice *C* is also unjustified since the author does not indicate that Alexander Hamilton's assistance was absolutely necessary. Choice *E* is incorrect because we don't know which particular presidents Washington would befriend. Choice *D* is correct because the passage states that Washington's farewell address clearly opposes political parties and partisanship. The author then notes that presidential elections often hit a fever pitch of partisanship. Thus, it follows that George Washington would probably not approve of modern political parties and their involvement in presidential elections.

2. E: The author finishes the passage by applying Washington's farewell address to modern politics, so the purpose probably includes this application. Choice *B* is incorrect because George Washington is already a well-established historical figure; furthermore, the passage does not seek to introduce him. Choice *C* is incorrect because the author is not fighting a common perception that Washington was merely a military hero. Choice *D* is incorrect because the author is not convincing readers. Persuasion does not correspond to the passage. Choice *E* states the primary purpose.

3. A: The tone in this passage is informative. Choice *B*, excited, is incorrect, because there are not many word choices used that would indicate excitement from the author. Choice *C*, bitter, is incorrect. Although the author does make a suggestion in the last paragraph to Americans, the statement is not necessarily bitter, but based on the preceding information. Choice *D*, comic, is incorrect, as the author does not try to make the audience laugh, nor do they make light of the situation in any way. Choice *E*, somber, is incorrect since the passage isn't sad or mournful.

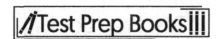

4. C: Interfering. Meddling means to interfere in something. Choice *A* is incorrect. One helpful thing would be to use the word in the sentence: "Washington warned Americans against 'supporting' in foreign affairs" does not make that much sense, so we can mark it off. Choice *B*, *speaking against*, is incorrect. This phrase would make sense in the sentence, but it goes against the meaning that is intended. George Washington warned against interference in foreign affairs, not speaking *against* foreign affairs. Choice *D* is also incorrect, because "gathering in foreign affairs" does not sound quite right. Choice *E*, *avoiding*, is incorrect because it is nearly the opposite of meddling. Choice *C*, *interfering*, is therefore the best choice for this question.

5. A: When Washington was offered a role as leader of the former colonies, he refused the offer. This is explained in the first sentence of the second paragraph. He did not simply ignore the offer, as he "famously" refused it. All of the other answer choices are incorrect and not mentioned in the passage.

6. D: The passage does not proceed in chronological order since it begins by pointing out Christopher Columbus's explorations in America, so Choice *A* does not work. Although the author compares and contrasts Erikson with Christopher Columbus, this is not the main way the information is presented; therefore, Choice *B* does not work. Neither does Choice *C*, because there is no mention of or reference to cause and effect in the passage. However, the passage does offer a conclusion (Leif Erikson deserves more credit) and premises (first European to set foot in the New World and first to contact the natives) to substantiate Erikson's historical importance. Thus, Choice *D* is correct. Choice *E* is incorrect because spatial order refers to the space and location of something or where things are located in relation to each other.

7. C: Choice *A* is incorrect because it describes facts: Leif Erikson was the son of Erik the Red and historians debate Leif's date of birth. These are not opinions. Choice *B* is incorrect; Erikson calling the land Vinland is a verifiable fact, as is Choice *D*, because he did contact the natives almost 500 years before Columbus. Choice *E* is also a fact and the passage mentions that there are several secondhand accounts (evidence) of their meetings. Choice *C* is the correct answer because it is the author's opinion that Erikson deserves more credit. Another person could argue that Columbus or another explorer deserves more credit, which makes it an opinion rather than a historical fact.

8. B: Choice *A* is incorrect because the author aims to go beyond describing Erikson as merely a legendary Viking. Choice *C* is incorrect because the author does not focus on Erikson's motivations, let alone name the spreading of Christianity as his primary objective. Choice *D* is incorrect because it is a premise that Erikson contacted the natives 500 years before Columbus, which is simply a part of supporting the author's conclusion. Choice *E* is incorrect because the author states at the beginning that he or she believes it can't be considered "discovering" if people already lived there. Choice *B* is correct because it accurately identifies the author's statement that Erikson deserves more credit than he has received for being the first European to explore the New World.

9. B: Choice *B* is correct because the author wants the reader to be informed about Leif Erikson's contribution to exploring the new world. While several other answers are possible options, Choice *B* is the strongest. Choice *A* is incorrect because the author is not in any way trying to entertain the reader. Choice *C* is incorrect because the nature of the writing does not indicate the author would be satisfied with the reader merely being alerted to Erikson's exploration; instead, the author is making an argument about the credit he should receive. Choice *D* is incorrect because the author goes beyond a mere suggestion; "suggest" is too vague.

198

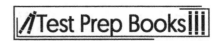

10. D: Choice *A* is incorrect because the author never addresses the Vikings' state of mind or emotions. Choice *B* is incorrect because the author does not elaborate on Erikson's exile and whether he would have become an explorer if not for his banishment. Choice *C* is incorrect because there is not enough information to support this premise. It is unclear whether Erikson informed the King of Norway of his findings. Although it is true that the king did not send a follow-up expedition, he could have simply chosen not to expend the resources after receiving Erikson's news. It is not possible to logically infer whether Erikson told him. Choice *E* is incorrect because the passage does not mention anything about Columbus' awareness of Erikson's travels. Choice *D* is correct because the uncertainty about Leif Erikson's birth year is an example of how historians have trouble pinning down important details in Viking history.

11. B: The author is opposed to tobacco. The author cites disease and deaths associated with smoking, and points to the monetary expense and aesthetic costs. Choices *A* and *C* are incorrect because they do not summarize the passage but rather are just premises. Choice *D* is incorrect because, while these statistics are a premise in the argument, they do not represent a summary of the piece. Choice *E* is incorrect because alternatives to smoking are not addressed in the passage. Choice *B* is the correct answer because it states the three critiques offered against tobacco and expresses the author's conclusion.

12. C: We are looking for something the author would agree with, so it should be anti-smoking or an argument in favor of quitting smoking. Choice *A* is incorrect because the author does not speak against means of cessation. Choice *B* is incorrect because the author does not reference other substances but does speak of how addictive nicotine, a drug in tobacco, is. Choice *D* is incorrect because the author would not encourage reducing taxes to encourage a reduction of smoking costs, thereby helping smokers to continue the habit. Choice *E* is wrong because the author states that according to the National Institute on Drug Abuse, nearly 35 million smokers expressed a desire to quit smoking in 2015. If the author had used the word "only" instead of "nearly" (and perhaps if the number was a lot lower) that would have changed the argument. Choice *C* is correct because the author is attempting to persuade smokers to quit smoking.

13. D: Here, we are looking for the author's opinion rather than a fact or statistic. Choice *A* is incorrect because quoting statistics from the CDC is stating facts, not opinions. Choice *B* is incorrect because it expresses the fact that cigarettes sometimes cost more than a few gallons of gas. It would be an opinion if the author said that cigarettes were not affordable. Choice *C* is incorrect because yellow stains are a known possible adverse effect of smoking. Choice *E* is incorrect because decreased life expectancy for smokers is a known fact because of the health problems it can create. Choice *D* is correct as an opinion because smell is subjective. Some people might like the smell of smoke rather than considering it "a pervasive nastiness," so this is the expression of an opinion.

14. B: The passage is cautionary, because the author warns about the hazards of smoking and uses the second-person *you* to offer suggestions, like "You would be wise to learn from their mistake." Choice *A*, objective, means that the passage would be totally without persuasion or suggestions, so this answer choice is incorrect. Choice *C*, indifferent, is incorrect because the author expresses an opinion and makes it clear they dislike smoking. Choice *D* is also incorrect; the passage is the opposite of admiring towards the subject of smoking. Finally, Choice *E*, philosophical, is incorrect, because this is a down-to-earth passage that presents facts and gives suggestions based on those facts, and there are no philosophical underpinnings here.

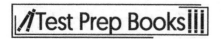

15. E: The word *pervasive* means "all over the place." The passage says that "The smell of smoke is all-consuming and creates a *pervasive* nastiness," which means a smell that is everywhere or all over. Choices *A* and *B*, pleasantly appealing and a floral scent, are too pleasant for the context of the passage. Choice *C* doesn't make sense in the sentence, as "to convince someone" wouldn't really describe the word *nastiness* like pervasive does. Choice *D* is also incorrect because that's the opposite of what the author is describing.

16. B: Choice *B* is correct because the author is trying to demonstrate the main idea, which is that heat loss is proportional to surface area, so they compare two animals with different surface areas to clarify the main point. Choice *A* is incorrect because the author uses elephants and anteaters to prove a point, that heat loss is proportional to surface area, not to express an opinion. Choice *C* is incorrect because though the author does use them to show differences, they do so in order to give examples that prove the above points. Choice *D* is incorrect because there is no language to indicate favoritism between the two animals. Choice *E* is incorrect because the passage is not about animals and only uses the elephant and the anteater to make a point.

17. C: Because of the way the author addresses the reader and the colloquial language the author uses (e.g., "let me explain," "so," "well," "didn't," "you would look stupid"), Choice *C* is the best answer because it has a much more casual tone than the usual informative article. Choice *A* may be a tempting choice because the author says the "fact" that most of one's heat is lost through their head is a "lie" and that someone who does not wear a shirt in the cold looks stupid. However, this only happens twice within the passage, and the passage does not give an overall tone of harshness. Choice *B* is incorrect because again, while not necessarily nice, the language does not carry an angry charge. The author is clearly not indifferent to the subject because of the passionate language that they use, so Choice *D* is incorrect. Choice *E* is incorrect because the author is not trying to show or use humor in the passage.

18. E: The author gives logical examples and reasons in order to prove that most of one's heat is not lost through their head; therefore, Choice *E* is correct. Choice *A* is incorrect because the author never mentions any specific experts as references. Choice *B* is incorrect because there is not much emotionally charged language in this selection, and even the small amount present is greatly outnumbered by the facts and evidence. Choice *C* is incorrect because there is no mention of ethics or morals in this selection. Choice *D* is incorrect because the author never qualifies himself as someone who has the authority to be writing on this topic.

19. C: *Gullible* means to believe something easily. The other answer choices could fit easily within the context of the passage: you can be angry toward, distrustful toward, frightened by, or happy toward authority. For this answer choice and the surrounding context, however, the author talks about a myth that people believe easily, so *gullible* would be the word that fits best in this context.

20. E: The whole passage is dedicated to debunking the head heat loss myth. The passage says that "each part of your body loses its proportional amount of heat in accordance with its surface area," which means an area such as the chest would lose more heat than the head because it's bigger. The other answer choices are incorrect.

21. E: The thesis is a statement that contains the author's topic and main idea. The main purpose of this article is to use historical evidence to provide counterarguments to anti-Stratfordians. Choice *A* is simply a definition; Choice *B* states part of the reasoning of the anti-Stratfordians; Choice *C* is a supporting detail, not a main idea; and Choice *D* represents an idea of anti-Stratfordians, not the author's opinion.

22. C: This requires readers to be familiar with different types of rhetorical devices. A rhetorical question is a question that is asked not to obtain an answer but to encourage readers to more deeply consider an issue.

23. B: This question asks readers to refer to the organizational structure of the article and demonstrate understanding of how the author provides details to support their argument. This particular detail can be found in the second paragraph where the author says, "even though he did not attend university, grade-school education in Shakespeare's time was actually quite rigorous."

24. A: This is a vocabulary question that can be answered using context clues. Other sentences in the paragraph describe London as "the most populous city in England" filled with "crowds of people," giving an image of a busy city full of people. Choice *B* is incorrect because London was in Shakespeare's home country, not a foreign one. Choice *C* is not mentioned in the passage. Choice *D* is not a good answer choice because the passage describes how London was a popular and important city, not an undeveloped one. Choice *E* is incorrect because quiet would be the opposite of how the city of London is described.

25. C: Shakespeare's father was a glove-maker. The passage states this fact in paragraph two, where it says "his father was a very successful glove-maker." The other answer choices are incorrect.

26. A: The author mentions St. Lucia a couple times throughout the passage. The other answer choices are incorrect.

27. C: Remember that supporting details help readers find out the main idea by answering questions like *who, what, where, when, why,* and *how.* In this question, cruises, local events, and cuisine are not talked about in the passage. However, family resorts and activities are talked about.

28. B: The last activity the speaker did was go for a hike up a mountain. We know this because the speaker "wanted to take one more walk" before the family left. The speaker did do Choices *A, C,* and *E*— swam with the sharks, lounged on the beach, and had a massage—but those weren't the last activities the speaker did. The speaker never said anything about surfing in the waves, so Choice *D* is incorrect.

29. E: To trek means to hike or walk, so Choice *E* is the best answer here. The other choices (ran, swam, sang, and drove) are incorrect because they do not reflect the hike mentioned earlier in the passage.

30. D: The author's attitude towards the topic is enthusiastic. We see the author's enthusiasm through the word choice such as *best vacation, enjoyed, beautiful,* and *peace.* We also see the author using multiple exclamation marks, which denotes excitement. Therefore, our best answer is Choice *D.* The author doesn't demonstrate any worry or resignation, except maybe a bit in the part where they have to go home soon, but the enthusiasm overrides these feelings in the rest of the passage. Choice *C,* objective, means to be fair and based in fact, and the author is far too enthusiastic toward St. Lucia, which creates some bias towards the topic. Choice *E* is incorrect because the author's apparent enthusiasm is the opposite of apathy, or a lack of interest.

31. D: Rain is the cause in this passage because it is why something happened. The effects of the rain are plants growing, rainbows, and puddle jumping. The author's trip was an element of the story but not what caused the listed effects.

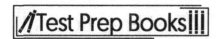

32. A: The author is comparing the plants, trees, and flowers. The author is showing how these things react the same to rain. They all get important nutrients from rain. If the author described the differences, then it would be contrasting, Choice *B*.

33. E: *Vital* can mean different things depending on the context or how it is used. In one sense, the word *vital* means full of life and energy. However, in this sentence, the word *vital* means necessary. Choices *A*, *B*, and *C* do not make sense in this context. Choice *D, dangerous,* is nearly an antonym of the word we are looking for, since the sentence says the nutrients are needed for growing. Something needed would not be dangerous. The best context clue is that it says the vital nutrients are needed, which tells us they are necessary.

34. C: This passage mentions several effects. Effects are the outcome of a certain cause. Remember that the cause here is rain, so Choice *A* is incorrect. Since the *cause* is rain, Choice *B*—brief spurts of sunshine—doesn't make sense because rain doesn't cause brief spurts of sunshine. Choice *C* makes the most sense because the effects of the rain in the passage are plants growing, rainbows, and puddle jumping. Choice *D*, weather, is not an effect of rain but describes rain in a general sense. Lastly, Choice *E*, thunderstorms, often accompany rain, but are not necessarily a cause or effect of it.

35. B: The author uses personal testimonies in this passage. We see this in the second and third paragraphs. The first time the author gives a personal testimony is when they talk about going on a trip across the United States and seeing all the rainbows. The second personal testimony we see is when the author goes outside after a storm to watch everyone play in the puddles. The other answer choices are not represented in the passage.

36. D: *Stealthily* means secretly, Choice *D*. Given the context of the passage, we probably can assume that Sylvia was trying her best to be secretive, since she was gathering bees while her father was away at work. *Hurriedly* might fit, Choice *A*, but it is not the best answer. *Begrudgingly*, Choice *B*, is incorrect, because if Sylvia was begrudging, or resentful, that she had to gather bees, she probably wouldn't have done it. Choice *C*, *confidently*, although it could fit in this context, is not the best choice for this definition. Finally, Choice *E*, *efficiently*, would mean Syliva collected them quickly or with little waste of effort, but this does not fit as well as *stealthily*.

37. C: The story is written in third-person point of view, which tells the story using *he, she, they*, etc. First-person narrative is used when the narrator is an *I* in the story, so it'll use language such as *I, we*, etc. There are no instances of *I* or *we* in the story, so Choice *A* is incorrect. Second person uses *you* to talk directly to the audience. However, *you* is not used in this manner in the narrative, so Choice *B* is incorrect. Finally, all stories have some kind of point of view, so Choices *D* and *E* are incorrect.

38. E: She wanted to keep them away from harm. Choice *A* is incorrect; the passage mentions nothing about a science experiment. Choice *B* is incorrect because doesn't indicate Sylvia is gathering the bees to learn beekeeping. Choice *C* is incorrect; the passage does not mention Sylvia wanting to give the bees to her father. Finally, Choice *D* is incorrect; although Sylvia's mother *is* terrified of the bees, this isn't her motivation for putting them inside a jar.

39. A: This passage is chronologically ordered, which means it goes from a beginning to an end in a logical way. Cause and effect order is when a topic goes from talking about a specific cause to its effects, and this is incorrect. Problem to solution is more of a formal paper where the narrative depicts a problem and then offers a solution at the end, so Choice *C* is incorrect. Sequential order is similar to

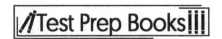

chronological order, but it is more like step-by-step instructions, so Choice *D* is incorrect. Order of importance places the most important information first to give it emphasis, so Choice *E* is incorrect.

40. C: If we had to choose one theme, it would probably be freedom. The theme is posed at the end of the passage, when Sylvia's mother basically asks her if she enjoys her own freedom playing outside. Sylvia realizes that she does and that the bees would probably enjoy that freedom as well, despite the dangers of being outdoors. The other answer choices are incorrect.

Verbal Section

Synonyms

1. B: The word *garish* means excessively ornate or elaborate, which is most closely related to the word *flashy*. The word *drab* is the opposite of *garish*. The word *gait* means a particular manner of walking, *hardy* means robust or sturdy, and *lithe* means graceful and supple.

2. D: The word *inane* means senseless or absurd. The word *ratify* means to approve, *illicit* means illegal, *uncouth* means crude, and *wry* means clever.

3. E: The word *solace* most closely resembles the word *comfort*. *Marred* means scarred, *induce* means to cause something, *depose* means to dethrone, and *inherent* means natural.

4. D: *Copious* is synonymous with the word *ample*. *Dire* means urgent or dreadful, *adept* means skillful, *indignant* means angered by injustice, and *nuance* means subtle difference.

5. C: *Supercilious* means arrogant. *Tenuous* means weak or thin, *waning* means decreasing, *placate* means to appease, and *extol* means to praise or celebrate.

6. A: *Lurid* most closely resembles the word *gruesome*. *Placid* means calm or mild, *irate* means angry, *quell* means defeat or suppress, and *torpor* means lethargy.

7. B: *Vanquish* means to *conquer*. *Saturate* means to soak, *reproach* means to scold, *parch* means to make dry, and *surrender* is the opposite of *vanquish*.

8. B: *Trite* is closest to the word *banal*, which means common. *Scanty* means barely sufficient, *polemical* means controversial, *indulgent* means lenient, and *eclectic* means from diverse sources.

9. E: *Divulge* means to admit or confess something. *Dupe* means to deceive, *flummox* means to confuse, *indulgent* means lenient, and *germinate* means to grow.

10. D: *Indolent* and *lackadaisical* both mean lazy or indifferent. *Adamant* means unyielding, *dour* means gloomy or grim, *noisome* means bad or offensive, and *remiss* means careless or thoughtless.

11. C: *Bolster* and *support* are both synonyms. *Bequeath* means to hand down through a will, *abate* means to lessen, *palliate* means to remove pain, and *tractable* means easily managed.

12. B: *Unwitting* and *unintentional* are synonyms. *Undermine* means weaken, *rife* means excessively abundant, *pernicious* means harmful, and *stolid* means apathetic or impassive.

13. A: *Ungainly* means awkward or clumsy. *Absurd* means ridiculous or senseless, *unruly* means boisterous, *tenuous* means flimsy, and *petulant* means irritable.

14. A: *Prattle* and *babble* are synonyms; they both mean to talk incessantly. *Prosaic* means lacking imagination, *deluded* means tricked or betrayed, *meddle* means to intervene, and *folly* means silliness.

15. D: *Prolific* is most closely related to the word *productive*. *Devoid* means lacking, *elusive* means difficult to define, *laconic* means concise, and *judicious* means fair.

16. E: *Fortitude* means courage. *Aura* means air or character, *disparage* means to criticize or belittle, *finesse* means tact or know-how, and *cowardice* is the opposite of fortitude.

17. B: *Acumen* is most closely related to the word *ingenuity*. *Diligent* means hardworking, *congenial* means pleasant, *embroiled* means to be involved in an argument, and *reverent* means respectful or pious.

18. C: *Relegate* means *demote* or transfer. *Relay* means to pass on or transmit. *Temporize* means delay or evade, *vigilant* means watchful and alert, and *spurn* means to reject with contempt.

19. B: *Curtail* means to cut short or *abridge*. *Covet* means to crave something someone else has, *foil* means to hinder or prevent, *construe* means to make sense of something, and *bilk* means to cheat someone.

20. D: *Conserve* is most closely related to the word *maintain*. *Constrain* means to force or restrain, *adjourn* means to stop a proceeding, *stipulate* means to designate, and *improve* means to become better.

21. D: *Ambivalent* means to be *conflicted* or doubtful. *Accosted* means to approach for solicitation, *engrossed* means preoccupied with something, *impartial* means fair or unprejudiced, and *convinced* is the opposite of *ambivalent*.

22. C: *Disrepute* is most closely related to the word *dishonor*. *Benevolent* means kind or generous. *Condone* means to overlook or approve. *Emit* means to discharge. *Postulate* means to assert.

23. A: *Instigate* is most closely related to *provoke*. *Renounce* means to give up. *Prescribe* means to command orders. To *modify* means to change or alter. To *diminish* means to become smaller.

24. E: A *maxim* is a saying or *adage*. *Discord* is a disagreement. *Clout* means special advantage or power. *Apex* means the peak or highest point of a thing. *Temperament* means usual feelings or mood.

25. D: *Presage* is most closely related to the word *prediction*. *Tactful* is an adjective meaning skilled at dealing with people. *Viability* means done in a useful way. *Vow* is the same as a promise. *Exploit* means to use selfishly or for profit.

26. C: *Onerous* means difficult or *arduous*. *Dubious* means doubtful. *Cultivate* means to foster growth. *Squalid* means run-down or decrepit. *Emphatic* means using emphasis.

27. B: *Munificent* means *generous*. To be *candid* means to be honest or blunt. *Livid* means filled with rage. *Suitable* means to be fit for something. *Malleable* means pliable or adaptable.

28. B: The closest synonym to *extant* is *surviving*. *Extant* means to be in existence. *Capitalize* means using to one's own advantage. *Foment* means to stir up. *Tentative* means not finalized yet. *Yield* means to surrender.

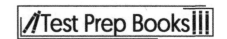

29. E: *Defunct* most nearly means *extinct*. *Simple* means not complex. *Potent* means to have a lot of influence. *Geriatric* is relating to old age, so this isn't the best answer. To *expend* means to use up.

30. B: *Cupidity* means *greed* or strong desire, so the rest of the words do not fit as synonyms here.

Verbal Analogies

31. C: This is a category analogy. Remember that we have to figure out the relationship between the first two words so that we can determine the relationship of the answer. Begonia is related to flower by type. Begonia is a type of flower, just as cardiologist is a type of doctor.

32. E: This is a synonym analogy. Notice that the word *malleable* is synonymous to the word *pliable*. Thus, in our answer, we should look for two words that have the same meaning. *Disparage* and *criticize* in Choice *E* have the same meaning, so this is the correct answer.

33. B: This is a part to whole analogy. The relationship between *cerebellum* and *brain* is that the cerebellum makes up part of the brain, while a *nucleus* makes up part of a *cell*.

34. A: Usually, a *whisk* is a cooking utensil used in the process of *baking*. As such, a *glove* is used in the sport of *boxing*. Both are objects used within a particular process.

35. C: This analogy relies on the logic of performer to related action. The original analogy says *umpires* (performer) *officiate* (action), which means to act as an official in a sporting event. In the same manner, a *counselor* (performer) *guides* (action) their clients toward well-being.

36. D: The analogy used here is degree/intensity. A *chuckle* is a giggle, while a *guffaw* is a burst of laughter. One is more intense than the other. *Whisper* is to talk softly, while *bellow* is to talk loudly. One is more intense than the other.

37. D: This analogy denotes a symbol and its representation. *Fire* can be representative of *passion*, while *ice* represents someone who is cold or *rigid*.

38. A: This is considered an antonym analogy. *Geriatric* means old age, and *youth* is the opposite of old age. Likewise, *transparent* means to see through something, while *opaque* means cloudy or muddy.

39. E: This is a cause and effect analogy. *Lying* causes *distrust*, while *hurricanes* cause *devastation*.

40. B: This is a synonym analogy. *Desolate* and *barren* both mean deserted. Likewise, *contend* and *maintain* are synonyms.

41. E: This is a part to whole analogy. Many *chapters* make up a *novel*, in the same way that many *strokes* make up a *painting*.

42. C: This is a performer to related action analogy. We know that *carpenters* perform *construction*, just as *wizards* perform *magic*.

43. C: This analogy relies on degree of intensity. *Tepid* means lukewarm, while *boiling* means extremely hot. In the same way, *rapacious* is an extreme form of *greed*.

44. C: This is a cause and effect analogy. To *read* is the cause or action, and a direct result that comes from reading is to *learn*. Likewise, when one *exercises* (cause), a direct result becomes better *health*.

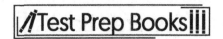

45. A: This is an antonym analogy. *Competent* means capable of something, while *impotent* means incapable of something. In the same way, *demur* means to object, which is the opposite of *accept*.

46. B: This is a category/type analogy. *Merengue* is a type of *music,* just as *tension* is a type of *headache*.

47. D: This is an object/function analogy. The *car* (object) has the function of *transporting* people from one place to the other. Likewise, the function of a *fireplace* is to *heat* up a room.

48. E: This is a symbol/representation analogy. In artistic images or literature, *flowers* usually represent *femininity*. Likewise, traditionally in art and religion, the image or presence of *light* represents *transcendence*.

49. A: This is a synonym analogy. *Principle* means assumption or *truth,* while *shabby* means *squalid*.

50. E: This is a degree of intensity analogy. *Fastidious* means to be very *careful*, while *lament* means to *grieve* deeply. The second word in each of these is more intense than the first.

51. C: This is a part to whole analogy. *Mantle* is part of the four layers that make up *earth*. Likewise, a *bun* is one of the things that makes up a *hamburger*.

52. B: This is a performer to related action analogy. A *maestro* is one who is an expert musician and who *conducts* a musical performance. Likewise, an *acupuncturist* deals with natural *healing* within the body.

53. E: This is an antonym analogy. Contentious means not agreeable, while *penurious* means stingy or ungenerous. The other pairs display synonymous relationships.

54. C: This is a category/type relationship. *Cumulus* is a type of *cloud,* just as *tortellini* is a type of *pasta*. *Rain* is a type of *weather*, but the relationship is presented in the wrong order. *Grapes* are used to make *wine*, but they are not a type of wine. *Elicit* and *snow* have no meaningful relationship. *Spanish* and *English* are two distinct languages.

55. A: This is an object/function analogy. One uses a *pot* to *boil.* Likewise, one uses a *belay* to *climb*. A *faucet* is not an action, so even though *water* comes out of one, it is not the correct completion to the analogy. Similarly, a *mirror* provides a *reflection*, but since reflection is a noun, it cannot be the correct answer choice. A *chef* is the person, not the object, who *cooks*. *Temper* is also not an object; therefore, even though it is associated with *rage*, it is not the correct answer.

56. B: This is a symbol/representation analogy. In Greek mythology, the *laurel* wreath is a symbol of *victory*. Additionally, in Christianity, a *dove* is used as a representation of *peace*. Though the other pairs contain words that are associated with each other, none of the options include one word that symbolically represents the other.

57. D: This is a synonym analogy. *Transient* and *ephemeral* both mean temporary or short-lived. *Sanguine* means *cheerful*. *Renounce* means give up one's claim to something, while *acknowledge* means admit or recognize. *Placate* means appease, and *subversive* means disruptive or rebellious. *Relinquish* means let go, while *vapid* means dull. *Verbose* means wordy, and *scarcity* means lack.

58. D: This is an antonym analogy. *Diverge* means to be at odds with, or the opposite of *agree*. Likewise, *antipathy* means a strong dislike or disgust, which is the opposite of *friendliness*. *Assail* means attack, but *belittle* means minimize or underestimate. *Dire* means very serious, and *folly* means foolishness.

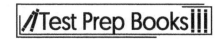

Lurid means bright, while *spartan* means arduous or bleak. *Waning* means diminishing, and *recant* means deny.

59. E: This is a category/type analogy. *Nitrogen* is a specific type of *element*, just as *calico* is a type of *cat*. *Canine* is a type of *species*, but the relationship is presented in the wrong order. None of the other answer choices represent words that have a category/type relationship.

60. C: This is a degree of intensity analogy. *Miniscule* is an extreme version of *small*, while *ailing* is an extreme version of *unhealthy*. *Chagrin* and *elusive* do not have a meaningful relationship, nor do *confined* and *rotten*. *Tall* is the opposite of *short*, and *cough* may be associated with *allergy*, but it does not represent a lesser degree.

Quantitative Reasoning 2

1. A: Compare each number after the decimal point to figure out which overall number is greatest. In Choices A (1.43785) and C (1.43592), both have the same tenths place (4) and hundredths place (3). However, the thousandths place is greater in Choice A (7), so A has the greatest value overall.

2. D: By rearranging and grouping the factors in Choice D, we can notice that $3 \times 3 \times 4 \times 2 = (3 \times 2) \times (4 \times 3) = 6 \times 12$, which is what we were looking for.

3. E: The total amount the company pays, y, equals the cost of the building ($50,000) plus the cost of the saws. Since the saws cost $40 each, the overall cost of the saws is $40 times x, where x is the number of saws. Putting all this together, we have $y = 50,000 + 40x$, which is equivalent to Choice D.

4. B: Since $850 is the price after a 20% discount, $850 represents 80% (or 0.8) of the original price. In other words, $850 = 0.8x$ (where x is the original price). Solving this, we find $x = \frac{850}{0.8} = 1,062.5$. Now, to find the savings, calculate the original price minus the sale price: $1,062.50 - $850 = $212.50.

5. A: To find the fraction of the bill that the first three people pay, the fractions need to be added, which means finding the common denominator. The common denominator will be 60:

$$\frac{1}{5} + \frac{1}{4} + \frac{1}{3} = \frac{12}{60} + \frac{15}{60} + \frac{20}{60} = \frac{47}{60}$$

The remainder of the bill is:

$$1 - \frac{47}{60} = \frac{60}{60} - \frac{47}{60} = \frac{13}{60}$$

6. C: To solve for the value of b, isolate the variable b on one side of the equation.

Start by moving the lower value of −4 to the other side by adding 4 to both sides:

$$5b - 4 = 2b + 17$$

$$5b - 4 + 4 = 2b + 17 + 4$$

$$5b = 2b + 21$$

207

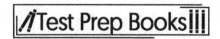

Then, subtract $2b$ from both sides:

$$5b - 2b = 2b + 21 - 2b$$

$$3b = 21$$

Then, divide both sides by 3 to get the value of b:

$$\frac{3b}{3} = \frac{21}{3}$$

$$b = 7$$

7. E: The total faculty is:

$$15 + 20 = 35$$

So, the ratio is $35 : 200$. Then, divide both of these numbers by 5, since 5 is a common factor to both, with a result of $7 : 40$.

8. C: Starting with 1, we get the next number in the sequence by adding 2, then 3, 4, 5, and 6. So to find the next number, we take our latest number and add 7, getting $21 + 7 = 28$.

9. C: To find what 85% of 20 questions is, multiply 20 by .85:

$$20 \times .85 = 17 \text{ questions}$$

10. D: This problem can be solved by setting up a proportion involving the given information and the unknown value. The proportion is:

$$\frac{21 \text{ pages}}{4 \text{ nights}} = \frac{140 \text{ pages}}{x \text{ nights}}$$

We can cross-multiply to get $21x = 4 \times 140$. Solving this, we find $x \approx 26.67$. Since this is not an integer, we round up to 27 nights because 26 nights would not give Sarah enough time to finish.

11. E: Using the conversion rate, multiply the projected weight loss of 25 lb by $0.45 \frac{\text{kg}}{\text{lb}}$ to get the amount in kilograms (11.25 kg).

12. D: First, subtract \$1,437 from \$2,334.50 to find Johnny's monthly savings; this equals \$897.50. Then, multiply this amount by 3 to find out how much he will have (in 3 months) before he pays for his vacation; this equals \$2,692.50. Finally, subtract the cost of the vacation (\$1,750) from this amount to find how much Johnny will have left: \$942.50.

13. B: To solve this correctly, keep in mind the order of operations with the mnemonic PEMDAS (Please Excuse My Dear Aunt Sally). This stands for Parentheses, Exponents, Multiplication & Division, Addition & Subtraction. Taking it step by step, start with the parentheses:

$$4 \times 7 + (4)^2 \div 2$$

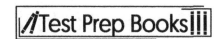

Then, apply the exponent:

$$4 \times 7 + 16 \div 2$$

Multiplication and division are both performed next:

$$28 + 8$$

Addition and subtraction are done last.

$$28 + 8 = 36$$

The solution is 36.

14. B: The variable y is directly proportional to x, which means that whenever x is multiplied by a number, y is multiplied by that same number. When x changes from 5 to 20, it is multiplied by 4, so the original y value must also be multiplied by 4. That means $y = 3 \times 4 = 12$.

15. E: We can use slope-intercept form, $y = mx + b$. We are told that the y-intercept (b) is 1, which gives us $y = mx + 1$. Now we can plug in the x and y values from our point, $(1,2)$, to find the slope: $2 = m(1) + 1$, so $m = 1$. This gives us $y = x + 1$.

16. E: To find the average of a set of values, add the values together and then divide by the total number of values. In this case, include the unknown value, x, of what Dwayne needs to score on his next test. The average must equal 90. Set up the equation and solve.

First, combine like terms:

$$\frac{78 + 92 + 83 + 97 + x}{5} = 90$$

$$\frac{350 + x}{5} = 90$$

Next, multiply both sides by 5:

$$(5)(\frac{350 + x}{5}) = (90)(5)$$

$$350 + x = 450$$

Lastly, subtract 350 from both sides:

$$350 + x - 350 = 450 - 350$$

$$x = 100$$

Dwayne would need to get a perfect score of 100 in order to get an average of at least 90.

Test this answer by substituting 100 back into the original formula.

$$\frac{78 + 92 + 83 + 97 + 100}{5} = 90$$

209

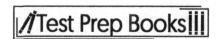

17. D: For an even number of total values, the *median* is calculated by finding the *mean*, or average, of the two middle values once all values have been arranged in ascending order from least to greatest. In this case, $\frac{83+92}{2}$ would equal the median 87.5, Choice *D*. Choice *A* is the lowest two values divided by 2, $\frac{78+83}{2} = 80.5$. Choice *B* is the first and third values divided by 2, $\frac{78+92}{2} = 85$. Choice *C* is the second and fourth values divided by 2, $\frac{83+97}{2} = 90$.

18. C: Follow the order of operations in order to solve this problem. Evaluate inside the parentheses first, being sure to follow the order of operations inside the parentheses as well. First, simplify the square roots:

$$(6 \times 4) - 3^2$$

Then, multiply inside the parentheses:

$$24 - 3^2$$

Next, simplify the exponent:

$$24 - 9$$

Finally, subtract to get 15, Choice *C*.

19. D: Three girls for every two boys can be expressed as a ratio: 3 : 2. This can be visualized as splitting the school into five groups: three girl groups and two boy groups. The number of students that are in each group can be found by dividing the total number of students by five:

$$\frac{650 \text{ students}}{5 \text{ groups}} = \frac{130 \text{ students}}{\text{group}}$$

To find the total number of girls, multiply the number of students per group (130) by the number of girl groups in the school (3). This equals 390, Choice *D*.

20. D: To solve for x, isolate the variables from the constants. First, subtract 13 from both sides:

$$13 - 13 - \frac{3x}{4} = -11 - 13$$

$$-\frac{3x}{4} = -24$$

Next, multiply both sides by 4 to eliminate the fraction:

$$-\frac{3x}{4} \times 4 = -24 \times 4$$

$$-3x = -96$$

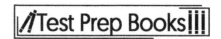

Finally, divide by -3 to solve for x:

$$\frac{-3x}{-3} = \frac{-96}{-3}$$

$$x = 32$$

Therefore, the value of x is 32.

21. C: Kimberley worked 4.5 hours at the rate of \$10/h and 1 hour at the rate of \$12/h. So the 4.5 hours would round up to 5 hours at the rate of \$10/h.

$$(5\text{h}) \times \left(\frac{\$10}{\text{h}}\right) + (1\text{h}) \times \left(\frac{\$12}{\text{h}}\right) = \$50 + \$12 = \$62$$

22. D:

$9x + x - 7 = 16 + 2x$	Combine $9x$ and x.
$10x - 7 = 16 + 2x$	
$10x - 7 + 7 = 16 + 2x + 7$	Add 7 to both sides to remove (-7).
$10x = 23 + 2x$	
$10x - 2x = 23 + 2x - 2x$	Subtract $2x$ from both sides to move it to the other side of the equation.
$8x = 23$	
$\dfrac{8x}{8} = \dfrac{23}{8}$	Divide by 8 to get x by itself.
$x = \dfrac{23}{8}$	

23. C: For each fraction, we can divide the numerator by the denominator to find a decimal value. $\frac{4}{5} = 0.8$, $\frac{2}{3} \approx 0.67$, and $\frac{91}{100} = 0.91$. Ordering these from least to greatest gives us 0.67, 0.8, 0.85, and 0.91, which matches Choice C.

24. B: First, calculate the difference between the larger value and the smaller value.

$$378 - 252 = 126$$

To calculate this difference as a percentage of the original value, and thus calculate the percentage *increase*, divide 126 by 252 to get 0.5, then multiply by 100 to reach the percentage 50%, Choice B.

25. B: When solving for x, add 3 to both sides to get $4x = 8$. Then, divide both sides by 4 to get $x = 2$.

Practice Writing Sample

Select one of the following two-story starters and write a creative story in the space provided. Make sure that your story has a beginning, middle, and end and is interesting for readers.

- The large red door was only partially closed, and Kurt could see light coming from inside the room.

- The blizzard howled outside, but a small figure could be seen trudging through the snow.

Quantitative Reasoning 1

1. What is $\frac{660}{100}$ rounded to the nearest integer?
   a. 67
   b. 66
   c. 60
   d. 6
   e. 7

2. Divide and reduce $\frac{5}{13} \div \frac{25}{169}$.
   a. $\frac{13}{5}$

   b. $\frac{65}{25}$

   c. $\frac{25}{65}$

   d. $\frac{5}{13}$

   e. $\frac{125}{2197}$

3. $5.88 \times 3.2 =$
   a. 18.816
   b. 16.44
   c. 20.352
   d. 17
   e. 1.8816

4. What is the length of the hypotenuse of a right triangle with one leg equal to 3 centimeters and the other leg equal to 4 centimeters?
   a. 7 cm
   b. 5 cm
   c. 25 cm
   d. 12 cm
   e. 49 cm

5. If a car can go 300 miles in 4 hours, how far can it go in an hour and a half?
   a. 100 miles
   b. 112.5 miles
   c. 135.5 miles
   d. 150 miles
   e. 165.5 miles

6. At the store, Jan buys $90 of apples and oranges. Apples cost $1 each and oranges cost $2 each. If Jan buys the same number of apples as oranges, how many oranges did she buy?
   a. 20 oranges
   b. 25 oranges
   c. 30 oranges
   d. 35 oranges
   e. 40 oranges

7. A box with rectangular faces is 5 feet long, 6 feet wide, and 3 feet high. What is its volume?
   a. 60 cubic feet
   b. 75 cubic feet
   c. 90 cubic feet
   d. 100 cubic feet
   e. 115 cubic feet

8. A train traveling 50 miles per hour takes a trip of 3 hours. If a map has a scale of 1 inch per 10 miles, how many inches apart are the train's starting point and ending point on the map?
   a. 10 inches
   b. 12 inches
   c. 13 inches
   d. 14 inches
   e. 15 inches

9. A traveler takes an hour to drive to a museum, spends three hours and 30 minutes there, and takes half an hour to drive home. What percentage of this time was spent driving?
   a. 15%
   b. 30%
   c. 40%
   d. 50%
   e. 60%

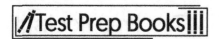

10. What is the value of x in the following triangle?

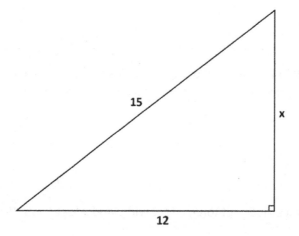

a. 19.2
b. 9
c. 3
d. 7.5
e. 81

11. If the sides of a cube are 5 centimeters long, what is its volume?
a. 10 cm³
b. 15 cm³
c. 50 cm³
d. 125 cm³
e. 25 cm³

12. Greg buys a $10 lunch with 5% sales tax. He leaves a $2 tip after his bill. How much money does he spend?
a. $12.00
b. $12.50
c. $13.00
d. $13.25
e. $16.00

13. Marty wishes to save $150 over a 4-day period. How much must Marty save each day on average?
a. $33.50
b. $35.00
c. $37.50
d. $40.00
e. $45.75

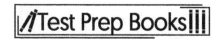

14. Bernard can make $80 per day. If he needs to make $300 and only works full days, how many days will this take?
    a. 2 days
    b. 3 days
    c. 4 days
    d. 5 days
    e. 6 days

15. A couple buys a house for $150,000. They sell it for $165,000. What percentage did the house's value increase?
    a. 10%
    b. 13%
    c. 15%
    d. 17%
    e. 19%

16. A map has a scale of 1 inch per 5 miles. A car can travel 60 miles per hour. If the distance from the start to the destination is 3 inches on the map, how long will it take the car to make the trip?
    a. 12 minutes
    b. 15 minutes
    c. 17 minutes
    d. 20 minutes
    e. 25 minutes

17. Taylor works two jobs. The first pays $20,000 per year. The second pays $10,000 per year. She donates 15% of her income to charity. How much does she donate each year?
    a. $4,500
    b. $5,000
    c. $5,500
    d. $6,000
    e. $6,500

18. A box with rectangular sides is 24 inches wide, 18 inches deep, and 12 inches high. What is the volume of the box in cubic feet?
    a. 2 cubic feet
    b. 3 cubic feet
    c. 4 cubic feet
    d. 5 cubic feet
    e. 6 cubic feet

19. Kristen purchases $100 worth of CDs and DVDs. The CDs cost $10 each and the DVDs cost $15 each. If she bought 4 DVDs, how many CDs did she buy?
    a. 1 CD
    b. 2 CDs
    c. 3 CDs
    d. 4 CDs
    e. 5 CDs

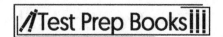

20. The total perimeter of a rectangle is 36 cm. If the length is 12 cm, what is the width?
    a. 3 cm
    b. 12 cm
    c. 6 cm
    d. 8 cm
    e. 9 cm

21. $\frac{14}{15} + \frac{3}{5} - \frac{1}{30} =$

    a. $\frac{19}{15}$

    b. $\frac{43}{30}$

    c. $\frac{4}{3}$

    d. $\frac{3}{2}$

    e. 3

22. Solve for x and y, given $3x + 2y = 8$ and $-x + 3y = 1$.
    a. $x = 2, y = 1$
    b. $x = 1, y = 2$
    c. $x = -1, y = 6$
    d. $x = 3, y = 1$
    e. $x = 4, y = 4$

23. What is the result of evaluating $\frac{1}{2}\sqrt{16}$?
    a. 0
    b. 1
    c. 2
    d. 4
    e. 8

24. The factors of $2x^2 - 8$ are:
    a. $2(4x^2)$
    b. $2(x^2 + 4)$
    c. $2(x + 2)(x + 2)$
    d. $2(x - 2)(x - 2)$
    e. $2(x + 2)(x - 2)$

25. Two of the interior angles of a triangle are 35° and 70°. What is the measure of the last interior angle?
    a. 60°
    b. 75°
    c. 90°
    d. 100°
    e. 105°

Reading Comprehension

1. At its easternmost part, Long Island opens like the upper and under jaws of some prodigious alligator; the upper and larger one terminating in Montauk Point. The bay that lies in here, and part of which forms the splendid harbor of Greenport, where the Long Island Railroad ends, is called Peconic Bay; and a beautiful and varied water is it, fertile in fish and feathered game. I, who am by no means a skillful fisherman, go down for an hour of a morning on one of the docks, or almost anywhere along shore, and catch a mess of black-fish, which you couldn't buy in New York for a dollar—large fat fellows, with meat on their bones that it takes a pretty long fork to stick through. They have a way here of splitting these fat black-fish and poggies, and broiling them on the coals, beef-steak-fashion, which I recommend your Broadway cooks to copy.

Which of the following is the best summary of this passage?
   a. Walt Whitman was impressed with the quantity and quality of fish he found in Peconic Bay.
   b. Walt Whitman preferred the fish found in restaurants in New York.
   c. Walt Whitman was a Broadway chef.
   d. Walt Whitman was frustrated because he was not a very skilled fisherman.
   e. Long Island reminded Walt Whitman of an alligator.

2. Evidently, our country has overlooked both the importance of learning history and the appreciation of it. But why is this a huge problem? Other than historians, who really cares how the War of 1812 began or who Alexander the Great's tutor was? Well, not many, as it turns out. So, is history really that important? Yes! History is critical for understanding the underlying forces that shape decisive events, preventing us from making the same mistakes twice, and giving us context for current events.

The above is an example of which type of writing?
   a. Expository
   b. Persuasive
   c. Narrative
   d. Poetry
   e. Drama

3. Although many Missourians know that Harry S. Truman and Walt Disney hailed from their great state, probably far fewer know that it was also home to the remarkable George Washington Carver. At the end of the Civil War, Moses Carver, the slave owner who owned George's parents, decided to keep George and his brother and raise them on his farm. As a child, George was driven to learn and he loved painting. He even went on to study art while in college but was encouraged to pursue botany instead. He spent much of his life helping others by showing them better ways to farm; his ideas improved agricultural productivity in many countries. One of his most notable contributions to the newly emerging class of Black farmers was to teach them the negative effects of agricultural monoculture (i.e., growing the same crops in the same fields year after year, depleting the soil of much needed nutrients and resulting in a lesser crop yield). Carver was an innovator, always thinking of new and better ways to do things, and is most famous for his over three hundred uses for the peanut. Toward the end of his career, Carver returned to his first love of art. Through his artwork, he hoped to inspire people to see the beauty around them and to do great things themselves. When Carver died, he left his money to help fund ongoing agricultural research. Today, people still visit and study at the George Washington Carver Foundation at Tuskegee Institute.

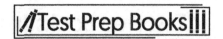

According to the passage, what was George Washington Carver's first love?
  a. Plants
  b. Art
  c. Animals
  d. Soil
  e. Education

4. Annabelle Rice started having trouble sleeping. Her biological clock was suddenly amiss, and she began to lead a nocturnal schedule. She thought her insomnia was due to spending nights writing a horror story, but then she realized that even the idea of going outside into the bright world scared her to bits. She concluded she was now suffering from heliophobia.

Which of the following most accurately describes the meaning of the underlined word in the sentence above?
  a. Fear of dreams
  b. Fear of sunlight
  c. Fear of strangers
  d. Generalized anxiety disorder
  e. Fear of the outdoors

5. A famous children's author recently published a historical fiction novel under a pseudonym; however, it did not sell as many copies as her children's books. In her earlier years, she had majored in history and earned a graduate degree in Antebellum American History, which is the timeframe of her new novel. Critics praised this newest work far more than the children's series that made her famous. In fact, her new novel was nominated for the prestigious Albert J. Beveridge Award but still isn't selling like her children's books, which fly off the shelves because of her name alone.

Which one of the following statements might be accurately inferred based on the above passage?
  a. The famous children's author produced an inferior book under her pseudonym.
  b. The famous children's author is the foremost expert on Antebellum America.
  c. The famous children's author did not receive the bump in publicity for her historical novel that it would have received if it were written under her given name.
  d. People generally prefer to read children's series rather than historical fiction.
  e. The famous author's book isn't selling because she published under her pseudonym.

6. In 2015, 28 countries, including Estonia, Portugal, Slovenia, and Latvia, scored significantly higher than the United States on standardized high school math tests. In the 1960s, the United States consistently ranked first in the world. Today, the United States spends more than $800 billion on education, which exceeds the next highest country by more than $600 billion. The United States also leads the world in spending per school-aged child by an enormous margin.

If the statements above are true, which of the following statements must be correct?
  a. Outspending other countries on education has benefits beyond standardized math tests.
  b. The United States' education system is corrupt and broken.
  c. The standardized math tests are not representative of American academic prowess.
  d. Spending more money does not guarantee success on standardized math tests.
  e. The United States' remains a top competitor in education across the globe.

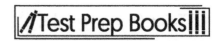

Please read the following two passages and then answer the question that follows.

Passage 1

In the modern classroom, cell phones have become indispensable. Cell phones, which are essentially handheld computers, allow students to take notes, connect to the web, perform complex computations, teleconference, and participate in surveys. Most importantly, though, due to their mobility and excellent reception, cell phones are necessary in emergencies. Unlike tablets, laptops, or computers, cell phones are a readily available and free resource—most school district budgets are already strained to begin with—and since today's student is already strongly rooted in technology, when teachers incorporate cell phones, they're "speaking" the student's language, which increases the chance of higher engagement.

Passage 2

As with most forms of technology, there is an appropriate time and place for the use of cell phones. Students are comfortable with cell phones, so it makes sense when teachers allow cell phone use at their discretion. Allowing cell phone use can prove advantageous if done correctly. Unfortunately, if that's not the case—and often it isn't—then a sizable percentage of students pretend to pay attention while surreptitiously playing on their phones. This type of disrespectful behavior is often justified by the argument that cell phones are not only a privilege but also a right. Under this logic, confiscating phones is akin to rummaging through students' backpacks. This is in stark contrast to several decades ago when teachers regulated where and when students accessed information.

7. With which of the following statements would both the authors of Passages 1 and 2 agree?
   a. Teachers should incorporate cell phones into the curriculum whenever possible.
   b. Cell phones are useful only when an experienced teacher uses them properly.
   c. Cell phones and, moreover, technology are a strong part of today's culture.
   d. Despite a good lesson plan, cell phone disruptions are impossible to avoid.
   e. Cell phone disruptions are easily avoidable.

8. The following exchange occurred after the baseball coach's team suffered a heartbreaking loss in the final inning:

   Reporter: The team clearly did not rise to the challenge. I'm sure that getting zero hits in 20 at-bats with runners in scoring position hurt the team's chances at winning the game. What are your thoughts on this devastating loss?

   Baseball Coach: Hitting with runners in scoring position was not the reason we lost this game. We made numerous errors in the field, and our pitchers gave out too many free passes. Also, we

219

did not even need a hit with runners in scoring position. Many of those at-bats could have driven in the run by simply making contact. Our team did not deserve to win the game.

Which of the following best describes the main point of dispute between the reporter and baseball coach?
- a. The loss was heartbreaking.
- b. Getting zero hits in 20 at-bats with runners in scoring position caused the loss.
- c. Numerous errors in the field and pitchers giving too many free passes caused the loss.
- d. The team deserved to win the game.
- e. There was no dispute between the reporter and the coach.

9. After looking for our perfect pet for several months, we adopted a dog from the local animal shelter last week. We wanted a dog that was not too old, but also past the puppy stage, so that training would be less time-intensive and so that we would give an older animal a home. Robin, as she's called, was a perfect match. We filled out our application and, upon approval, were permitted to bring her home. Her physical exam and lab work all confirmed she was healthy. We went to the pet store and bought all sorts of bedding, food, toys, and treats to outfit our house as a dog-friendly and fun place. The shelter told us she liked dry food only, which is a relief because wet food is expensive and pretty off-putting. We even got fencing and installed a dog run in the backyard for Robin to roam unattended. Then we took her to the vet to make sure she was healthy. Next week, she starts the dog obedience class that we enrolled her in with a discount coupon from the shelter. It will be a good opportunity to bond with her and establish commands and dominance. When we took her to the park the afternoon after we adopted her, it was clear that she is a sociable and friendly dog, easily playing cohesively with dogs of all sizes and dispositions.

Which of the following is out of sequence in the story?
- a. After looking for our perfect pet for several months, we adopted a dog from the local animal shelter last week.
- b. Robin, as she's called, was a perfect match. We filled out our application and, upon approval, were permitted to bring her home.
- c. Her physical exam and lab work all confirmed she was healthy.
- d. Next week, she starts the dog obedience class that we enrolled her in with a discount coupon from the shelter.
- e. It will be a good opportunity to bond with her and establish commands and dominance.

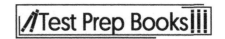

10. While scientists aren't entirely certain why tornadoes form, they have some clues into the process. Tornadoes are dangerous funnel clouds that occur during a large thunderstorm. When warm, humid air near the ground meets cold, dry air from above, a column of the warm air can be drawn up into the clouds. Winds at different altitudes blowing at different speeds make the column of air rotate. As the spinning column of air picks up speed, a funnel cloud is formed. This funnel cloud moves rapidly and haphazardly. Rain and hail inside the cloud cause it to touch down, creating a tornado. Tornadoes move in a rapid and unpredictable pattern, making them extremely destructive and dangerous. Scientists continue to study tornadoes to improve radar detection and warning times.

The main purpose of this passage is to:
   a. Show why tornadoes are dangerous.
   b. Explain how a tornado forms.
   c. Compare thunderstorms to tornadoes.
   d. Explain what to do in the event of a tornado.
   e. Explain that tornadoes are not dangerous.

11. There are two major kinds of cameras on the market right now for amateur photographers. Camera enthusiasts can either purchase a digital single-lens reflex (DSLR) camera or a compact system camera (CSC). The main difference between a DSLR and a CSC is that the DSLR has a full-sized sensor, which means it fits in a much larger body. The CSC uses a mirrorless system, which makes for a lighter, smaller camera. While both take quality pictures, the DSLR generally has better picture quality due to the larger sensor. CSCs still take very good quality pictures and are more convenient to carry than a DSLR. This makes the CSC an ideal choice for the amateur photographer looking to step up from a point-and-shoot camera.

The main difference between the DSLR and CSC is:
   a. The picture quality is better in the DSLR.
   b. The CSC is less expensive than the DSLR.
   c. The DSLR is a better choice for amateur photographers.
   d. The DSLR's larger sensor makes it a bigger camera than the CSC.
   e. The CSC has better picture quality.

12. When selecting a career path, it's important to explore the various options available. Many students entering college may shy away from a major because they don't know much about it. For example, many students won't opt for a career as an actuary because they aren't exactly sure what it entails. They would be missing out on a career that is very lucrative and in high demand. Actuaries work in the insurance field and assess risks and premiums. The average salary of an actuary is $100,000 per year. Another career option students may avoid, due to lack of knowledge of the field, is a hospitalist. This is a physician that specializes in the care of patients in a hospital, as opposed to those seen in private practices. The average salary of a hospitalist is upwards of $200,000. It pays to do some digging and find out more about these lesser-known career fields.

An actuary is:
   a. A doctor who works in a hospital
   b. The same as a hospitalist
   c. An insurance agent who works in a hospital
   d. A person who assesses insurance risks and premiums
   e. A person who researches actual facts

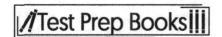

13. Many people are unsure of exactly how the digestive system works. Digestion begins in the mouth where teeth grind up food and saliva breaks it down, making it easier for the body to absorb. Next, the food moves to the esophagus, and it is pushed into the stomach. The stomach is where food is stored and broken down further by acids and digestive enzymes, preparing it for passage into the intestines. The small intestine is where the nutrients are absorbed from food and passed into the bloodstream. Other essential organs like the liver, gall bladder, and pancreas aid the stomach in breaking down food and absorbing nutrients. Finally, food waste is passed into the large intestine where it is eliminated by the body.

The purpose of this passage is to:
    a. Explain how the liver works.
    b. Show why it is important to eat healthy foods.
    c. Explain how the digestive system works.
    d. Show how nutrients are absorbed by the small intestine.
    e. Explain how the esophagus works.

14. Hard water occurs when rainwater mixes with minerals from rock and soil. Hard water has a high mineral count, including calcium and magnesium. The mineral deposits from hard water can stain hard surfaces in bathrooms and kitchens as well as clog pipes. Hard water can stain dishes, ruin clothes, and reduce the life of any appliances it touches, such as hot water heaters, washing machines, and humidifiers.

One solution is to install a water softener to reduce the mineral content of water, but this can be costly. Running vinegar through pipes and appliances and using vinegar to clean hard surfaces can also help with mineral deposits.

From this passage, it can be concluded that:
    a. Hard water can cause a lot of problems for homeowners.
    b. Calcium is good for pipes and hard surfaces.
    c. Water softeners are easy to install.
    d. Vinegar is the only solution to hard water problems.
    e. There are no solutions for hard water problems.

Questions 15 and 16 are based on the following passage:

Dear Brand-X Employees:

Over the past 10 years, Brand-X has been happy to provide free daycare to Brand-X employees. Based on the dedication, long workdays, and professionalism shown daily, it's the least Brand-X management can do. Brand-X wouldn't be where it is today without the hard work of countless unsung heroes and is truly blessed to have such an amazing staff.

Unfortunately, Brand-X is subject to the same economic forces as any other company. We regret to inform you that, beginning March 15th, Brand-X has decided to discontinue the childcare program. This was a difficult decision to make, one that was arrived at only with the greatest of deliberation. Many other options were discussed, and this seemed to be the only one that allowed Brand-X to still stay competitive while not reducing staff.

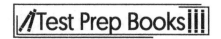

Fortunately, all other programs—employee rewards, vacation and sick days, retirement options, volunteer days—have not been impacted. In addition, on Friday we'll be hosting a free lunch buffet. Employees are welcome to wear jeans.

Hope to see you there,

Brand-X Management

15. Which of the following words best describe the tone in the first, second, and third paragraphs?
    a. Relieved; conciliatory; ominous
    b. Conciliatory; ominous; relieved
    c. Proud; apologetic; placating
    d. Placating; apologetic; proud
    e. Aggravated; terse; cheerful

16. "Unfortunately, Brand-X is subject to the same economic forces as any other company." This line was most likely provided to do what?
    a. Emphasize that Brand-X is no worse than other companies.
    b. Redirect blame from Brand-X to outside forces.
    c. Encourage staff to look for work elsewhere.
    d. Intimidate staff into cooperating.
    e. Ask for suggestions on ways to solve this problem.

Questions 17–20 are based on the following passage:

Knowing that Mrs. Mallard was afflicted with heart trouble, great care was taken to break to her as gently as possible the news of her husband's death.

It was her sister Josephine who told her, in broken sentences; veiled hints that revealed in half concealing. Her husband's friend Richards was there, too, near her. It was he who had been in the newspaper office when intelligence of the railroad disaster was received, with Brently Mallard's name leading the list of "killed." He had only taken the time to assure himself of its truth by a second telegram, and had hastened to forestall any less careful, less tender friend in bearing the sad message.

She did not hear the story as many women have heard the same, with a paralyzed inability to accept its significance. She wept at once, with sudden, wild abandonment, in her sister's arms. When the storm of grief had spent itself she went away to her room alone. She would have no one follow her.

There stood, facing the open window, a comfortable, roomy armchair. Into this she sank, pressed down by a physical exhaustion that haunted her body and seemed to reach into her soul.

She could see in the open square before her house the tops of trees that were all aquiver with the new spring life. The delicious breath of rain was in the air. In the street below a peddler was crying his wares. The notes of a distant song which some one was singing reached her faintly, and countless sparrows were twittering in the eaves.

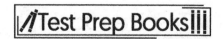

There were patches of blue sky showing here and there through the clouds that had met and piled one above the other in the west facing her window.

She sat with her head thrown back upon the cushion of the chair, quite motionless, except when a sob came up into her throat and shook her, as a child who has cried itself to sleep continues to sob in its dreams.

She was young, with a fair, calm face, whose lines bespoke repression and even a certain strength. But now there was a dull stare in her eyes, whose gaze was fixed away off yonder on one of those patches of blue sky. It was not a glance of reflection, but rather indicated a suspension of intelligent thought.

There was something coming to her and she was waiting for it, fearfully. What was it? She did not know; it was too subtle and elusive to name. But she felt it, creeping out of the sky, reaching toward her through the sounds, the scents, the color that filled the air.

Now her bosom rose and fell tumultuously. She was beginning to recognize this thing that was approaching to possess her, and she was striving to beat it back with her will— as powerless as her two white slender hands would have been. When she abandoned herself a little whispered word escaped her slightly parted lips. She said it over and over under her breath: "free, free, free!" The vacant stare and the look of terror that had followed it went from her eyes. They stayed keen and bright. Her pulses beat fast, and the coursing blood warmed and relaxed every inch of her body.

She did not stop to ask if it were or were not a monstrous joy that held her. A clear and exalted perception enabled her to dismiss the suggestion as trivial. She knew that she would weep again when she saw the kind, tender hands folded in death; the face that had never looked save with love upon her, fixed and gray and dead. But she saw beyond that bitter moment a long procession of years to come that would belong to her absolutely. And she opened and spread her arms out to them in welcome.

Excerpt from "The Story of an Hour" by Kate Chopin, 1894

17. What point of view is the above passage told in?
   a. First person
   b. Second person
   c. Third person omniscient
   d. Third person limited
   e. Third person objective

18. What kind of irony are we presented with in this story?
   a. The way Mrs. Mallard reacted to her husband's death
   b. The way in which Mr. Mallard died
   c. The way in which the news of her husband's death was presented to Mrs. Mallard
   d. The way in which nature is compared with death in the story
   e. The way Mrs. Mallard looked before and after the news of her husband's death

19. Kate Chopin is the author of *The Awakening*. *The Awakening* and this excerpt from "The Story of an Hour" have which of the following themes in common?
    a. Horrors of war and soldiers' deaths
    b. Romantic love and familial love
    c. Terminal illness and loneliness
    d. Family life and friendship
    e. Liberation from marriage and cultural limitations

20. What is the best summary of the passage above?
    a. Mr. Mallard, a soldier during World War I, is killed by the enemy and leaves his wife widowed.
    b. Mrs. Mallard understands the value of friendship when her friends show up for her after her husband's death.
    c. Mrs. Mallard combats mental illness daily and will perhaps be sent to a mental institution soon.
    d. Mrs. Mallard suffers from a heart condition and her friends are worried for her health.
    e. Mrs. Mallard, a newly widowed woman, finds unexpected relief in her husband's death.

Questions 21–26 are based on the following passage:

My Good Friends—When I first imparted to the committee of the projected Institute my particular wish that on one of the evenings of my readings here the main body of my audience should be composed of working men and their families, I was animated by two desires; first, by the wish to have the great pleasure of meeting you face to face at this Christmas time, and accompany you myself through one of my little Christmas books; and second, by the wish to have an opportunity of stating publicly in your presence, and in the presence of the committee, my earnest hope that the Institute will, from the beginning, recognise one great principle—strong in reason and justice—which I believe to be essential to the very life of such an Institution. It is, that the working man shall, from the first unto the last, have a share in the management of an Institution which is designed for his benefit, and which calls itself by his name.

I have no fear here of being misunderstood—of being supposed to mean too much in this. If there ever was a time when any one class could of itself do much for its own good, and for the welfare of society—which I greatly doubt—that time is unquestionably past. It is in the fusion of different classes, without confusion; in the bringing together of employers and employed; in the creating of a better common understanding among those whose interests are identical, who depend upon each other, who are vitally essential to each other, and who never can be in unnatural antagonism without deplorable results, that one of the chief principles of a Mechanics' Institution should consist. In this world a great deal of the bitterness among us arises from an imperfect understanding of one another. Erect in Birmingham a great Educational Institution, properly educational; educational of the feelings as well as of the reason; to which all orders of Birmingham men contribute; in which all orders of Birmingham men meet; wherein all orders of Birmingham men are faithfully represented—and you will erect a Temple of Concord here which will be a model edifice to the whole of England.

Contemplating as I do the existence of the Artisans' Committee, which not long ago considered the establishment of the Institute so sensibly, and supported it so heartily, I earnestly entreat the gentlemen—earnest I know in the good work, and who are now

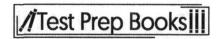

among us,—by all means to avoid the great shortcoming of similar institutions; and in asking the working man for his confidence, to set him the great example and give him theirs in return. You will judge for yourselves if I promise too much for the working man, when I say that he will stand by such an enterprise with the utmost of his patience, his perseverance, sense, and support; that I am sure he will need no charitable aid or condescending patronage; but will readily and cheerfully pay for the advantages which it confers; that he will prepare himself in individual cases where he feels that the adverse circumstances around him have rendered it necessary; in a word, that he will feel his responsibility like an honest man, and will most honestly and manfully discharge it. I now proceed to the pleasant task to which I assure you I have looked forward for a long time.

This excerpt is an adaptation from Charles Dickens' speech in Birmingham in England on December 30, 1853 on behalf of the Birmingham and Midland Institute.

21. Which word is most closely synonymous with the word *patronage* as it appears in the following statement?

"that I am sure he will need no charitable aid or condescending patronage"

a. Auspices
b. Aberration
c. Acerbic
d. Adulation
e. Admiration

22. Which term is most closely aligned with the definition of the term *working man* as it is defined in the following passage?

"You will judge for yourselves if I promise too much for the working man, when I say that he will stand by such an enterprise with the utmost of his patience, his perseverance, sense, and support"

a. Athlete
b. Viscount
c. Entrepreneur
d. Bourgeois
e. Champion

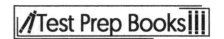

23. Which of the following statements most closely correlates with the definition of the term *working man* as used in the following passage?

> "You will judge for yourselves if I promise too much for the working man, when I say that he will stand by such an enterprise with the utmost of his patience, his perseverance, sense, and support"

  a. A working man is not someone who works for institutions or corporations but rather someone who is well versed in the workings of the soul.
  b. A working man is someone who is probably not involved in social activities because the physical demand for work is too high.
  c. A working man is someone who works for wages among the middle class.
  d. The working man has historically taken to the field, to the factory, and now to the screen.
  e. The working man is a man of noble birth who also works in agriculture.

24. Based upon the contextual evidence provided in the passage above, what is the meaning of the term *enterprise* in the third paragraph?
  a. Company
  b. Courage
  c. Game
  d. Plan
  e. Cause

25. The speaker addresses his audience as "My Good Friends." What function does this salutation serve for the speaker?
  a. The speaker is an employer addressing his employees, so the salutation is a way for the boss to bridge the gap between himself and his employees.
  b. The speaker's salutation is one from an entertainer to his audience and uses the friendly language to connect to his audience before a serious speech.
  c. The salutation gives the serious speech that follows a somber tone, as it is used ironically.
  d. The speech is one from a politician to the public, so the salutation is used to grab the audience's attention.
  e. The way the speaker addresses his audience shows that he is an expert in his field, and the audience should pay attention to what he says.

26. According to the passage, what is the speaker's second desire for his time in front of the audience?
  a. To read a Christmas story
  b. To support the idea that the working man should have a say in an institution that is designed for his benefit
  c. To have an opportunity to stand in their presence
  d. For the life of the institution to be essential to the audience as a whole
  e. To reinforce the barriers between employees and employers

Questions 27–31 are based upon the following passage:

> Insects as a whole are preeminently creatures of the land and the air. This is shown not only by the possession of wings by a vast majority of the class, but by the mode of breathing to which reference has already been made, a system of branching air-tubes carrying atmospheric air with its combustion-supporting oxygen to all the insect's

227

tissues. The air gains access to these tubes through a number of paired air-holes or spiracles, arranged segmentally in series.

It is of great interest to find that, nevertheless, a number of insects spend much of their time under water. This is true of not a few in the perfect winged state, as for example aquatic beetles and water-bugs ('boatmen' and 'scorpions') which have some way of protecting their spiracles when submerged, and, possessing usually the power of flight, can pass on occasion from pond or stream to upper air. But it is advisable in connection with our present subject to dwell especially on some insects that remain continually under water till they are ready to undergo their final moult and attain the winged state, which they pass entirely in the air. The preparatory instars of such insects are aquatic; the adult instar is aerial. All may-flies, dragon-flies, and caddis-flies, many beetles and two-winged flies, and a few moths thus divide their life-story between the water and the air. For the present we confine attention to the Stone-flies, the May-flies, and the Dragon-flies, three well-known orders of insects respectively called by systematists the Plecoptera, the Ephemeroptera, and the Odonata.

In the case of many insects that have aquatic larvae, the latter are provided with some arrangement for enabling them to reach atmospheric air through the surface-film of the water. But the larva of a stone-fly, a dragon-fly, or a may-fly is adapted more completely than these for aquatic life; it can, by means of gills of some kind, breathe the air dissolved in water.

Excerpt adapted from The Life-Story of Insects, by Geo H. Carpenter

27. Which statement best details the central idea in this passage?
   a. It describes the life cycle of insects.
   b. It delves into entomology, especially where gills are concerned.
   c. It defines what constitutes insects' breathing.
   d. It invites readers to have a hand in the preservation of insects.
   e. It introduces certain insects that transition from water to air.

28. Which definition most closely relates to the usage of the word *moult* in the passage?
   a. An adventure of sorts, especially underwater
   b. Mating act between two insects
   c. The act of shedding part or all of the outer shell
   d. Death of an organism that ends in a revival of life
   e. A respiratory opening in the body of an insect

29. What is the purpose of the first paragraph in relation to the second paragraph?
   a. The first paragraph serves as a cause, and the second paragraph serves as an effect.
   b. The first paragraph serves as a contrast to the second.
   c. The first paragraph is a description for the argument in the second paragraph.
   d. The first and second paragraphs are merely presented in a sequence.
   e. The first and second paragraphs are steps in a process.

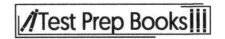

30. What does the following sentence most nearly mean?

> The preparatory instars of such insects are aquatic; the adult instar is aerial.

   a. The volume of water is necessary to prep the insect for transition rather than the volume of the air.

   b. The abdomen of the insect is designed like a star in the water as well as the air.

   c. The early stages in between periods of molting are acted out in the water, while the last stage is in the air.

   d. These insects breathe first in the water through gills yet continue to use the same organs to breathe in the air.

   e. Some insects prefer to live in water, while others thrive in the air.

31. Which of the statements reflects information that one could reasonably infer based on the author's tone?

   a. The author's tone is persuasive and attempts to call the audience to action.

   b. The author's tone is passionate due to excitement over the subject and personal narrative.

   c. The author's tone is informative and exhibits interest in the subject of the study.

   d. The author's tone is somber, depicting some anger at the state of insect larvae.

   e. The author's tone is narrative, providing a story about how different insects interact.

Questions 32 and 33 are based upon the following passage:

> Four score and seven years ago our fathers brought forth on this continent, a new nation, conceived in liberty, and dedicated to the proposition that all men are created equal.
>
> Now we are engaged in a great civil war, testing whether that nation, or any nation so conceived and so dedicated, can long endure. We are met on a great battlefield of that war. We have come to dedicate a portion of that field, as a final resting place for those who here gave their lives that this nation might live. It is altogether fitting and proper that we should do this.
>
> But, in a larger sense, we cannot dedicate, we cannot consecrate, we cannot hallow this ground. The brave men, living and dead, who struggled here, have consecrated it, far above our poor power to add or detract. The world will little note, nor long remember what we say here, but it can never forget what they did here. It is for us the living, rather, to be dedicated here to the unfinished work which they who fought here have thus far so nobly advanced. It is rather for us to be here and dedicated to the great task remaining before us—that from these honored dead we take increased devotion to that cause for which they gave the last full measure of devotion—that we here highly resolve that these dead shall not have died in vain—that this nation, under God, shall have a new birth of freedom—and that government of the people, by the people, for the people, shall not perish from the earth.

Address by Abraham Lincoln, delivered at the dedication of the cemetery at Gettysburg, November 19, 1863

229

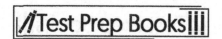

32. What message is the speaker trying to convey through this address?
    a. The audience should perpetuate the ideals of freedom that the soldiers died fighting for.
    b. The audience should honor the dead by establishing an annual memorial service.
    c. The audience should form a militia that would overturn the current political structure.
    d. The audience should forget the lives that were lost and discredit the soldiers.
    e. The audience should join a political party to advocate changes in the country.

33. What is the effect of Lincoln's statement in the following passage?

> But, in a larger sense, we cannot dedicate—we cannot consecrate—we cannot hallow—this ground. The brave men, living and dead, who struggled here, have consecrated it, far above our poor power to add or detract.

    a. His comparison emphasizes the great sacrifice of the soldiers who fought in the war.
    b. His comparison serves as a reminder of the inadequacies of his audience.
    c. His comparison serves as a catalyst for guilt and shame among audience members.
    d. His comparison suggests that the dedication ceremony was inappropriate.
    e. His comparison casts blame upon opposing political factions for the deaths.

Read the following passage and then answer questions 34-38:

The Old Man and His Grandson

There was once a very old man, whose eyes had become dim,

his ears dull of hearing, his knees trembled, and when he sat at

table he could hardly hold the spoon, and spilt the broth upon

the table-cloth or let it run out of his mouth. His son and his

son's wife were disgusted at this, so the old grandfather at last

had to sit in the corner behind the stove, and they gave him his

food in an earthenware bowl, and not even enough of it. And he

used to look towards the table with his eyes full of tears. Once,

too, his trembling hands could not hold the bowl, and it fell to

the ground and broke. The young wife scolded him, but he said

nothing and only sighed. Then they brought him a wooden

bowl for a few half-pence, out of which he had to eat.

They were once sitting thus when the little grandson of four

years old began to gather together some bits of wood upon the

ground. 'What are you doing there?' asked the father. 'I am

230

making a little trough,' answered the child, 'for father and

mother to eat out of when I am big.'

The man and his wife looked at each other for a while, and

presently began to cry. Then they took the old grandfather to

the table, and henceforth always let him eat with them, and

likewise said nothing if he did spill a little of anything.

(Grimms' Fairy Tales, p. 111)

34. Which of the following most accurately represents the theme of the passage?
    a. Respect your elders.
    b. Children will follow their parents' example.
    c. You reap what you sow.
    d. Loyalty will save your life.
    e. Life is not fair.

35. How is the content in this selection organized?
    a. Spatially
    b. Problem and solution
    c. Compare and contrast
    d. Order of importance
    e. Chronologically

36. Which character trait most accurately reflects the son and his wife in this story?
    a. Compassionate
    b. Understanding
    c. Cruel
    d. Impatient
    e. Loving

37. Where does the story take place?
    a. In the countryside
    b. In America
    c. In a house
    d. In a forest
    e. In a castle

38. Why do the son and his wife decide to let the old man sit at the table?
    a. Because they felt sorry for him
    b. Because their son told them to
    c. Because the old man would not stop crying
    d. Because they saw their own actions in their son
    e. Because he kept breaking his bowl

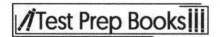

Questions 39 and 40 refer to the passage below:

I believe that this was the first moving line ever installed. The idea came in a general way from the overhead trolley that the Chicago packers use in dressing beef. We had previously assembled the fly-wheel magneto in the usual method. With one workman doing a complete job he could turn out from thirty-five to forty pieces in a nine-hour day, or about twenty minutes to an assembly. What he did alone was then spread into twenty-nine operations; that cut down the assembly time to thirteen minutes, ten seconds. Then we raised the height of the line eight inches—this was in 1914—and cut the time to seven minutes. Further experimenting with the speed that the work should move at cut the time down to five minutes. In short, the result is this: by the aid of scientific study one man is now able to do somewhat more than four did only a comparatively few years ago. That line established the efficiency of the method and we now use it everywhere. The assembling of the motor, formerly done by one man, is now divided into eighty-four operations—those men do the work that three times their number formerly did. In a short time we tried out the plan on the chassis.

Excerpt from *My Life and My Work* by Henry Ford, 1922

39. According to the passage, which one of the following best describes the primary economic benefit of this innovation?
    a. The innovation increased workers' ability to multitask.
    b. The innovation decreased labor costs per worker.
    c. The innovation increased productivity in terms of both speed and quantity.
    d. The innovation decreased the size of the industrial workforce.
    e. The innovation increased workers' wages.

40. According to the passage, how did this new method of production improve over time?
    a. The method improved by adopting the exact practices of other industries.
    b. The method improved after it was applied to the chassis.
    c. The method improved by continually increasing the number of operations per product.
    d. The method improved progressively through experimentation.
    e. The method improved using expert advice from a team of scientists.

Verbal Section

Synonyms

1. WEARY
    a. Tired
    b. Clothing
    c. Happy
    d. Hot
    e. Whiny

2. VAST
   a. Rapid
   b. Expansive
   c. Small
   d. Ocean
   e. Uniform

3. DEMONSTRATE
   a. Tell
   b. Show
   c. Build
   d. Complete
   e. Make

4. ORCHARD
   a. Flower
   b. Fruit
   c. Grove
   d. Peach
   e. Farm

5. TEXTILE
   a. Fabric
   b. Document
   c. Mural
   d. Ornament
   e. Knit

6. INSPIRE
   a. Motivate
   b. Impale
   c. Exercise
   d. Patronize
   e. Collaborate

7. NOMAD
   a. Munching
   b. Propose
   c. Wanderer
   d. Conscientious
   e. Blissful

8. MALEVOLENT
   a. Evil
   b. Concerned
   c. Maximum
   d. Cautious
   e. Crazy

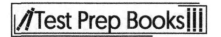

9. PERPLEXED
    a. Annoyed
    b. Vengeful
    c. Injured
    d. Confused
    e. Prepared

10. LYRICAL
    a. Whimsical
    b. Vague
    c. Fruitful
    d. Expressive
    e. Playful

11. IRATE
    a. Anger
    b. Knowledge
    c. Tired
    d. Confused
    e. Taciturn

12. LUXURIOUS
    a. Faded
    b. Bright
    c. Lavish
    d. Inconsiderate
    e. Overwhelming

13. IMMOBILE
    a. Fast
    b. Slow
    c. Eloquent
    d. Vivacious
    e. Sedentary

14. MENDACIOUS
    a. Earnest
    b. Bold
    c. Criminal
    d. Liar
    e. Humorous

15. CHIVALROUS
    a. Fierce
    b. Annoying
    c. Rude
    d. Dangerous
    e. Courteous

234

16. RETORT
   a. Conversation
   b. Jest
   c. Counter
   d. Flexible
   e. Erudite

17. SUBLIMINAL
   a. Subconscious
   b. Transportation
   c. Underground
   d. Substitute
   e. Penumbral

18. INCITE
   a. Understanding
   b. Illumination
   c. Rally
   d. Judgment
   e. Compose

19. MONIKER
   a. Name
   b. Mockery
   c. Umbrella
   d. Insult
   e. Burden

20. SERENDIPITOUS
   a. Creation
   b. Sympathy
   c. Unfortunate
   d. Calm
   e. Coincidental

21. OVERBEARING
   a. Neglect
   b. Overacting
   c. Clandestine
   d. Formidable
   e. Amicable

22. PREVENT
   a. Avert
   b. Rejoice
   c. Endow
   d. Fulfill
   e. Ensure

23. REPLENISH
    a. Falsify
    b. Hindsight
    c. Dwell
    d. Refresh
    e. Nominate

24. REGALE
    a. Remember
    b. Grow
    c. Outnumber
    d. Entertain
    e. Bore

25. ABATE
    a. Anger
    b. Forlorn
    c. Withdraw
    d. Excellent
    e. Crazed

26. OFFSPRING
    a. Bounce
    b. Parent
    c. Music
    d. Child
    e. Skip

27. PERMIT
    a. Law
    b. Parking
    c. Crab
    d. Jail
    e. Allow

28. WOMAN
    a. Man
    b. Lady
    c. Women
    d. Girl
    e. Mother

29. ROTATION
    a. Wheel
    b. Year
    c. Spin
    d. Flip
    e. Orbit

30. CONSISTENT
    a. Stubborn
    b. Contains
    c. Sticky
    d. Texture
    e. Steady

Verbal Analogies

31. Cow is to milk as
    a. Horse is to cow
    b. Egg is to chicken
    c. Chicken is to egg
    d. Glass is to milk
    e. Milk is to glass

32. Web is to spider as
    a. Arctic is to fox
    b. Living room is to den
    c. Den is to fox
    d. Tarantula is to spider
    e. Spider is to fly

33. Sad is to blue as
    a. Happy is to glad
    b. Cheerful is to yellow
    c. Glad is to smiling
    d. Happy is to laugh
    e. Excited is to calm

34. Door is to store as
    a. Money is to store
    b. Open is to close
    c. Frame is to house
    d. Deal is to wheel
    e. Door is to house

35. Dog is to veterinarian as
    a. Child is to daycare
    b. Baby is to mother
    c. Puppy is to dog
    d. Lion is to zookeeper
    e. Baby is to pediatrician

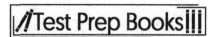

36. Cat is to paws as
   a. Giraffe is to neck
   b. Elephant is to ears
   c. Horse is to hooves
   d. Snake is to skin
   e. Turtle is to shell

37. Dancing is to rhythm as
   a. Singing is to pitch
   b. Essay is to brevity
   c. Sound is to loud
   d. Speaking is to speed
   e. Drum is to beat

38. Towel is to dry as
   a. Jacket is to cold
   b. Warm is to earmuffs
   c. Wet is to coat
   d. Hat is to cover
   e. Top is to hat

39. Books are to reading as
   a. Movies are to making
   b. Shows are to watching
   c. Poetry is to writing
   d. Scenes are to performing
   e. Concerts are to music

40. Cereal boxes are to rectangular prisms as
   a. Balls are to circles
   b. Cylinders are to cans
   c. Spokes are to wheels
   d. Globes are to spheres
   e. Squares are to cubes

41. Backpacks are to textbooks as
   a. Houses are to people
   b. Fences are to trees
   c. Plates are to food
   d. Chalkboards are to chalk
   e. Computers are to mice

42. Storm is to rainbow as
   a. Wind is to clouds
   b. Sunrise is to fog
   c. Morning is to breakfast
   d. Day is to night
   e. Sunset is to stars

238

43. Falcon is to mice as
    a. Giraffe is to leaves
    b. Zebra is to lion
    c. Tiger is to cat
    d. Antelope is to grasslands
    e. Bear is to omnivore

44. Car is to motorcycle as
    a. Plane is to wings
    b. Speedboat is to jet ski
    c. Sailboat is to steam train
    d. Bicycle is to roller skates
    e. Canoe is to oar

45. Mechanic is to repair as
    a. Mongoose is to cobra
    b. Rider is to bicycle
    c. Tree is to grow
    d. Food is to eaten
    e. Doctor is to heal

46. Whistle is to blow horn as
    a. View is to art
    b. Criticize is to literature
    c. Painting is to sculpture
    d. Painter is to paintbrush
    e. Art is to museum

47. Paddle is to boat as
    a. Doors are to unlock
    b. Garages are to cars
    c. Lights are to illuminate
    d. Keys are to piano
    e. Bikes are to wheels

48. Monotonous is to innovative as
    a. Gorgeous is to beautiful
    b. Ancient is to archaic
    c. Loquacious is to silent
    d. Sturdy is to fortified
    e. Spectacular is to grandiose

49. Mountain is to peak as
    a. River is to bed
    b. Hill is to valley
    c. Current is to ocean
    d. Cone is to volcano
    e. Wave is to crest

239

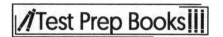

50. Ambiguous is to indecisive as
    a. Uncertain is to indefinite
    b. Doubtful is to certain
    c. Flippant is to engaged
    d. Brave is to fearful
    e. Positive is to helpful

51. Fluent is to communication as
    a. Crater is to catastrophe
    b. Gourmet is to cooking
    c. Ink is to pen
    d. Crow is to raven
    e. Whistle is to whistler

52. Winter is to autumn as
    a. Halloween is to Christmas
    b. Snow is to melt
    c. Summer is to spring
    d. March is to April
    e. Spring is to blooming

53. Penguin is to lemur as
    a. Eagle is to howler monkey
    b. Pelican is to osprey
    c. Slug is to warthog
    d. Zebra is to lion
    e. Antelope is to reindeer

54. Fiberglass is to surfboard as
    a. Bamboo is to panda
    b. Capital is to D.C.
    c. Copper is to penny
    d. Flint is to knapping
    e. Wind is to windmill

55. Myth is to explain as
    a. Narrative is to genre
    b. Read is to enjoy
    c. Story is to setting
    d. Laughter is to funny
    e. Joke is to amuse

56. Clock is to time as
    a. Ruler is to length
    b. Jet is to speed
    c. Alarm is to sleep
    d. Drum is to beat
    e. Watch is to wrist

57. Wire is to electricity as
    a. Power is to lamp
    b. Pipe is to water
    c. Fire is to heat
    d. Heat is to fire
    e. Water is to pipe

58. Executive branch is to president as:
    a. Judicial branch is to Supreme Court justice
    b. Legislative branch is to judge
    c. Cabinet is to senator
    d. Federal branch is to lawyer
    e. Congress is to congressmen

59. Flour is to cake as
    a. Spoon is to soup
    b. Oven is to casserole
    c. Yeast is to bread
    d. Salad is to lettuce
    e. Hot fudge is to ice cream

60. Grief is to sadness as
    a. Celebration is to birthday
    b. Merriment is to happiness
    c. Vexation is to reconciliation
    d. Tears are to crying
    e. Joy is to emotion

Quantitative Reasoning 2

1. A square field has an area of 400 square feet. What is its perimeter?
    a. 100 feet
    b. 80 feet
    c. $40\sqrt{2}$ feet
    d. 40 feet
    e. 2 feet

2. $\frac{5}{3} \times \frac{7}{6} =$
    a. $\frac{3}{5}$

    b. $\frac{18}{3}$

    c. $\frac{45}{31}$

    d. $\frac{17}{6}$

    e. $\frac{35}{18}$

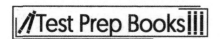
3. One apple costs $2. One papaya costs $3. If Samantha spends $35 and gets 15 pieces of fruit, how many papayas did she buy?
   a. 3 papayas
   b. 4 papayas
   c. 5 papayas
   d. 6 papayas
   e. 7 papayas

4. If $x^2 - 6 = 30$, then one possible value for x is:
   a. -6
   b. -4
   c. 3
   d. 5
   e. 8

5. A cube has a side length of 6 inches. What is its volume?
   a. 6 cubic inches
   b. 36 cubic inches
   c. 144 cubic inches
   d. 200 cubic inches
   e. 216 cubic inches

6. A square has a side length of 4 inches. A triangle has a base of 2 inches and a height of 8 inches. What is the total area of the square and triangle?
   a. 24 square inches
   b. 28 square inches
   c. 32 square inches
   d. 36 square inches
   e. 40 square inches

7. $-\frac{1}{3}\sqrt{81} =$
   a. -9
   b. -3
   c. 0
   d. 3
   e. 9

8. Simplify $(2x - 3)(4x + 2)$.
   a. $8x^2 - 8x - 6$
   b. $6x^2 + 8x - 5$
   c. $-4x^2 - 8x - 1$
   d. $4x^2 - 4x - 6$
   e. $5x^2 + 4x + 3$

9. $\frac{11}{6} - \frac{3}{8} =$

    a. $\frac{5}{4}$

    b. $\frac{51}{36}$

    c. $\frac{35}{24}$

    d. $\frac{3}{2}$

    e. $\frac{39}{16}$

10. Which is closest to 17.8×9.9?

    a.   140
    b.   180
    c.   200
    d.   350
    e.   400

11. 6 is 30% of what number?

    a.   18
    b.   22
    c.   24
    d.   26
    e.   20

12. $3\frac{2}{3} - 1\frac{4}{5} =$

    a. $1\frac{13}{15}$

    b. $\frac{14}{15}$

    c. $2\frac{2}{3}$

    d. $\frac{4}{5}$

    e. $1\frac{2}{3}$

13. What is $\frac{420}{98}$ rounded to the nearest integer?

    a.   7
    b.   3
    c.   5
    d.   6
    e.   4

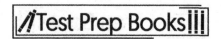

14. Which of the following values is the largest?
 a. 0.45
 b. 0.096
 c. 0.3
 d. 0.313
 e. 0.078

15. 20 is 40% of what number?
 a. 50
 b. 8
 c. 200
 d. 5,000
 e. 80

16. Which of the following expressions is equivalent to this expression?

$$\frac{2xy^2 + 4x - 8y}{16xy}$$

 a. $\frac{y}{8} + \frac{1}{4y} - \frac{1}{2x}$

 b. $8xy + 4y - 2x$

 c. $xy^2 + \frac{x}{4y} - \frac{1}{2x}$

 d. $\frac{y}{8} + 4y - 8y$

 e. $\frac{y}{8} - 4y + 8y$

17. Simplify the following expression:

$$(3x + 5)(x - 8)$$

 a. $3x^2 - 19x - 40$
 b. $4x - 19x - 13$
 c. $3x^2 - 19x + 40$
 d. $3x^2 + 5x - 3$
 e. $4x - 5x + 9$

18. It costs Chad $12 to produce three necklaces. If he can sell each necklace for $20, how much profit would he make if he sold 60 necklaces?
 a. $240
 b. $360
 c. $960
 d. $1,200
 e. $720

19. This chart indicates how many sales of CDs, vinyl records, and MP3 downloads occurred over the last year. Approximately what percentage of the total sales was from CDs?

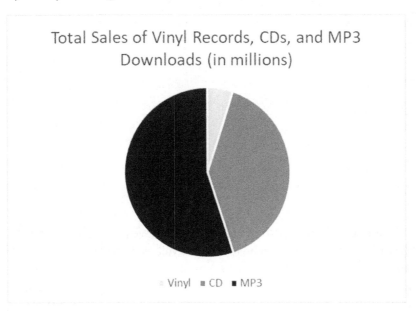

Total Sales of Vinyl Records, CDs, and MP3 Downloads (in millions)

Vinyl ■ CD ■ MP3

- a. 55%
- b. 25%
- c. 40%
- d. 5%
- e. 75%

20. A family purchases a vehicle in 2005 for $20,000. In 2010, they decide to sell it for a newer model. They are able to sell the car for $8,000. By what percentage did the value of the family's car drop?
- a. 40%
- b. 68%
- c. 60%
- d. 33%
- e. 67%

21. On May 1, 2010, a couple purchased a house for $100,000. On September 1, 2016, the couple sold the house for $93,000 so they could purchase a bigger one to start a family. How many months did they own the house?
- a. 76 months
- b. 54 months
- c. 85 months
- d. 93 months
- e. 72 months

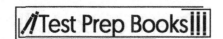

22. In an office, there are 50 workers. A total of 60% of the workers are women. 50% of the women are wearing skirts. If no men wear skirts, how many workers are wearing skirts?
    a. 12 workers
    b. 15 workers
    c. 16 workers
    d. 20 workers
    e. 21 workers

23. 32 is 25% of what number?
    a. 64
    b. 128
    c. 12.65
    d. 8
    e. 155

24. A piggy bank contains 12 dollars' worth of nickels. A nickel weighs 5 grams, and the empty piggy bank weighs 1,050 grams. What is the total weight of the full piggy bank?
    a. 1,110 grams
    b. 1,200 grams
    c. 2,150 grams
    d. 2,250 grams
    e. 2,500 grams

25. Last year, the New York City area received approximately $27\frac{3}{4}$ inches of snow. The Denver area received approximately three times as much snow as New York City. How much snow fell in Denver?
    a. $71\frac{3}{4}$ inches

    b. $27\frac{1}{4}$ inches

    c. $89\frac{1}{4}$ inches

    d. $83\frac{1}{4}$ inches

    e. $64\frac{3}{4}$ inches

Answer Explanations #2

Quantitative Reasoning 1

1. E: Dividing by 100 means shifting the decimal point of the numerator to the left by 2. The result is 6.6, which rounds to 7.

2. A: First, set up the division problem.

$$\frac{5}{13} \div \frac{25}{169}$$

Flip the second fraction and multiply.

$$\frac{5}{13} \times \frac{169}{25}$$

Simplify and reduce with cross-multiplication.

$$\frac{1}{1} \times \frac{13}{5}$$

Multiply across the top and across the bottom to solve.

$$\frac{1 \times 13}{1 \times 5} = \frac{13}{5}$$

3. A: This problem can be multiplied as 588×32, except at the end, the decimal point needs to be moved three places to the left (because in the problem, we have a total of three digits after decimal points: 88 and 2). Performing the multiplication will give 18,816, and moving the decimal point over three places results in 18.816.

4. B: Choice *B* is correct because $3^2 + 4^2$ is $9 + 16$, which is 25. The square root of 25 is 5. Choice *A* is not the correct answer because that is $3 + 4$. Choice *C* is not the correct answer because that is stopping at $3^2 + 4^2$ is $9 + 16$, which is 25. Choice *D* is not the correct answer because that is 3×4. Choice *E* is incorrect because that is $(3 + 4)^2$.

5. B: 300 miles in four hours is $\frac{300}{4} = 75$ miles per hour. In 1.5 hours, the car will go 1.5×75 miles, or 112.5 miles.

6. C: One apple/orange pair costs $3 total. Jan therefore bought $\frac{90}{3} = 30$ total pairs, and hence 30 oranges.

7. C: The volume of a box with rectangular sides is equal to the length times width times height, so:

$$5 \times 6 \times 3 = 90 \text{ cubic feet}$$

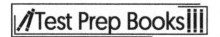

8. E: First, the train's journey in the real world is:

$$3 \text{ h} \times 50\frac{\text{mi}}{\text{h}} = 150 \text{ mi}$$

On the map, 1 inch corresponds to 10 miles, so that is equivalent to:

$$150 \text{ mi} \times \frac{1 \text{ in}}{10 \text{ mi}} = 15 \text{ in}$$

Therefore, the start and end points are 15 inches apart on the map.

9. B: The total trip time is:

$$1 + 3.5 + 0.5 = 5 \text{ hours}$$

The total time driving is:

$$1 + 0.5 = 1.5 \text{ hours}$$

So, the fraction of time spent driving is $\frac{1.5}{5}$, or $\frac{3}{10}$. To convert this to a percentage, multiply the top and bottom by 10 to make the denominator 100. We find $\frac{3}{10} \times \frac{10}{10} = \frac{30}{100}$. Since the denominator is 100, the numerator is our percentage: 30%.

10. B: This problem can be solved using the Pythagorean theorem. The triangle has a hypotenuse of 15 and one leg of 12. These values can be substituted into the Pythagorean formula to yield:

$$12^2 + b^2 = 15^2$$

$$144 + b^2 = 225$$

$$81 = b^2$$

$$b = 9$$

In this problem, b is represented by x, so $x = 9$ is the correct answer.

11. D: The formula for the volume of a cube is $V = s^3$, where V is the volume and s is the side length. Here, $s = 5$ cm, so $V = (5 \text{ cm})^3 = 125 \text{ cm}^3$.

12. B: The tip is not taxed, so he pays 5% tax only on the $10. To find 5% of $10, calculate $0.05 \times \$10 = \$0.50$. Add up $10 + $0.50 + $2 to get $12.50.

13. C: Divide the total amount by the number of days: $\frac{150}{4} = 37.5$. She needs to save an average of $37.50 per day.

14. C: The number of days can be found by taking the total amount Bernard needs to make and dividing it by the amount he earns per day:

$$\frac{300}{80} = \frac{30}{8} = \frac{15}{4} = 3.75$$

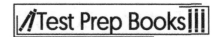

Bernard will need to work four days since he is only working full days and three days is not enough time.

15. A: The value went up by:

$$\$165,000 - \$150,000 = \$15,000$$

Out of $150,000, this is:

$$\frac{15,000}{150,000} = \frac{1}{10}$$

If we multiply the top and bottom by 10 to give us a denominator of 100, the result is $\frac{10}{100}$, or 10%.

16. B: The journey will be:

$$5 \times 3 = 15 \text{ miles}$$

A car traveling at 60 miles per hour is traveling at 1 mile per minute. The resulting equation would be:

$$\frac{15 \text{ mi}}{1 \text{ mi/min}} = 15 \text{ min}$$

Therefore, it will take 15 minutes to make the journey.

17. A: Taylor's total income is $20,000 + $10,000 = $30,000. 15 percent as a fraction is $\frac{15}{100} = \frac{3}{20}$. So:

$$\frac{3}{20} \times \$30,000 = \frac{\$90,000}{20} = \frac{\$9,000}{2}$$

$$\frac{\$9,000}{2} = \$4,500$$

18. B: Since the answer will be in cubic feet rather than inches, start by converting from inches to feet for the dimensions of the box. There are 12 inches per foot, so the box is $\frac{24}{12} = 2$ ft wide, $\frac{18}{12} = 1.5$ ft deep, and $\frac{12}{12} = 1$ ft high. The volume is the product of these three together:

$$2 \times 1.5 \times 1 = 3 \text{ cubic feet}$$

19. D: Kristen bought 4 DVDs, which would total a cost of:

$$4 \times 15 = \$60$$

She spent a total of $100, so she spent $100 - $60 = $40 on CDs. Since they cost $10 each, she must have purchased $\frac{40}{10} = 4$ CDs.

20. C: The formula for the perimeter of a rectangle is $P = 2l + 2w$, where P is the perimeter, l is the length, and w is the width. The first step is to substitute all of the data into the formula:

$$36 = 2(12) + 2w$$

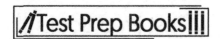

Simplify by multiplying 2×12:

$$36 = 24 + 2w$$

Simplifying this further by subtracting 24 on each side, which gives:

$$36 - 24 = 24 - 24 + 2w$$

$$12 = 2w$$

Divide by 2:

$$6 = w$$

The width is 6 cm. Remember to test this answer by substituting this value into the original formula:

$$36 = 2(12) + 2(6)$$

21. D: Start by taking a common denominator of 30.

$$\frac{14}{15} = \frac{28}{30}, \frac{3}{5} = \frac{18}{30}, \frac{1}{30} = \frac{1}{30}$$

Add and subtract the numerators for the next step and simplify.

$$\frac{28}{30} + \frac{18}{30} - \frac{1}{30}$$

$$\frac{28 + 18 - 1}{30} = \frac{45}{30} = \frac{3}{2}$$

22. A: From the second equation, add x to both sides and subtract 1 from both sides:

$$-x + 3y + x - 1 = 1 + x - 1$$

With the result of $3y - 1 = x$, substitute this into the first equation and get:

$$3(3y - 1) + 2y = 8 \text{ or } 9y - 3 + 2y = 8$$

$$11y = 11$$

$$y = 1$$

Putting this into $3y - 1 = x$ gives $3(1) - 1 = x$, or $x = 2$. This makes the final answer $x = 2, y = 1$.

23. C: The square root of 16 is 4, so this expression simplifies to:

$$\frac{1}{2}\sqrt{16} = \frac{1}{2}(4) = 2$$

Therefore, Choice *C* is correct.

24. E: The easiest way to approach this problem is to factor out a 2 from each term.

$$2x^2 - 8 = 2(x^2 - 4)$$

250

Use the formula $x^2 - y^2 = (x + y)(x - y)$ to factor:

$$x^2 - 4 = x^2 - 2^2 = (x + 2)(x - 2)$$

So,

$$2(x^2 - 4) = 2(x + 2)(x - 2)$$

25. B: The total of the interior angles of a triangle must be 180°. The sum of the first two is 105°, so the remaining is:

$$180° - 105° = 75°$$

Reading Comprehension

1. A: Choice *A* is correct because there is evidence in the passage to support it, specifically when he mentions catching "a mess of black-fish, which you couldn't buy in New York for a dollar—large fat fellows, with meat on their bones that it takes a pretty long fork to stick through." There is no evidence to support the other answer choices.

2. B: Persuasive is the correct answer because the author is clearly trying to convey the point that history education is very important. Choice *A* is incorrect because expository writing is more informative and less emotional. Choice *C* is incorrect because narrative writing involves storytelling. Choice *D* is incorrect because this is a piece of prose, not poetry.

3. B: The passage begins by describing Carver's childhood fascination with painting and later returns to this point when it states that at the end of his career, "Carver returned to his first love of art." For this reason, all the other answer choices are incorrect.

4. B: The passage indicates that Annabelle has a fear of going outside into the daylight. Thus, *heliophobia* must refer to a fear of bright lights or sunlight.

5. C: We are looking for an inference—a conclusion that is reached on the basis of evidence and reasoning—from the passage that will likely explain why the famous children's author did not achieve her usual success with the new genre (despite the book's acclaim). Choice *A* is wrong because the statement is false according to the passage. Choice *B* is wrong because, although the passage says the author has a graduate degree on the subject, it would be an unrealistic leap to infer that she is the foremost expert on Antebellum America. Choice *D* is wrong because there is nothing in the passage to lead us to infer that people generally prefer a children's series to historical fiction. In contrast, Choice *C* can be logically inferred since the passage speaks of the great success of the children's series and the declaration that the fame of the author's name causes the children's books to "fly off the shelves." Thus, we can infer that she did not receive any bump from her name since she published the historical novel under a pseudonym, which makes Choice *C* correct.

6. D: Outspending other countries on education could have other benefits, but there is no reference to this in the passage, so Choice *A* is incorrect. Choice *B* is incorrect because the author does not mention corruption. Choice *C* is incorrect because there is nothing in the passage stating that the tests are not genuinely representative. Choice *D* is accurate because spending more money has not brought success. The United States already spends the most money, and the country is not excelling on these tests. Choice *D* is the correct answer.

251

7. C: Despite the opposite stances in Passages 1 and 2, both authors establish that cell phones are a strong part of culture. In Passage 1 the author states, "Today's student is already strongly rooted in technology." In Passage 2 the author states, "Students are comfortable with cell phones." The author of Passage 2 states that cell phones have a "time and place." The author of Passage 2 would disagree with the statement that teachers should incorporate cell phones into curriculum whenever possible. While Passage 2 implies that cell phones are useful only when an experienced teacher uses them properly, the author in Passage 1 says cell phones are "indispensable." In other words, no teacher can do without them. The statement from Choice *D* is not supported by either passage. Even though the author in the second passage is more cautionary, the author states, "This can prove advantageous if done correctly." Therefore, there is a possibility that a classroom can run properly with cell phones.

8. B: Both passages mention the at-bats with runners in scoring position. The reporter asserts that the team lost due to the team failing to get such a hit. In contrast, the coach identifies several other reasons for the loss, including fielding and pitching errors. Additionally, the coach disagrees that the team even needed a hit in those situations.

9. C: The passage is told in chronological order; it details the steps the family took to adopt their dog. The narrator mentions that Robin's physical exam and lab work confirmed she was healthy before discussing that they brought her to the vet to evaluate her health. It is illogical that lab work would confirm good health prior to an appointment with the vet when, presumably, the lab work would be collected.

10. B: The main point of this passage is to show how a tornado forms. Choice *A* is incorrect because while the passage does mention that tornadoes are dangerous, it is not the main focus of the passage. While thunderstorms are mentioned, they are not compared to tornadoes, so Choice *C* is incorrect. Choice *D* is incorrect because the passage does not discuss what to do in the event of a tornado.

11. D: The passage directly states that the larger sensor is the main difference between the two cameras. Choices *A* and *B* may be true, but these answers do not identify the major difference between the two cameras. Choice *C* states the opposite of what the paragraph suggests is the best option for amateur photographers, so it is incorrect.

12. D: An actuary assesses risks and sets insurance premiums. While an actuary does work in insurance, the passage does not suggest that actuaries have any affiliation with hospitalists or working in a hospital, so all other choices are incorrect.

13. C: The purpose of this passage is to explain how the digestive system works. Choice *A* focuses only on the liver, which is a small part of the process and not the focus of the paragraph. Choice *B* is off-track because the passage does not mention healthy foods. Choices *D* and *E* each only focus on one part of the digestive system.

14. A: The passage focuses mainly on the problems of hard water. Choice *B* is incorrect because calcium is not good for pipes and hard surfaces. The passage does not say anything about whether water softeners are easy to install, so Choice *C* is incorrect. Choice *D* is also incorrect because the passage does offer other solutions besides vinegar.

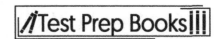

15. C: Brand-X Management uses a proven technique to deliver bad news: sandwich it between good. The first paragraph extolls the virtue of its employees: "Brand-X wouldn't be where it is today without the hard work of countless unsung heroes and is truly blessed to have such an amazing staff." The management of Brand-X is proud of its employees. The second paragraph delivers the bad news. Along with the announcement of the termination of the childcare program, Brand-X management provides several reasons why, such as they're "subject to the same economic forces as any other company" and their decision "allowed Brand-X to still stay competitive while not reducing staff." The passage implies that they didn't want to—they had to. The tone of the second paragraph is apologetic. The third paragraph ends on a positive note. Management reminds staff that other services—employee rewards, vacation and sick days, retirement options, volunteer days—have not been impacted, and on Friday employees will have a luncheon and be allowed to wear jeans. This passage is there to not only remind employees why it's still beneficial to work there but also to provide evidence that Brand-X wants its employees to be happy by hosting luncheons and letting employees wear jeans. It's designed to reduce their hostilities about cancelling the program or, in other words, placate or appease them.

16. B: "Unfortunately, Brand-X is subject to the same economic forces as any other company." This line was most likely provided to redirect blame from Brand-X to outside forces. Throughout the second paragraph, Brand-X consistently defends its decision to cancel the childcare program. Based on the context of the paragraph, it's continually implied that management was left with no choice. While it might be true that Brand-X is no worse than other companies (others are forced to do the same), this statement supports the idea that it's beyond their control, a message reiterated throughout the paragraph. Nowhere in the paragraph does Brand-X encourage employees to look for work elsewhere. In fact, management does the opposite by reminding employees why they want to continue working there: employee rewards, vacation and sick days, retirement options, and volunteer days. The tone of the passage is not intimidating. No threats are made, implied or otherwise. For example, when management makes reference to reducing staff, it's described as an undesirable choice, not a viable option. It does not appear that the company is looking for input from staff concerning this decision as it appears the decision has already been made and is final.

17. C: The passage is narrated in third person omniscient point of view. We know this because the story starts out with us knowing something that the character does not know: that her husband has died. Mrs. Mallard eventually comes to know this, but we as readers know this information before it is broken to her. In third person limited, Choice *D*, we would only see and know what Mrs. Mallard herself knew, and we would find out the news of her husband's death when she found out the news, not before.

18. A: The irony in this story is called situational irony, which means the situation that takes place is different than what the audience anticipated. At the beginning of the story, we see Mrs. Mallard react with a burst of grief to her husband's death. However, once she's alone, she begins to contemplate her future and says the word "free" over and over. This is quite a different reaction from Mrs. Mallard than what readers expected from the beginning of the story.

19. E: Liberation from marriage and cultural limitations are common themes of both texts. The other answer choices may be touched upon in one or both of the texts, but they are not the central themes of both texts. *The Awakening* is the story of a woman who awakens slowly to her desire to live a life true to herself. She craves freedom from convention and in search of this, creates conflict with those around her. "The Story of an Hour" is also about craving freedom from convention (from marriage) and is an instant awakening to this desire instead of a progressive one.

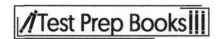

20. E: A summary is a brief explanation of the main point of a story. The story mostly focuses on Mrs. Mallard and her reaction to her husband's death, especially in the room when she's alone and contemplating the present and future. Choice *B* is briefly mentioned in the story; however it is not the main focus of the story. Choice *D* is also mentioned in the story, but it is only a small part of the story.

21. A: The word *patronage* most nearly means auspices, which means protection or support. Choice *B*, *aberration*, means abnormality and does not make sense within the context of the sentence. Choice *C*, *acerbic*, means sour or sharply critical, and it also does not make sense in the sentence. Choices *D* and *E*, *adulation* and *admiration*, both have a positive meaning, and thus do not fit with the word *condescending* in the sentence.

22. D: *Working man* is most closely aligned with Choice *D*, *bourgeois.* In the context of the speech, the word *bourgeois* means working or middle class. Choice *A*, *athlete*, does suggest someone who works hard, but it does not make sense in this context. Choice *B*, *viscount*, is a European title used to describe a specific degree of nobility. Choice *C*, *entrepreneur*, is a person who operates their own business. Choice *E*, *champion*, is someone who has succeeded against all others in a particular field.

23. C: In the context of the speech, the term *working man* most closely correlates with Choice *C*, a working man is someone who works for wages among the middle class. Choice *A* is not mentioned in the passage and is off-topic. Choice *B* may be true in some cases, but it does not reflect the sentiment described for the term *working man* in the passage. Choice *D* is not a definition, and the topics of the field, factory, and screen are not mentioned in the passage. Choice *E* is incorrect because a working man in this context is not a member of the nobility.

24. E: *Enterprise* most closely means cause. Choices *A*, *B*, *C*, and *D* are all related to the term *enterprise*. However, Dickens speaks of a cause here, not a company, courage, game, or plan. "He will stand by such an enterprise" is a call to stand by a cause to enable the working man to have a certain autonomy over his own economic standing. The very first paragraph ends with the statement that the working man "shall...have a share in the management of an institution which is designed for his benefit."

25. B: Recall from the first paragraph that the speaker is there to "accompany [the audience] ... through one of my little Christmas books," making him an author there to entertain the crowd with his own writing. The speech preceding the reading is the passage itself, and, as the tone indicates, it is a serious speech addressing the working man. Although the passage speaks of employers and employees, the speaker himself is not an employer of the audience, so Choice *A* is incorrect. Choice *C* is also incorrect, as the salutation is not used ironically, but sincerely, as the speech addresses the wellbeing of the crowd. Choice *D* is incorrect because the speech is given by a writer, not a politician. Choice *E* is incorrect because the friendly language does not indicate that the speaker is trying to demonstrate his expert knowledge.

26. B: Choice *A* is incorrect because that is the speaker's first desire, not his second. Choices *C* and *D* are tricky because the language of both of these is mentioned after the word *second*. However, the speaker doesn't get to the second wish until the next sentence. Choices *C* and *D* are merely preliminary remarks before the statement of the main clause. Choice *E* is the opposite of what the speaker is trying to put forward.

27. E: The central idea of this passage is to introduce certain insects that transition from water to air. Choice *A* is incorrect because while certain aspects of insect life cycle are mentioned, that is not the central message of the passage. Choice *B* is incorrect because although the passage talks about gills, it is

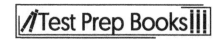

not the central idea of the passage. Choices *C* and *D* are incorrect because the passage does not define insect breathing or invite readers to participate in insect preservation. Rather, the passage serves as an introduction to stoneflies, dragonflies, and mayflies and their transition from water to air.

28. C: The term *moult* refers to the act of shedding part or all of the outer shell. Choices *A, B, D,* and *E* are incorrect.

29. B: Notice how the first paragraph goes into detail describing how insects are able to breathe air. The second paragraph acts as a contrast to the first by stating, "[i]t is of great interest to find that, nevertheless, a number of insects spend much of their time under water." Watch for transition words such as *nevertheless* to help find what type of passage you're dealing with.

30: C: Instars are the phases between two periods of molting, and the text explains when these transitions occur. The preparatory stages are acted out in the water, while the last stage is in the air. Choices *A, B, D,* and *E* are all incorrect.

31. C: Overall, the author presents us with information on the subject. One moment where personal interest is depicted is when the author states, "It is of great interest to find that, nevertheless, a number of insects spend much of their time under water."

32. A: The speaker is trying to convey that the audience should perpetuate the ideals of freedom that the soldiers died fighting for. Lincoln doesn't address any of the topics outlined in Choices *B, C, D,* or *E.* Therefore, Choice *A* is the correct answer.

33. A: Choice *A* is correct because Lincoln's intention was to memorialize the soldiers who had fallen as a result of war as well as celebrate those who had put their lives in danger for the sake of their country. Choices *B* and *C* are incorrect because Lincoln's speech was supposed to foster a sense of pride among the members of the audience while connecting them to the soldiers' experiences. Choice *D* is incorrect because Lincoln's comparison does not suggest that the dedication ceremony was inappropriate but rather that the soldiers' great sacrifice was worth remembering. Choice *E* is incorrect because Lincoln does not use this speech to try and lay blame for the soldiers' death on anyone or any party.

34. B: Choice *B* fits most appropriately with the primary purpose because the son and wife realize that, when they grow old, their child is planning on treating them the same cruel way that they treat the grandfather. Choice *A* is incorrect because even though the parents are treating the grandfather with disrespect, the purpose of the passage is more about how children respond to their parents' actions. Choice *C*, to "reap what you sow," means that there are repercussions for every action, yet the parents receive no punishment other than their own sorrow. Choice *D* is incorrect because, even though it may be argued that the boy is being loyal to his grandfather, this does not fit with the primary purpose. Choice *E* is incorrect because although the parents were not being fair to the elder, the story does not end there.

35. E: Choice *E* is correct because it follows a series of events that happen in order, one right after the other. First the grandfather spills his food, then his son puts him in a corner, then the child makes a trough for his parents to eat out of when he's older, and finally the parents welcome the old man back to the table. Choice *A* is incorrect because a spatial text structure involves describing a room or space. Choice *B* is incorrect. Although it could be argued that the way they treat the old man is a problem, there really isn't a solution to the problem, even though they stop treating him badly. Also, problem and solution styles generally do not follow a chronological timeline. Choice *C* is incorrect because events in

Answer Explanations #2

the passage are not compared and contrasted; this is not a primary organizational structure of the passage. Choice *D* is incorrect because there is no language to indicate that one person or event is more important than the other.

36. C: Choice *C* is correct because it condenses the terrible actions of the son and his wife into a single, appropriate word. Choice *A* is incorrect because although they show him compassion in the end, it is only out of a selfish realization that they will be treated the same way when they are older. Choice *B* is incorrect because the son and his wife neither understand nor care about the grandfather's aging troubles. Choice *D* may be tempting to pick as they are impatient with him, but it is not the best answer. People can be impatient without being cruel. Choice *E* is incorrect because the son and his wife show the grandfather very little love.

37. C: Choice *A* is incorrect as there is no descriptive language to indicate that they are in the countryside. Choice *B* is incorrect because the passage has no language or descriptions to indicate they are in America. Choice *C* is correct because the setting contains elements of a house: a table, a stove, and a corner. Choice *D* may be tempting as there is mention of "bits of wood upon the ground," but as there are no other elements of a forest in the story, this is not the correct answer. Choice *E* is incorrect as the story does not indicate in any way that the setting is a castle.

38. D: The parents allow the old man to sit at the table because their son starts to make them a trough, so their motivation in letting him eat at the table is not because they feel sorry for him but rather because they don't want their son to treat them that way when they are old. This makes Choice *A* incorrect. Their son did not tell them to let the old man sit at the table, so Choice *B* is incorrect. In the story, it mentions that even after the old man has eyes full of tears, the wife gave him a cheap wooden bowl to eat out of, so clearly his crying did not make them stop treating him badly, making Choice *C* incorrect. Choice *D* is correct because the parents let the old man sit at the table as a result of the boy mimicking their behavior. Choice *E* is incorrect; one of the reasons the grandfather was not allowed to sit at the table was because he kept spilling and breaking his bowl.

39. C: The innovation's primary economic benefit was to increase productivity in terms of both speed and quantity. The passage contains several examples of how the assembly increased the production of fly-wheel magnetos and motors. For example, at the end of the passage, Ford claims that the assembly line tripled the productivity for motors. Thus, Choice *C* is the correct answer. The innovation is that each worker is assigned one single operation to be completed on every product, which is the opposite of multitasking. So, Choice *A* is incorrect. Although the innovation might have decreased labor costs by standardizing tasks, the passage doesn't reference labor costs. Therefore, Choice *B* is incorrect. Choice *D* is the second-best answer choice. Ford mentions that men can perform three times the amount of work, but it's unclear whether this means the workforce decreased. In other words, the workforce could've remained the same or even increased to support mass production. As such, Choice *D* is incorrect. Choice *E* is incorrect because the workers' wages are not mentioned in the passage.

40. D: The method improved progressively through experimentation. Ford describes how he first got the idea from the overhead trolley used by Chicago beef packers and then they later elevated the height of the assembly line. In addition, the passage explicitly references "experimenting with the speed" of the line and making use of "scientific study." Thus, Choice *D* is the correct answer. Choice *A* is the second best answer choice because the Chicago beef packing industry influenced Ford. However, Ford claims it was only loosely based on the beef industry's overhead trolley, and he repeatedly describes experimenting with the height and speed. So, Choice *A* is incorrect. The passage ends with Ford stating his intention to test the new method on a chassis, which is the automobile's frame. As such, the chassis

256

This material is provided for exam preparation purposes only and does not indicate an endorsement of any specific scientific, political, or religious point of view. © TPB Publishing. You have been licensed one copy of this document for personal use only. Any other reproduction or redistribution is strictly prohibited. All rights reserved.

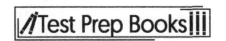

didn't improve the method as described in the passage, so Choice B is incorrect. Choice C is incorrect because the increased number of operations was a consequence of Ford's experimentation; the method didn't improve simply because the number of operations increased. So, Choice C is incorrect. Choice E is incorrect because a team of scientists did not assist in improving the method.

Verbal Section

Synonyms

1. A: *Weary* most closely means tired. Someone who is weary and tired may be whiny, but they do not necessarily mean the same thing.

2. B: Something that is vast is far-reaching and expansive. Choice D, *ocean*, may be described as vast, but the word alone doesn't mean vast. The heavens or skies may also be described as vast. Someone's imagination or vocabulary can also be vast.

3. B: To demonstrate something means to show it. The word *demonstration* comes from demonstrate, and a demonstration is a modeling or show-and-tell type of example that is usually visual.

4. C: An orchard is most like a grove because both are areas like plantations that grow different kinds of fruit. Peach is a type of fruit that may be grown in an orchard, but it is not a synonym for *orchard*. Many citrus fruits are grown in groves, but either word can be used to describe many fruit-bearing trees in one area. Choice E, *farm*, may have an orchard or grove on the property, but they are not the same thing, and many farms do not grow fruit trees.

5. A: *Textile* is another word for fabric. The most confusing alternative choice in this case is *knit* because some textiles are knit. However, *textile* and *knit* are not synonyms, and plenty of textiles are not knit.

6. A: If someone is inspired, they are motivated to do something. Someone who is an inspiration motivates others to follow their example.

7. C: Nomadic tribes are those who, throughout history and even today, prefer to wander their lands instead of settling in any specific place. *Wanderer* best describes these people.

8. A: *Malevolent* literally means bad or evil-minded. The clue is also in the Latin root *mal-*, which translates to bad.

9. D: *Perplexed* means baffled or puzzled, which are synonymous with confused.

10. D: *Lyrical* is used to refer to something being poetic or song-like, characterized by showing enormous imagination and description. While the context of lyrical can be playful or even whimsical, the best choice is expressive, since whatever emotion lyrical may be used to convey in its context will be expressive in nature.

11. A: *Irate* means being in a state of anger. Clearly this is a negative word that can be paired with another word in kind. The closest word to match this is obviously anger. Research would also reveal that *irate* comes from the Latin *ira*, which means anger.

12. C: *Lavish* is a synonym for *luxurious*. Both words describe elaborate, elegant lifestyles and/or settings.

13. E: *Immobile* means being unable to move. The two best selections are sedentary and slow. However, slow still implies some form of motion, whereas sedentary has the connotation of complete inactivity for a significant period of time.

14. D: *Mendacious* describes dishonesty or lying in several ways. This is another word of classical lineage. *Mendacio* in Latin means *liar*. While *liar* lacks the Latin root, the meanings fit.

15. E: *Chivalrous* reflects showing respect and courtesy toward others, particularly women.

16. C: *Retort* is a verb that means to answer back, usually in a sharp manner. This term embodies the idea of a response, emphasized by the *re-* prefix meaning back or again. While a retort can be used in a conversation or as a jest, neither term embodies the idea of addressing someone again. *Counter*, however, means to respond in opposition when used as a verb.

17. A: *Subliminal* and *subconscious* share the Latin prefix *sub-*, meaning under or below, or more commonly used when talking about messages the sender doesn't want the receiver to consciously take note of. The word *subliminal* means beneath the consciousness. Thus, subconscious is the perfect match.

18. C: Although *incite* usually has negative connotations, leaders can incite their followers to benevolent actions as well. In both cases, people rally to support a cause.

19. A: While a moniker commonly refers to a title, this is technically a designated name. Monikers can be mockeries, insults, and/or burdens, but none of these are direct forms of a title or identification.

20. E: Events that occur through serendipity happen purely by chance. *Serendipitous* conveys the idea of something unplanned yet potentially desirable. *Coincidental* is defined as happening by chance.

21. B: *Overbearing* refers to domineering or being oppressive. This is emphasized in the *over* prefix, which emphasizes an excess in definitions. This prefix is also seen in *overacting*. Similar to overbearing, *overacting* reflects an excess of action.

22. A: The *pre* prefix describes something that occurs before an event. *Prevent* means to stop something before it happens. This leads to a word that relates to something occurring beforehand and, in a way, is preventive—wanting to stop something. *Avert* literally means to turn away or ward off an impending circumstance, making it the best fit.

23. D: *Refresh* is synonymous with *replenish*. Both words mean to restore or refill. Additionally, these terms do share the *re-* prefix as well.

24. D: *Regale* literally means to amuse someone with a story. This is a very positive word; the best way to eliminate choices is to look for a term that matches regale in both positive context/sound and definition. *Entertain* is both a positive word and a synonym of regale.

25. C: *Abate* is defined as something becoming less intense and fading. The only word that matches abate is *withdraw*, which means to go back or draw away from a particular position.

26. D: Offspring are the children of parents. This word is especially common when talking about the animal kingdom, although it can be used with humans as well. *Offspring* does have the word *spring* in it, although it has nothing to do with bouncing or jumping. The other answer choice, *parent*, may be somewhat tricky because parents have offspring, but for this reason, they are not synonyms.

258

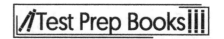

27. E: *Permit* can be a verb or a noun. As a verb, it means to allow or give authorization for something. As a noun, it generally refers to a document or something that has been authorized like a parking permit or driving permit, allowing the authorized individual to park or drive under the rules of the document.

28. B: A woman is a lady. Test takers must read carefully and remember the difference between *woman* and *women*. *Woman* refers to an individual lady or one person who is female, while *women* is the plural form and refers to more than one, or a group, of ladies. A woman may be a mother but not necessarily, and these words are not synonyms. A girl is a child and not yet a woman.

29. C: *Rotation* means to spin or turn, such as a wheel rotating on a car, although *wheel* does not mean rotation.

30. E: Something that is consistent is steady, predictable, reliable, or constant. *Consistent* comes from the word *consist,* which means to contain, Choice *B*. Test takers must be discerning readers and knowledgeable about vocabulary to recognize the difference in these words and look for the true synonym of *consistent.*

Verbal Analogies

31. C: Cows produce milk, so the question is looking for another pair that has a producer and their product. Horses don't produce cows, Choice *A*, glasses don't produce milk, Choice *D*, and milk doesn't produce a glass, Choice *E*. The correct choice is *C*: chicken is to egg. The tricky one here is Choice *B*, egg is to chicken, because it has the correct words but the wrong order, and therefore it reverses the relationship. Eggs don't produce chickens, so it doesn't work with the first part of the analogy: cow is to milk.

32. C: The first part of the analogy—web is to spider—describes the home (web) and who lives in it (spider), so the question is looking for what animal lives in a den. The best choice is *C*, fox. Living room is another word or a synonym for a den.

33. A: *Sad* and *blue* are synonyms because they are both describing the same type of mood. The word *blue* in this case is not referring to the color; therefore, although yellow is sometimes considered a "cheerful" color, the question isn't referring to colors, and *yellow* and *cheerful* are not synonyms. Someone who is glad or happy may laugh or smile, but these words are not synonyms. Lastly, someone who is excited will not generally be calm so these two are not synonyms.

34. D: The key to answering this question correctly is to recognize that the relationship between *door* and *store* is that the words rhyme. One may at first consider the fact that stores have doors, but after reviewing the other choices, he or she should notice that none of the other words have this relationship. Instead, the answer choice should be one that has rhyming words. *Wheel* and *deal*, although spelled differently, are rhyming words, and therefore the correct answer is *D*.

35. E: This question relies on the test takers' knowledge of occupations. Dogs are taken care of by veterinarians, so the solution is looking for that relationship. However, this level of detail is not yet specific enough. Veterinarians take care of sick dogs and act as a medical doctor for pets. Therefore, with this higher level of specificity and detail, test takers should select Choice *E* because pediatricians are doctors for babies and children.

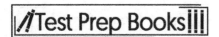

36. C: This is a part/whole analogy. The common thread is what animals walk on. Choices *A*, *B*, and *E* all describe signature parts of animals, but paws are not the defining feature of cats. While snakes travel on their skins, they do not walk.

37. A: This is a characteristic analogy. The connection lies in what observers will judge a performance on. The other choices do not reflect the same connection.

38. D: This is a use/tool analogy. The analogy focuses on an item's use. While hats are worn when it's cold with the goal of making the top of your head warm, this is not always guaranteed—their primary use is to provide cover. There is also the fact that not all hats are used to keep warm, but all hats cover the head.

39. B: This is a tool/use analogy. The common thread is audience response to an art form. Choices *A*, *C*, and *D* deal with the creation of artwork instead of its consumption. Choice *E* describes a form of art instead of the audience engagement with such.

40. D: This is a characteristic analogy and is based on matching objects to their geometric shapes. Choice *A* is not correct because balls are three-dimensional, whereas circles exist in two dimensions. Choice *B* is incorrect because this analogy switches the object and the geometric shape. Choice *C* is incorrect because spokes are just parts of wheels. Choice *E* is incorrect because rather than comparing objects to their geometric shapes, it compares two-dimensional shapes to three-dimensional shapes.

41. A: This is a tool/use analogy. The key detail of this analogy is the idea of enclosing or sealing items/people. When plates are filled with food, there is no way to enclose the item. While trees can be inside a fence, they can also be specifically outside of one.

42. E: This is a sequence of events analogy. The common thread is celestial cause-and-effect. Just like rainbows can be seen after a storm, stars can be seen after dark.

43. A: This is a provider/provision analogy. The theme of this analogy is pairing a specific animal to their food source. Falcons prey on mice. Giraffes are herbivores and often eat leaves.

44. B: This is a category analogy. The common thread is motorized vehicles. None of the other choices have a common thread similar to car and motorcycle.

45. E: This is a provider/provision analogy. This analogy looks at professionals and what their job is. Just as a mechanic's job is to repair machinery, a doctor works to heal patients.

46. C: This is a category analogy. Both whistles and blow horns are devices used to project/produce sound. Therefore, the analogy is based on finding something of a categorical nature. Sculpture is another form of art and expression, just like painting.

47. D: This is a part/whole analogy. This analogy examines the relationship between two objects. Specifically, this analogy examines how one object connects to another object, with the first object(s) being the means by which people use the corresponding object to produce a result directly. People use a paddle to steer a boat, just as pressing keys on a piano produces music.

48. C: This is an antonym analogy. The common thread is opposite meanings. Monotonous refers to being dull or being repetitive, while innovative means new and bringing in changes. All of the other

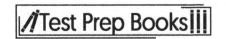

choices reflect synonymous word pairs. However, *loquacious*, which means talkative, is the opposite of silent.

49. E: This is a part/whole analogy. This analogy focuses on natural formations and their highest points. The peak of a mountain is its highest point, just as the crest is the highest rise in a wave.

50. A: This is a negative connotations analogy. Essentially all of the given words in the example express the same idea of uncertainty or not taking a definitive stance. *Ambiguous* means open to possibilities, which parallels to not being able to make a decision, which describes indecisive as well as uncertain. *Uncertain* also means not definite, which not only relates to the given words but also directly to indefinite.

51. B: This is an intensity analogy. Fluent refers to how well one can communicate, while gourmet describes a standard of cooking. The analogy draws on degrees of a concept.

52. C: This is a sequence of events analogy. This analogy pairs one season with the season that precedes it. Winter is paired with autumn because autumn actually comes before winter. Spring, of course, is the season that comes before summer, making it the right answer.

53. A: This is a pairs analogy. To find the analogy, the way that each term is paired should be analyzed. Penguin, a bird, is paired with lemur, which is a primate. The only logical analogy to be made is to find another primate to pair with a bird, which is an eagle and a howler monkey.

54. C: This is a source/comprised of analogy. This analogy focuses on pairing a raw material with an object that it's used to create. Fiberglass is used to build surfboards, just as copper is used in the creation of pennies. While wind powers a windmill, there is no physical object produced, like with the fiberglass/surfboard pair.

55. E: This is an object/function analogy. The common thread between these words is that one word describes a kind of story, and it is paired with the purpose of the story. A myth is/was told in order to explain fundamental beliefs and natural phenomena. The purpose of telling a joke is to amuse the audience, thus making *E* the right choice.

56. A: The relationship in the first half of the analogy is that clocks are used to measure time, so the second half of the analogy should have a tool that is used to measure something followed by what it measures. Rulers can be used to measure length, so that is the best choice. Remember that the key to solving analogies is to be a good detective. Some of the other answer choices are related to clocks and time but not to the relationship between clocks and time.

57. B: Wires are the medium that carry electricity, allowing the current to flow in a circuit. Pipes carry water in a similar fashion, so the best choice is Choice *B*. Test takers must be careful to not select Choice *E*, which reverses the relationship between the components. Choices *A*, *C*, and *D* contain words that are related to one another but not in the same manner as wires and electricity.

58. A: This question pulls from social studies knowledge and the understanding of the basic roles and positions of the three branches of the government. The president serves in the executive branch, and the Supreme Court justices serve in the judicial branch.

59. C: This is a part/whole analogy. Flour is an ingredient of cake, just as yeast is an ingredient of bread. Spoons and ovens are instruments that are typically associated with soup and casseroles, but they are

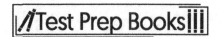
not ingredients. Lettuce is an ingredient of salad, but the relationship is presented in the wrong order. Hot fudge is a topping, not an ingredient, of ice cream.

60. B: This is a synonym analogy. *Grief* and *sadness* mean the same thing, as do *merriment* and *happiness*. Though a birthday is a cause for celebration, the two words are not synonymous. *Vexation* means anger, while *reconciliation* typically refers to bringing together that which was previously separated. Tears are a manifestation of the action of crying. *Joy* is a type of *emotion*, but the words are not synonymous since there are many emotions other than joy.

Quantitative Reasoning 2

1. B: The length of the side will be $\sqrt{400}$. The calculation is performed a bit more easily by breaking this into the product of two square roots:

$$\sqrt{400} = \sqrt{4 \times 100}$$

$$\sqrt{4} \times \sqrt{100} = 2 \times 10 = 20 \text{ feet}$$

However, there are 4 sides, so the total perimeter is $20 \times 4 = 80$ feet.

2. E: To take the product of two fractions, just multiply the numerators and denominators:

$$\frac{5}{3} \times \frac{7}{6} = \frac{5 \times 7}{3 \times 6} = \frac{35}{18}$$

The numerator and denominator have no common factors, so this is simplified completely.

3. C: Let a be the number of apples purchased, and let p be the number of papayas purchased. There is a total of 15 pieces of fruit, so one equation is:

$$a + p = 15$$

The total cost is \$35, which in terms of the total apples and papayas purchased can be written as:

$$2a + 3p = 35$$

If we multiply the first equation by 2 on both sides, it becomes:

$$2a + 2p = 30$$

We then subtract this equation from the second equation:

$$2a + 3p - (2a + 2p) = 35 - 30$$

$$p = 5$$

So, 5 papayas were purchased.

4. A: This equation can be solved as follows:

$$x^2 = 30 + 6$$

$$x^2 = 36$$

262

$$x = \pm\sqrt{36} = \pm 6$$

Only -6 shows up in the list.

5. E: The volume of a cube is given by cubing the length of its side.

$$6^3 = 6 \times 6 \times 6$$

$$= 216 \text{ in}^3$$

6. A: The area of the square is the square of its side length, so $4^2 = 16$ square inches. The area of a triangle is half the base times the height. So,

$$\frac{1}{2} \times 2 \times 8 = 8 \text{ square inches}$$

The total area is $16 + 8 = 24$ square inches

7. B: $-\frac{1}{3}\sqrt{81} = -\frac{1}{3}(9) = -3$

8. A: Multiply each of the terms in the first parentheses with each of the terms in the second parentheses.

$$(2x - 3)(4x + 2)$$

$$2x(4x) + 2x(2) - 3(4x) - 3(2)$$

$$8x^2 + 4x - 12x - 6$$

$$8x^2 - 8x - 6$$

9. C: Use a common denominator of 24.

$$\frac{11}{6} - \frac{3}{8}$$

$$\frac{44}{24} - \frac{9}{24}$$

$$\frac{44 - 9}{24} = \frac{35}{24}$$

10. B: Instead of multiplying these out, we can estimate the product by using $18 \times 10 = 180$.

11. E: This can be set up as an equation:

$$0.30x = 6$$

That equation is asking, "30% of what number equals 6?" Working out the problem gives us:

$$x = \frac{6}{0.3}$$

$$x = 20$$

263

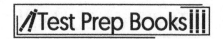

12. A: First, these numbers need to be converted to improper fractions: $\frac{11}{3} - \frac{9}{5}$. Take 15 as a common denominator:

$$\frac{11}{3} - \frac{9}{5} = \frac{55}{15} - \frac{27}{15} = \frac{28}{15} = 1\frac{13}{15}$$

13. E: Dividing by 98 can be approximated by dividing by 100, which would mean shifting the decimal point of the numerator to the left two places. The result is 4.2, which rounds to 4.

14. A: To figure out which value is the largest, look at the first nonzero digits. Answer *B* and *E*'s first nonzero digit is in the hundredths place. The other three all have nonzero digits in the tenths place, so it must be Choice *A*, *C*, or *D*. Of these, Choice *A*'s first nonzero digit is the largest.

15. A: Setting up a proportion is the easiest way to represent this situation. The proportion is $\frac{20}{x} = \frac{40}{100}$, and cross-multiplication can be used to solve for x. Here, $40x = 2,000$, so $x = 50$.

16. A: First, separate each element of the numerator with the denominator as follows:

$$\frac{2xy^2}{16xy} + \frac{4x}{16xy} - \frac{8y}{16xy}$$

Simplify each expression accordingly, reaching Choice *A*:

$$\frac{y}{8} + \frac{1}{4y} - \frac{1}{2x}$$

17. A: When parentheses are around two expressions, they need to be multiplied. In this case, separate each expression into its parts (separated by addition and subtraction) and multiply by each of the parts in the other expression. Remember that when multiplying a positive integer by a negative integer, it will remain negative. Then, add the products together:

$$(3x)(x) + (3x)(-8) + (+5)(x) + (+5)(-8)$$

$$3x^2 - 24x + 5x - 40$$

Then add $-24x$ and $5x$ together to get the final simplified expression $3x^2 - 19x - 40$, Choice *A*.

18. C: In order to calculate the profit, we need to create an equation that models the total income minus the cost of the materials.

$$60 \times \$20 = \$1,200 \text{ total income}$$

$$60 \div 3 = 20 \text{ sets of materials}$$

$$20 \times \$12 = \$240 \text{ cost of materials}$$

$$\$1,200 - \$240 = \$960 \text{ profit}$$

19. C: Looking at the pie chart, we can see that the slice for CDs is less than half the circle (50%) but more than one-fourth of the circle (25%). The only answer choice that meets both requirements is 40%.

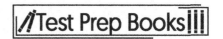

20. C: To find the drop in value, subtract the new value from the old value. To see what percentage of the initial value this is, divide the difference by the initial value, then multiply by 100.

$$\frac{20,000 - 8,000}{20,000} = 0.6$$

$$(.60) \times 100 = 60\%$$

21. A: The question only asks how long they owned the house, so ignore the extra details about prices.

There are 6 years between May 1, 2010 and May 1, 2016. There are another 4 months between May 1, 2016 and September 1, 2016. Therefore, they owned the house for a total of 6 years and 4 months. Each year has 12 months, so the total number of months is $(6 \times 12) + 4 = 72 + 4 = 76$ months.

22. B: If 60% of 50 workers are women, then there are 30 women working in the office. If half of them are wearing skirts, then that means 15 women wear skirts. Since nobody else wears skirts, this means there are 15 people wearing skirts.

23. B: This question involves the percent formula:

$$\frac{32}{x} = \frac{25}{100}$$

Cross-multiply to get $25x = 32 \times 100 = 3,200$. We can solve for x by calculating $x = 3,200 \div 25 = 128$.

As an alternative, we could recall that 25% is $\frac{1}{4}$ and simply multiply 32 by 4 to get 128.

24. D: A dollar contains 20 nickels. Therefore, if there are 12 dollars' worth of nickels, there are:

$$12 \times 20 = 240 \text{ nickels}$$

Each nickel weighs 5 grams. Therefore, the weight of the nickels is $240 \times 5 = 1,200$ grams.

To find the total weight of the filled piggy bank, add the weight of the nickels and the weight of the empty bank:

$$1,200 + 1,050 = 2,250 \text{ grams.}$$

25. D: To find Denver's total snowfall, 3 must be multiplied by $27\frac{3}{4}$. In order to easily do this, the mixed number should be converted into an improper fraction.

$$27\frac{3}{4} = \frac{27 \times 4 + 3}{4} = \frac{111}{4}$$

Therefore, Denver had approximately $\frac{3 \times 111}{4} = \frac{333}{4}$ inches of snow. The improper fraction can be converted back into a mixed number through division.

$$\frac{333}{4} = 83\frac{1}{4} \text{ inches}$$

SSAT Upper Practice Tests #3 & #4

To keep the size of this book manageable, save paper, and provide a digital test-taking experience, the 3rd and 4th practice tests can be found online. Scan the QR code or go to this link to access it:

testprepbooks.com/bonus/ssat-upper

The first time you access the tests, you will need to register as a "new user" and verify your email address.

If you have any issues, please email support@testprepbooks.com

Index

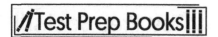

Dear SSAT Upper Test Taker,

Thank you for purchasing this study guide for your SSAT Upper exam. We hope that we exceeded your expectations.

Our goal in creating this study guide was to cover all of the topics that you will see on the test. We also strove to make our practice questions as similar as possible to what you will encounter on test day. With that being said, if you found something that you feel was not up to your standards, please send us an email and let us know.

We would also like to let you know about other books in our catalog that may interest you.

PSAT 8/9

amazon.com/dp/1637756747

SAT

amazon.com/dp/1637754051

ACT

amazon.com/dp/1637758596

ACCUPLACER

amazon.com/dp/1637756356

CLEP College Composition

amazon.com/dp/163775129X

We have study guides in a wide variety of fields. If the one you are looking for isn't listed above, then try searching for it on Amazon or send us an email.

Thanks Again and Happy Testing!
Product Development Team
info@studyguideteam.com

FREE Test Taking Tips Video/DVD Offer

To better serve you, we created videos covering test taking tips that we want to give you for FREE. **These videos cover world-class tips that will help you succeed on your test.**

We just ask that you send us feedback about this product. Please let us know what you thought about it—whether good, bad, or indifferent.

To get your **FREE videos**, you can use the QR code below or email freevideos@studyguideteam.com with "Free Videos" in the subject line and the following information in the body of the email:

   a. The title of your product
   b. Your product rating on a scale of 1-5, with 5 being the highest
   c. Your feedback about the product

If you have any questions or concerns, please don't hesitate to contact us at info@studyguideteam.com.

Thank you!

Made in United States
North Haven, CT
02 November 2024

59775516R00154